# GLIMPSES OF REAL LIFE

AS SEEN IN THE

## THEATRICAL WORLD AND IN BOHEMIA.

AN ARCHON BOOK ON POPULAR ENTERTAINMENTS

A. H. Saxon, *General Editor*

# GLIMPSES OF REAL LIFE

AS SEEN IN THE

# THEATRICAL WORLD AND IN BOHEMIA:

BEING

## THE CONFESSIONS OF PETER PATERSON,

A STROLLING COMEDIAN.

"*Hamlet.* Good my lord, will you see the players well bestowed !
"*Polonius.* My lord, I will use them according to their desert.
"*Hamlet.* Odd's bodikins, man, much better."
SHAKSPEARE.

## ARCHON BOOKS

### Hamden, Connecticut

1979

*Library of Congress Cataloging in Publication Data*

Bertram, James Glass, 1824-1892.
Glimpses of real life as seen in the theatrical world and in Bohemia.

(An Archon book on popular entertainments)
Reprint of the 1864 ed. published by W. P. Nimmo, Edinburgh.
1. Bertram, James Glass, 1824-1892.
2. Actors—Great Britain—Biography.
3. Theater—Great Britain—History—19th century.
I. Title. II. Series.
PN2598.B59A3 1979    792′.028′0924    [B -]    79-4126
ISBN 0-208-01812-3
*(James Glass Bertram used the pseudonym*
*of "Peter Paterson" in writing this book)*

First published 1864 in Edinburgh
by William P. Nimmo.
This facsimile edition published 1979
as an Archon Book, an imprint of
The Shoe String Press, Inc.,
Hamden, Connecticut 06514
Foreword © A. H. Saxon 1979
Printed in the United States of America

TO

# CHARLES DICKENS, ESQ.,

AUTHOR OF "NICHOLAS NICKLEBY,"

THE CREATOR OF MR VINCENT CRUMMLES,

AND

"THE INFANT PHENOMENON,"

This Narrative,

IN ADMIRATION OF THAT GENTLEMAN'S LITERARY POWER,

IS RESPECTFULLY INSCRIBED,

BY HIS HUMBLE SERVANT,

PETER PATERSON,
STROLLING PLAYER AND BOHEMIAN.

# FOREWORD

ANY number of triumphant memoirs have been written by actors who, commencing their careers under the most adverse circumstances, eventually rose to positions of eminence in their profession—very few by those who, after engaging in the same heart-breaking struggle, utterly failed to achieve their goal. Among the latter are the recollections of the Scottish writer James Glass Bertram, or, as he preferred to call himself on the title page of the following work, "Peter Paterson." Born in 1824 in the border village of Tillsmouth, at the age of thirteen he entered the service of William Tait, the proprietor of *Tait's Edinburgh Magazine,* and within a few short years rose to the position of managing clerk and cashier. This much one learns from the anonymous sketch of his life prefacing his posthumously published *Some Memories of Books, Authors, and Events* (1893), a work that deals almost exclusively with his apprentice years in Edinburgh and contains no reference whatever to his later association with the theatre, although the author does admit to being stage-struck at an early age and to the "fearful joy" he felt whenever a visit to the theatre or circus was contemplated.

As the same sketch informs us, it was around the time
he attained his majority that Bertram abandoned his
career in publishing to make a three-year attempt upon
the stage. Failing to gain his living as an actor, he
returned to the world of journalism and, besides contrib-
uting articles to such publications as *Chambers's Journal, Hogg's Instructor,* and *Baily's Magazine,* served as
editor, and for a time proprietor, of the penny newspaper
the *North Briton* from 1855 to 1873. A number of other
periodicals also engaged his attention, among them the
*Scottish Thistle* and the Conservative morning paper the
*Glasgow News.* Meanwhile, he wrote a three-volume
novel entitled *The Stolen Heir;* a pantomime, *The House
That Jack Built,* produced at the Dundee Theatre Royal;
and several works on angling and fisheries, including
*The Harvest of the Sea,* an important contribution to the
subject of fishery economy, originally published in 1865,
which went through numerous editions. Under a variety
of pseudonyms Bertram also wrote on other topics. As
the "Rev. Wm. M. Cooper, B.A.," for instance, he was the
author of *Flagellation and the Flagellants: A History of
the Rod in All Countries from the Earliest Period to the
Present Time,* which also went through several editions;
as "Ellangowan," *Out-Door Sports in Scotland* and
*Sporting Anecdotes;* and as "Louis Henry Curzon," *The
Blue Ribbon of the Turf* and *A Mirror of the Turf; or, The
Machinery of Horse-Racing Revealed,* with the last appearing shortly after his death on 3 March 1892. According to Lowe, he was also the author of *The Way to the
Stage; or, How to Become an Actor and Get an Engage-
ment,* published in 1852, whose title page contains the

cautionary "Advice to persons about to go upon the stage—DON'T!"

The same warning, it will be noted, forms the conclusion of the present work, which began its career, as a forty-two page publication entitled *The Confessions of a Strolling Player; or Three Year's Experience in Theatres Rural,* in the same year. After being expanded nearly four-fold, it sallied forth again, in 1858, as *Behind the Scenes: Being the Confessions of a Strolling Player;* and in 1864, following another considerable augmentation consisting mainly of new chapters that, in the interval, had appeared in such magazines as *Chambers's Journal* and *All the Year Round,* attained its final form under the present title. *Glimpses of Real Life as Seen in the Theatrical World and in Bohemia* presents a fascinating picture of the little-known and seamy world of theatrical booths and "fit-up" theatres, of venal critics and unscrupulous agents, of barnstorming strollers and their day-to-day struggles in the face of ill-attended (and, in truth, often ill-prepared) performances, miserable theatres and even more wretched wardrobes, and the always present dangers of poverty, the bottle, and actual starvation. More than this, it presents a truly "behind-the-scenes" view of the workings of early tenting circuses, in one of which the author appeared for a time as a clown; the operation of booth theatres at country fairs, where the actors, after going "on parade" to advertise themselves, blithely ran through such plays as *Richard III* and *The Castle Spectre* in as little as twelve or thirteen minutes, depending on the number of spectators waiting outside for the next performance; the mysteries of getting up a Christmas

pantomime; and the various cheats of showmen and
others, in which Bertram himself, who at one time set up
as a fortune-teller, confesses to having participated.
Along the way one encounters a succession of well-
known characters of the period, including the eccentric
Glasgow theatrical manager John Henry Alexander, his
Edinburgh counterpart William Henry Murray, and pre-
sumably the circus proprietors Bertram refers to as the
"Brothers Chirper," but whom contemporary readers
would have immediately recognized as George and John
Sanger, the leading men in their field in the second half
of the nineteenth century.

Apropos of these last, it would seem the author occasionally thought it advisable to thinly veil the true identi-
ties of those he was writing about; and in fact it would
appear Bertram introduced the names of the "Chirpers"
merely to lend some topicality to his expanded narrative,
since in the earlier 1858 version he writes that the circus
he joined was actually that of "Fankey Swartha," a
patent reference to the Negro equestrian and circus manager known to the public as Pablo Fanque, but whose
real name was William Darby. Fanque possessed a celebrated black mare named Beda and at one time engaged
the stage manager William D. Broadfoot, both of whom
are mentioned by Bertram, the former under the name of
"Bella." At other times it seems possible such changes
are attributable to spelling errors—as when Bertram
writes "Woodford" for Woolford, a well-known circus
family in the nineteenth century, or "Gimrack" for Jam-
rach, the famous London animal dealer.

Despite these minor errors and inconsistencies, there

can be little doubt Bertram was writing from his own observations and experiences, as when he describes his brief career at a Manchester "tavern-theatre" or complains of being cheated and kept on starvation wages by the itinerant manager "Podger." His comments on the decline of family troupes and the provincial theatre in general are also of considerable interest, for Bertram was in at the end of these traditions, and was also a witness to the rise of the music hall, whose attractions for both patrons and performers, as he realized, promised devastating competition for the legitimate theatre. All told, the picture he paints appears to be an authentic one. And for this reason his book stands as a rare and valuable glimpse into the shadowy, peripheral areas of the nineteenth-century theatre, as well as into those rival entertainments that, increasingly, were threatening to displace it.

A. H. Saxon

*General Editor*

# CONTENTS.

CONTENTS.

# PROLOGUE.

In bygone times—in the days of Garrick, for instance, and even later—it was the strict rule to have a prologue to every play, and a preface to every book; but this practice is not now observed, especially in reference to plays —scarcely any of modern production having the old-fashioned prologue and epilogue. To books, however, it is still the custom to affix a preface, which, after all, is, in most instances, mere words; and these, if not full of sound and fury, usually signify nothing, or, at least, very, very little: but a prologue to the adventures and confessions of so interesting a vagabond as a strolling player and Bohemian must not be allowed to degenerate into anything so commonplace.

What the Editor has principally to do in reference to the reader in this preface is, to warn him not to expect anything particularly exciting in the following true, if rather literal, narrative. The old days of romantic adventure, and of wonderful incident "by flood and field," so far as they relate to "the diverting varlets who act profane and immoral stage plays," have long passed away. There were times—but it is many years ago—when strolling was a necessity, and the poor player used then to meet

with adventures that would have delighted the novelist
—adventures of love and gallantry, and " hairbreadth
'scapes" as well. The unromantic railway, however, has
ended the days of the stroller *par excellence*—George
Stephenson having, many years ago, made it cheaper to
ride than to walk.

Besides, the ideal strolling player of the present day is
a great man—a star of the first magnitude, in fact, who
travels in a *coupé* and keeps a secretary. In other words,
it is only great actors who can afford to travel now—a
man or woman of repute in the profession engages some
half-dozen subordinates, and makes a series of tours
every year. In this way country managers are being
taught that a small resident company of " utility people"
will serve their purpose, and as good stars are always safe
to draw, by pursuing this line of policy they put money
in their purses. Again, some of the more " knowing" of
our dramatic authors are becoming rich after a similar
fashion—they send out one or two parties of actors with
a sensation play, so that country managers need take no
trouble either in organising a company or in providing
performances. Our strolling stars do both.

But we can remember the days when the old strolling player was an institution of the country—as, indeed,
in some remote parts he still is—and when the annual
visit of the strolling company would awaken the curiosity
of " the town." Then, when the wonderfully smart-look-
ing gentleman, dressed in the sharply-defined hat, the
tight-fitting but very threadbare coat, which had the merit
of buttoning up to the chin, and who wore ingeniously

patched but still presentable "continuations," accompanied by his lady and family, all attired in similar style as regarded the fashion and quality of their apparel, would drop down into the little market-town, which was honoured with our residence, as if from the clouds—for no one that we knew (and, being curious about the matter, we often inquired) ever saw them arrive,—straightway the glad tidings were bruited for miles around, on the strength of their arrival, especially among the juveniles,—"The theatre has come again." This wonderful looking gentleman and his lady were usually the forerunners of the company, and were sent in advance to secure an eligible barn—or, if fortune and the magistrates were kind, the town-hall or court-room—in which to fit up the theatre-rural for a few weeks, and to spot out such lodgings as the suspicious townspeople, ever afraid of "the players," could be induced to let, for the entertainment of their companions, whom they were anxious, of course, to see well bestowed. Anon the waggon would lumber into the town with the wonderful scenery, machinery, dresses, decorations, and other paraphernalia, on which, in those days, we used to gaze with great awe and reverence. *Richard's* truncheon we knew was in the property-box, as were also *Hamlet's* foils ; and the tripod "kail-pot," which did occasional duty as the witches' caldron in "Macbeth," and in which an itinerant scene-painter sometimes mixed his paint, we knew, from ancient experience, was also there ; and so, we likewise knew, was the flail with which *Jock Howison* used to succour, with such earnest good will, the *King* in the farce of " Cramond

Brig." And there was a countless host of odds-and-ends besides these: the whole furnishing forth of *Macbeth's* banquet might be espied in another little wooden box in the waggon; and there were swords also—little short ones, and long ones slender and sharp; and there were also to be seen *Mattie's* lantern, *Lady Macbeth's* "cruzie;" and in addition to all these things we could discern saw-dust-stuffed legs of mutton, and a tin box filled with dry rose-pink, which a well-informed juvenile friend assured us was the principal ingredient in stage blood. A large trunk did duty as a wardrobe, and held the ermined robes in which the mimic kings and queens of the boards strutted and fretted their brief hour on the village stage. *Hamlet's* shirt and *Rob Roy's* kilt lay in that receptacle, and were peacefully rolled up along with *Bailie Nicol Jarvie's* cocked hat and *Rolla's* sandals, awaiting their time to be of use. We knew that they were all there, and that in due time—so soon, in fact, as the company got the theatre fitted up, and when we could scrape together the necessary sixpence—we should see them in all their glory, when the mysterious green curtain rolled aside, and "Act I., scene 1," in all its wonder-inspiring magnificence, opened up to our restless imagination a new fairyland.

Those scenes! how familiar they became by the successive visits of the strollers. In time we learned them as a book. That blue drawing-room—that cut wood—those battlements—"the Castle of Elsineur"—that "street in Verona;" yes, or anywhere else,—even now they rise before our mind's eye, phantom-like, and we can realise

them still. The fine scenery of all the great theatres of
Europe has failed to blot from our memory the daubs
which filled with wonder the playgoers upon whom our
strollers conferred the sunshine of their countenance.

A few days would elapse from the appearance of its
harbingers ere the little company were all gathered together; but gradually the strollers arrived at head-quarters, having strolled perhaps a matter of seventeen miles.
First came the low comedian—a grave-looking individual,
but with a little twinkle in his eye that made a smile inevitable—always carrying an umbrella, with its point a
far way in advance of himself, as if to keep off those
mobs of urchins whom he had on sundry occasions made
to roar with delight at what he called his "mugs," and
who would insist upon congregating round him, at such
times as they could safely indulge in a gratuitous view
of his stolid, but, to them, wonderful face. The "heavy
man" was next in importance—semi-respectable, pompous, a widower, but the father of three "foine childer,"
(the heavy man in a provincial *corps* is often an Irishman,) used as the infant phenomena—the Crummelses of
the company. The leading man was a "great creature,"
who usually rejoiced in a fine name, as Mortimer, De
Courcy, or Fontenay, and always carried about a book of
the play with him. It was a "point" of his, and had
perhaps an ultimate effect on what he called, in his moments of unbending, "my ben," which, we may be allowed
to explain to the uninitiated, meant his benefit. Two
"utility men," who officiated principally as "walking
gentlemen;" together with the first arrival, now, we

believe, called "a go-a-head," but then a kind of secretary, combining light comedy and fiddling, made up the male part of the company. The ladies were in keeping; but there were only two of them in addition to the manager's own family—for his eldest and second daughter selected the best parts, and were, of course, looked upon as the stars of the company. *They* had always great benefits, much, no doubt, to the chagrin of the other ladies; but as one of them, a very old stager, used to say, "What can you expect? it is cheek, not acting, that is wanted now-a-days; but it was different twenty years ago—there was acting wanted then, ay, that there was."

After sundry interviews with the printer, occasioning much journeying to and fro upon the part of the aforesaid secretary and fiddler, who seemed the thorough man of many parts, the first bill made its appearance, after having been eagerly expected for a day or two previous. The bill of the play! surely there was greater magic in its large clumsy letters in those days than there is now? How tenderly we used to gaze upon and con it over, and wonder about "The Poor Gentleman," and "The Ploughman turned Lord," and such other pieces as we were then ignorant of. The opening play was invariably national— "Macbeth," "Rob Roy," or at least "Wallace," for your little company is sure to fix upon the largest pieces, requiring, in consequence, no end of "doubles" on the part of the utility folks—and the house was crowded. How happy, when a fortnight's rigid economy enabled us to say that *we* were present, our hoardings having accomplished the necessary seat in the back row. Great was the three hours' delight afforded us by the strolling company. What cared *we* that the witches' caldron had to be drawn off by means of ropes, and *would* stick before it gained the wing? —we could see nothing wrong in that—with us 'twas included in the bill, and was paid for as a part of the play —it had no sin in it that we could then discern. But we used to tire even of "Rob Roy" and "Macbeth," because, of course, being what were called stock pieces, they were so often performed that everybody in our town had seen them at least half-a-score of times. We preferred the mysterious and romantic creations of obscurer authors— plays that had a murder or two in them, and in which every scene ended with a combat of four, and where, at the end, the mysterious stranger, who brought on the *dénouement*, used to make a sudden entrance in a black cloak, the back of which was kilted up by his protruding sword. How it did thrill us, and how we did start our eyes, when he commenced his speech:—"Hold, villain, your hour has come! There is an eye above that watches over the innocent and points out the guilty. Your villany is detected. Your crimes have fallen upon your own head —behold, I am the rightful heir!" These were the pieces for our sixpences.

The strollers soon run through their *répertoire;* the houses dwindle away, and at length the manager is compelled to sound the note of approaching departure, and the strollers again commence their stroll to the next town on the circuit, where the same course is once more run in a way similar to that we have described ; or this time, perhaps, the company may break up altogether—always, of

course, excepting the family nucleus—and away bounds
some Mr Alfred Gushington of the company, promoted to a
higher position, having the fortune to be engaged by the
manager of a regular circuit ; or, better still, by some
happy stroke of fortune, called to the nearest metropolis,
where, mayhap, he makes a " hit," and straightway finds
himself on the high road to fortune, becoming, in a few
years, " the great creature" of the day ; having pieces
written for him, having managers writing for his terms,
and the papers writing him up to the third heaven of
greatness.

But there are always two sides to the canvas. That is
one side of the picture ; but the fate of the poor stroller is
too often less happy, as the following simple narrative
will shew :—Thirty years ago, when autumn was fading
into winter, and just

> " When the wan leaf frae the birk-tree was fa'ing,"

a poor strolling player, accompanied by his wife and two
children—a fine boy and girl—arrived at Lairg, in the
county of Sutherland, where the inhabitants of the district
are " few and far between," and separated on all sides by
rugged mountains, which impart a feeling of terrible soli-
tude to the grandeur of the scene. A cluster of cottages
lie about the manse, on the south side of Loch Shine, and
there are also huts scattered among the hills, which, though
they at first elude observation, are rife with inmates. The
player resolved to try a performance, but, it being Saturday
evening, he determined to rest over Sunday, and accord-

ingly deferred astonishing the simple people till Monday or Tuesday. The poor wanderer, however, was destined never to gratify the people of Lairg by "fretting his hour" upon their stage. He set out on the Monday towards Altna-harrow to rouse the country and collect an audience, taking with him his son to bear him company over the mountain. Neither of them returned; the "play" was, of course, postponed; and day after day passed without bringing any tidings of the actor or his boy. The wife and daughter departed, and the circumstance became forgotten, when, some weeks after, on a solitary part of the farm of Shines, the bodies of a man and boy were discovered in a state of great decomposition, and the mouldering remains were identified by the people of Lairg as those of the poor player and his son. They had lost their way among the hills, and were overtaken by a storm which they had not strength to resist. They had apparently sunk down on the ground exhausted; the boy's head was supported by his father, over which he had, with parental fondness, thrown a part of his coat as a protection from the night and the storm. The man's name and history are unknown; and thus, in a land of strangers, far from the crowded haunts of mankind, perished the lone outcast of the drama, with his unfortunate son. Alas! poor stroller! "After life's fitful fever, he sleeps well."

That was a dark fate for the friendless player; and generally, as will be seen from the following pages, the stroller's career is a grotesque mixture of sunshine and

storm; smiles and tears alternate in his daily career; but
for all that, let us give a

> " Hail to the Theatre ! where genius' thoughts,
>     Depicted on the stage's mimic world,
>     Raise the rapt soul to their own standard high
>     Of intellectual loveliness."

# CHAPTER I.

THERE is a peculiar fascination incidental to the acted
drama which, year after year, draws a number of young
men and women within its attractive vortex; and he who
would attempt to account for the strange longings and
restless disposition which give victims to the stage, must
be prepared to solve a very curious problem,—so curious,
indeed, that I will not myself attempt to meddle with it.
The gaudy attire of the players—the inspiring music—the
beautiful scenery—the feverish excitement—the brilliant
lights—the pleasure of the moment, and the happy and
admiring audience, no doubt lay siege to the senses of
youthful beholders, and tempt them to entertain notions
of penetrating into that mysterious region from which
they are separated by the yawning orchestra.

A nightly attendance in the stalls of the playhouse
strengthens the desire to go "behind" and see for one's
self, at the sacrifice even of being lured into the net, till
it becomes a *furor*. A course of reading, composed of
" Lives of the Players," " Our Actresses," and what is
usually denominated " Theatrical Criticism," in the pages
of obscure penny publications devoted to the drama, and
bedaubed with "noisy" woodcuts of distinguished per-

formers, in favourite characters and in striking attitudes, is not calculated to allay the unhealthy desire. Neither did my historical inquiries into the origin and history of the acted drama tend to cure the fever which had begun to rage; as from these studies I learned that Thespis had originated the dramatic art some five or six hundred years before the Christian era; also, that Thespis had been a strolling player, and that the sages of ancient Greece had listened to his declamation; and more than that, that he had earned money at the rate of £45 per day. This reminded me that Edmund Kean had been, like Thespis, his master, a strolling player,—that John Kemble had been in difficulties,—that his sister, Mrs Siddons, had been a domestic servant,—and that Macready and all the great stars that ever shone in the theatrical horizon had been at one time poor and needy, although afterwards great stars and very wealthy,—and "stars" at that time, and strollers as well, with the romantic stories incidental to their career, were my constant study and meditation. All these facts—and the stage is well garnished with such—naturally impel the imagination to conjure up a finger-post which points out the path to "the boards,"—and many there be who travel along the fascinating road, albeit it is a *via dolorosa*,—

> " Youths foredoom'd their fathers' souls to cross,
>   By spouting Shakspeare when they should engross."

To help me in this resolve, I had in my possession, among other theatrical literature, that finger-post to young actors, "Leman Rede's Guide to the Stage,"—or, as some severe parents designate it, "Rede's Road to Ruin,"—with its instruction to novices,—its catalogue of managers,—its list of theatrical salaries,—its chapters on benefits, and on making superior engagements. There was no point of interest to the stage-struck left unelucidated in "Leman Rede's Guide to the Stage." The aspirant was even told "how to colour the face for the representation of Moors, Negroes," &c., and also instructed how to put a little oil in the palm of his hand to take away the paint, when he had suddenly to appear pale. Then there were hints about how to "make up," as well as a chapter about the method of expressing the various "passions, emotions," &c.; likewise directions as to where to obtain dresses and wigs, and a complete list of the indispensable requisites as regards a theatrical wardrobe for an outset in the profession; besides a great variety of useful and peculiar information,— the whole giving the book a value, in the eyes of the stage-struck, which no other work could have. I must, I fear, set down much of my stage madness to dramatic literature. I can never otherwise account for the hallucination which, like a wicked *ignis fatuus*, lighted me on that path which had already been trodden by so many, and induced me to enlist, a *raw* enough recruit, under the banner of that immortal Thespis about whom I had been reading. It must have been a kind of mesmeric attraction that ultimately impelled me to "smell the lamps;" for when the notion once took possession of me, the very devil himself could not have blotted from my mind the idea that I was destined to be a John Kemble, or a second Garrick,—in fact, the greatest tragic actor of my day; certain to become in time, like the heroes I worshipped, a future subject for the biographer, and destined, undoubtedly, to have my portrait circulated by thousands in the periodicals I so much admired.

It is good for us that we can only paint our future career as we would wish it to be, and are denied a prevision of it as it will in reality occur. The high spirit of youth, glowing with ruddy health, the pulsation dancing through a vigorous frame, looks ever on the bright side of the picture,—the restless mind ever cries onward,—and so youth's day-dreams are ever sunny, delighting to contemplate the exalted position which, in the mind's eye, has been fixed as the climax of an ambitious career. It was thus that, in the company of a chosen band of companions—all ambitious, although in a different path from myself—I used to dilate on the glorious position of a great actor, and would bombastically picture myself as being in time the ornament of the stage, *the* tragedian of the day, the observed of all observers. Truly, we know what we are, but what we may become can only be settled at the end of our journey.

As usual with all afflicted by a similar monomania, I spouted on every occasion, proper or improper. As a friend said, of recitation I never could have my fill. Nothing came amiss; I could

> " All parts alike with equal pleasure take :
>     To die like *Richard,* or like *Jack* and *Gill.*"

I walked about with favourite passages from Shakspeare on my tongue's end; and when I met a friend, he was invariably accosted in a select sentence of blank verse. Evening parties were a perfect godsend—for at these I was certain to be asked to spout; and "Rolla's Address," or "Is this a dagger?" bring rich rewards of flattery to sucking Garricks. On such occasions I was in my glory, and the lines came rolling forth with all the ignorance and pomposity common to that infatuated class of 'block-heads denominated "theatrical amateurs," and of whom, I regret to say, there are generally one or two in each little coterie,—often a funny man, with imitations of Buckstone, T. P. Cooke, or Charles Matthews; also a heavier spirit, intent on "doing" Kean or Macready, in a turn-over collar, and with very long hair. But I sinned in pure ignorance, having no idea that I was not per-fectly sublime; and the admiring applause of partial friends gave me no hint that I had become a downright nuisance, known at many tea-parties as the "spouting bore." How ridiculous all this was never occurred to me then, but I often laugh now at these absurd cantrips; and when age dulls the glow and tames the impetuosity of youth, and the spectacles of prudence and propriety are balanced upon the nose, we are all of us very apt to shake our wise heads at such juvenile absurdities.

In such a manner did the fates beckon me on. I be-came at length quite "the theatrical young gentleman," —"Sir Oracle," to those who would listen, on the births, deaths, and marriages of all the actors and actresses who had flourished from the time of Roscius, to the days of the great Alfred Bunn. In fact, to be considered a walking cyclopædia of all matters pertaining to the British drama,

—an authority on everything theatrical, from the best way to put on rouge, to the newest reading in "Hamlet," was a part of my ambition. All this was the more extraordinary, as I had the good fortune to hold an excellent situation, which my unfortunate propensity led me to give up. I was happy in every respect, had a comfortable home and troops of friends, who, melancholy to record, upheld me in my determination to make a fool of myself. In time, as my theatrical *furor* grew with what it fed on, I neglected my office, and got into disgrace with my employer, who threatened to discharge me. This was a stunning blow to my vanity ; and as I had hitherto prided myself on the proper manner in which I performed all the duties required of me, I determined to shake off the trammels of day-book and ledger, and fix upon the stage as my future occupation, and at once to become an actor. The lamp of my theatrical genius must at this period have burned with almost supernatural brightness to sustain me in such a course of folly.

As most stage-struck fools commence their career with the determination of becoming tragedians, it may readily be supposed that I formed no exception to the rule. The whole tenor of my theatrical reading might have pointed out the absurdity of such a method of procedure; for it is notorious that all the best actors begin at the beginning, and serve a regular apprenticeship to the profession, in the course of which they obtain ample opportunity to find out for what line of " business " nature may have fitted them. As is usual with theatrical aspirants, nothing but the sublimity of tragedy would suit my ardent spirit; and to give my genius the fullest scope, *Hamlet* was fixed upon as my opening character, and I determined upon embellishing the part with several new and pet readings which had occurred to me in the course of my studies. After making due inquiry at one or two public-houses which were much frequented by the members of the sock and buskin, I found that I might obtain an opening in the theatre of a well-known manufacturing town in the West of Scotland, which, if the courteous reader please, he may call Threadham. A call upon the manager settled this point at once, and the intervening period between that visit and my *début* found me making elaborate preparations for my launch into this new sphere of life. During my brief preliminary visit I obtained a glimpse of the internal resources of a fourth-class provincial theatre; but, having previously been on the stage, and seen the appliances of the Edinburgh and Glasgow houses, I was much astonished to find how things were dwarfed in the temple of the drama at Threadham. The stage, to my ambitious eye—and at the time I felt myself *Hamlet* — seemed but a span in breadth; the scenery looked like that of a toy theatre; and the aspect of the whole was desolate and gloomy, which tended, in some degree, to chill the ardour of my tragic aspirations. "But stop," said the manager, to whom I had disclosed my feelings—"stop till we light up, my boy, you will feel more at home then; the lights are half the battle, man; this gas was a glorious invention for the stage; it puts a new face on everything theatrical."

I had assiduously collected a stock of hares' feet, a

great number of burnt corks, some pearl powder and rouge, and many accessories of the costumier. My supply of tights, collars, boots, shape-shoes, russet and velvet, shape-hats, swords, Roman and Highland, and various other "props," as "properties" are usually designated by most actors, was perfectly *en règle;* and thus accoutred, and fully "up in my part," I started for the scene of action, determined "to conquer or die,"—resolved, at all events, to make such a hit in the character of the "inky Dane" as would spread my fame through all the theatres of Great Britain and Ireland.

# CHAPTER II.

CONTAINS ONE MORE EXEMPLIFICATION OF THE OLD PRO-
VERB, THAT "THE BEST-LAID SCHEMES O' MICE AND
MEN GANG AFT AGLEY."

ON my arrival at the scene of (as I thought it would
be) triumph, my eyes were delighted with the large
placards announcing, in letters of gigantic size, that a
new tragedian was about to blaze upon the world. At
least six times between the railway-station and the theatre
did I stop to look at the bills containing the " caste," and
read—"The character of *Hamlet*, by *a gentleman;* his
first appearance on any stage." This was indeed a fore-
taste of my future greatness! The manager was kind
enough to have two rehearsals on my account, and I got
through *them* pretty well. The company was more select
than numerous, the principal members consisting of a few
old stagers, who were required to make themselves very
useful, and who had, in consequence, often enough to play
several parts in one play. They were men who had
figured in many a hard theatrical campaign—who had
drunk in full of the strollers' bitters, but who had also, at
times, even drawn sweets from the vagabondism of the
strolling players' varied existence.

The eventful night at last arrived, big with the fate
of the new *Hamlet* and my future fortunes. After par-

taking of dinner, and a small modicum of generous liquor
to lend its aid in the way of inspiration, I again, for the
last time, looked over my part, with a view to impress it
thoroughly on my memory; then summoning up all my
courage, and confident of success, I set out for the playhouse, and arrived at that building exactly at six o'clock,
and for the first time was ushered into the dressing-
room.

The dressing-room! Let the courteous reader recall
to his mind's eye the picture of Hogarth's "Strollers,"
and he will have a faint idea of the sight which met my
astonished eyes. There was only one tiring-room, and it
was used in common by all the company—all the gentlemen, I mean; for, as usual, the ladies had a room to
themselves. Hitherto I had only seen the sunny side of
things *before* the curtain—now I was introduced to the
seedy side *behind* the curtain. We had rehearsed "Hamlet" in our everyday clothes; but in the evening I saw
the company in *déshabillé*.

The scene is absolutely quite indescribable, or could
only be reproduced by the graphic pen of a Boz. "Motley's your only wear" may be a motto among actors at all
times, both on and off the stage. Here, at any rate, I saw
many of the shifts and dodges to which the poor player
must resort to keep up appearances in a small country
town. The whole of the "gentlemen" constituting the
male part of the company were before me, numbering
eight individuals in all. In one corner was the individual
who was to play *Laertes*, apologising for *again* being
minus his shirt, it having been sent this time to get a

new breast put in—last time, it was away getting retailed. In the middle of the floor stood the *King*, a fine
" ould " Irishman, who, while arranging his robes (and
this was no easy matter, as they would not button upon
him) kept bewailing the loss of an *illigant* pair of
" toights," and a huge box of books, which had gone the
way of all theatrical properties, (*i.e.*, been lent to " my
uncle,") in a bad season at Clonmel, where Paddy had
been manager of a strolling company—a family company,
most of his children having been celebrated as infant
phenomena. in various country theatres. We may as
well mention, by way of parenthesis, that all players have
great losses to mourn over, and it is particularly at
dressing-time that they give vent to their lamentations,
as it is at that hour they most feel the want of them. I
never yet, in the whole round of my travels, met an actor
who had not been ruined and robbed over and over again,
both of his " props " and books,—in fact, such calamities
occurred so frequently, that the sufferers, like the eels,
must have been quite accustomed to them,—so accustomed
as to lead me to suppose that they would almost like the
process. The general public would smile if they knew
at times what is done with " properties." A great actor
has often told, that when he was a stroller he frequently
breakfasted on his boots, dined on his coat, supped on one
of his swords, and obtained his gin and water by means
of his hat, a style of feeding which poor Paddy, with his
insatiable thirst for a " dhrop of the crathur," had often
to have recourse to—hence his wailing over the " illigant
toights." Next to the *King* was *Hamlet's* friend, *Horatio,*

who was patiently endeavouring to close up a rent which, much to his chagrin, had made its appearance in a prominent part of one of his most necessary vestments, and that, too, at a very inappropriate moment—viz., when he was kneeling on the previous evening, according to the stage direction, to pay his addresses to a lady in a comic drama, in which he acted the lover. The *First Actor* was a *mauvais sujet*, steaming with raw whisky, and boasting of how many glasses, or rather cupfuls, he had drunk during the day. He was beseeching the previous newcomer, a novice like myself, for the loan of a collar (his own being, as was usual, lent.) *Polonius* was taking huge pinches of snuff, and scattering it all over the wig he was engaged in dressing. The *First Gravedigger*, next to the manager, the low comedian of the company, a quiet, unostentatious fellow, seemed the best provided of all the motley crew, and, for a consideration, he hired out some of his dresses to those of the company who required them ; but it is really quite wonderful with how little an actor will make a good appearance. The *Ghost* (he was the wit of the company) stood before the fire eating a small mutton-pie, as he said he could not be hollow enough in the voice unless he was quite full in the stomach.

The dressing-room was a large, bare apartment, over one part of the stage ; a wooden board or shelf ran round two sides of it, and each individual had a share of this dresser. At dressing-time there was always a great borrowing of chalk, rouge, hares' feet, whiting, &c., &c. Sometimes, too, a gent would inconsiderately get into some other gent's tights, or by accident put on his neighbour's boots; and occasionally there would be a fight for the possession of a tunic that was considered a good one,—the wardrobe of the theatre only furnished tunics and cloaks; each actor had to provide his own tights, boots, collars, hats, &c. Then would come a *row*, when everybody spoke at once, and the gent had to step out of the stolen tights, amid the titter of those of his brethren who, having their own, could afford to be honest in the matter of such " indispensables."

One actor in this company being for a time without boots—he had lost the whole of his wardrobe in a disastrous season just concluded at Londonderry—was obliged to borrow, and had to be accommodated as well as possible by those whose turn it was to be " off" the stage. When every person had to be on, this gentleman, who acted a prominent character in the play—he was our light comedian, in fact—persuaded some one who could stand in the shade to lend him his boots or shoes, in order that he might be quite *en règle*. I have seen him make narrow escapes; once, in a particular play, he had to speak a speech at the wing, while in the act of pulling on a pair of very tight boots: that speech was mixed up with a great many " Ah's," and " Oh's," and " Hang it's," which were not set down by the author.

Having achieved the important feat of dressing, we all descended to the stage a few minutes before the rising of the curtain, and as there was no green-room, we generally had a strut about and some gossip—the staple conversation being almost invariably the " miseries of the profes-

sion." Paddy, on such occasions, was usually the most
eloquent of the company. "Och, me boy," he would exclaim, "take a faather's advoice, and don't be a player!"
and then he would wish that he had had a bason of boiling-
hot porridge in his boots when he became an "acthor," and
many more of the group held similar views, which they
did not hesitate to proclaim. Most of their remarks, as
I very keenly felt, were levelled at myself, intending to
deter me from the stage. They fell, however, on an un-
willing ear—my shoulders had rubbed the scene, and, in
short, "he would be an actor."

As the evening advanced, the shouts of the manager
"gave dreadful note of preparation," and my *Horatio*, who
also officiated in the capacity of prompter, was speedily at
his post. A broken tea-cup, containing a gill of raw
whisky mixed with sugar, stood on a convenient shelf near
enough at hand to be frequently appealed to. The music
had been rung in, a great house had assembled, and the
busy hum of an expectant audience was heard on the
other side of the curtain. The company, I noticed, was
greatly interested in the appearance of the house, and each
actor in turn took a peep through a small hole in the
curtain, in order, as they called it, to "take stock" of the
audience. I could note that the manager, for one, was very
well pleased; for full houses are frequently few and far between in a country circuit. In the meantime, "Richard the
Buster," as the prompter was called, bustled about, getting
the stage cleared, and directing the first scene; and his
broad and peculiar oaths, all of which were given in the
genuine Scottish dialect, were highly characteristic. At

length the overture was played out, and Richard, having drained his cup of the last mouthful of whisky, had borrowed fourpence to get it replenished preparatory to the rising of the " hippen," as he called the curtain.

Now came the eventful moment ; " Clear the stage," was shouted by the manager, and at last the curtain was rung up. All this time, from the minute I left the dressing-room, and while the ladies and gentlemen of the company strutted about in the costume appropriate to their part, I began to experience a growing queerness, and felt the coming on of that awful sensation which I had so often ridiculed in others, known to the initiated as " stage fright." As the first brief scene went on, and *Francisco* spoke about the weather, &c., the feeling increased ; and when I was pushed into my place to be " discovered," along with the *Queen* and court, I felt much inclined to run away, and leave histrionic greatness to be achieved by others who had more nerve. But there they all were—escape impossible ; besides, I question if the state of my knees would have permitted my legs to have performed their functions.

When the stony ramparts of Elsineur drew asunder, and the audience beheld " *Scene II.—A Room of State in the Castle*"—there was a welcoming round of applause in honour of the new *Hamlet*, who all the time was standing as if in instant expectation of being hanged. The state of my feelings during these brief minutes cannot be described ; I felt unutterably helpless. All the combined evils that ever were heaped on the devoted head of any poor human being could, I thought, be nothing to what I

suffered at the moment when it came to my turn to speak.
I was letter-perfect in the part of *Hamlet,* and had frequently galloped over every word of it from beginning to
end; indeed, I knew the whole tragedy by heart—every
sentence was coursing vividly before me—but I was suddenly struck dumb, and could make no utterance. Cold
drops of sweat ran down my back, my head felt on fire,
my knees were decidedly uneasy, my eyes grew glassy, the
sea of human heads before me seemed converted into one
great petrified face—and oh! how terribly hard it looked
at me—seeming to read-my very soul. I tried to shut
my eyes, but the gigantic head, with hundreds of penetrating eyes, still glared on me; at one moment it seemed
as if it would melt with compassion, and then it became
fixed with an icy contemptuous smile that seemed to refuse all sympathy, and mock at me. Then a new feeling
came over me. I felt as if all that was taking place was
no concern of mine—nothing to me individually. I did
not understand it. I was in a region of unconsciousness
—far away in dreamland—and my mind was blank; I did
not even think—I had become a statue immovable, but
with just the breath of life in me. In a moment again I
woke up—I tried to concentrate my thoughts—my eyes
brightened, and I gazed into the audience; tried to look
unusually mild, philosophic, and intellectual. I succeeded
to some extent in this, as I fancied; but, as I have since
been told, I only attained the drunkard-like position of
looking unutterably foolish. Again and again my cue
was given, but I heeded it not. Answer made he none—
no sound issued from the deep chest of the "inky Dane."

He was too silent. My lips moved, but my voice was frozen. I felt choked up ; my legs quivered and quavered, and silently danced a quick, shaky kind of movement. The prompter cried out the beginning of my part several times—

" A little more ——"

but my only reply was a hopeless, helpless stare. I looked, and looked, and better looked at the audience—but the fact was—all memory had fled. I *felt* what I had to say, but could not speak it. The audience began to get impatient, and hiss. All at once a thought of home came vividly across me ; and glancing at my sombre dress, I said to myself, as I thought, " What would my mother say if she saw me making such an infernal fool of myself ? "

I shall never forget the roar that took place ; for, instead of merely thinking these words, I had spoken them—they unwittingly found vocal expression—and the audience shouted with excitement. The company, losing all sense of propriety, first tittered, and then joined heartily in the general roar ; and I, looking first one way and then another, bolted off the stage as hard as my rather shaky legs would allow me, amid a renewed shout from the whole audience.

And so ended my first appearance on any stage.

# CHAPTER III.

AFTER the curtain had fallen on my unfortunate attempt at *Hamlet*, it became necessary to appease the offended audience by a few words of apology. This was not difficult; for, to say the truth, the good weavers of Threadham were rather amused than otherwise at the affair, and quite inclined, after their hearty laugh, to be in a forgiving disposition. The gentleman who was to do the *Ghost* was sent on to make a suitable speech, appealing, in the wonted stock phrases, to the generous sympathies of the audience, and begging the usual indulgence for the manager on account of their unlooked-for disappointment. The speech was well received, and after a substitute for the novice had been provided, the play went on, the manager thus retaining all the cash which had come into the house—rather a pleasing fact for him, considering that it was a crowded one.

As to my own feelings immediately after my escape from the stage, I cannot now recollect what they were. Covered with perspiration, I staggered away to the dressing-room, and from intense mental excitement, fell in huddle on the floor in a deep faint. I recovered, however, in a short time, and found myself surrounded by the company, who were kindly ministering to me. All signs of merriment by this time had vanished; they, no doubt, fancied it might turn out too serious an affair for a joke. As for myself, after I had taken a glass of water, I felt considerably relieved; and although I forced myself to laugh at the absurd termination of all my schemes, I wished at the time to have a good cry, could I have wept in secret.

The gentleman who acted old *Polonius* told me to keep up my spirits and not be cast down. "Try again, my boy," said he; "one failure is nothing. Let me honestly advise you, however, not to fly at such high game as *Hamlet;* stick to little bits; what you can get, in fact —you will thus gain practice and confidence together, and opportunities of murdering *Hamlet* will no doubt frequently occur. In the meantime, I may venture to prophesy, from your face, that comedy will be your *forte,* and you may throw tragedy to the dogs as soon as you please." "Oich, me boy," said the *King,* in his best brogue, "don't moind yer leetle failure. I have done the same meself when I was a novice, an' here I am, ye sees, play'n the *King* in this abominable dress that I can't get to fit me any how; bedad, now I wish me boots had been filled with chips of my own glass when I tuk to acting; but thry it again, me lad, thry it again!"

Having a strong impression that my advisers were in the right, and thanking them kindly for their good

advice, I resolved to profit by it ; and it is advice so good
that I would here impress it upon all stage-struck heroes
—a class of people who invariably fancy that tragedy
alone is the line of business that will suit them best, as is
evinced by the mistake committed in this respect by many
of the great actors of former times, and also of the present
day, who, at the outset of their career, strutted in their
buskins, having ultimately, however, to get them altered
into a pair of socks.

I may as well mention here, that the only instance I
recollect to have heard of a person speaking his thoughts
on the stage in the same manner as I had unwittingly
done, much to the amusement of my audience, took place
in this very theatre. The play was " Hamlet" also, and
great amusement was afforded by a little bit of eccen-
tricity in the principal performer, an amateur from a
Glasgow dramatic club. This gentleman had acquired a
great habit of *quoting* Shakspeare, and invariably, after
a recitation, out came the customary " Shakspeare." He
became so forgetful of being in the middle of " Hamlet,"
that, after one of his best soliloquies, as usual the quota-
tion must be given, and in a moment, to the astonishment
of both audience and brother actors, there rolled from his
mouth the sonorous mark indicative of his author—
" Shakspeare." The effect of such a thing cannot be
given on paper, but it was excessively ludicrous.

The morning after my failure, Watkins (that was the
manager's name) sent a message for me to call upon him
at his lodgings. I went, of course, and he received me
with great kindness.

"I have been thinking," he said, "that you would be the better of a little more experience, and a great deal more practice, before you try *Hamlet* again. Now, if you like to stay with me till the end of the season at Shippham, you will get some nice little parts, and be put up to the business of the stage in a regular way; and you know the profession of an actor must be learned just like any other. Of course, you know, my boy, I won't be able to afford you a salary for the first few weeks, as you are quite a novice, but you will get your choice of the 'little business,' and I have no doubt you will get on well if you take pains. We open at Shippham in a week, and if you think these terms (I did not think them *terms* at all) suitable, you can join us there."

"You'll get some nice 'business' to play," chimed in Mrs W.; "and when we go to our next town, I've no doubt Mr Watkins will give you a salary."

Now, had I been a wise young man, I would at once have given up going a-acting, and gone home once more to my mother's apron-strings, but the demon of pride stepped in to prevent this, and I accepted Watkins's offer. I did not certainly relish the idea of working without any salary, but I gulped down the affront, and resolved to make the best of the intentions of the fates regarding me. It is quite usual to entrap beginners thus, and as they have generally a capital supply of dresses and properties, they are an acquisition; for as there must be a certain number of persons in a company, in order to look the characters in a play if they cannot act them, it is clear that even a well-dressed dummy, when he is procured at the cheap price of nothing, is just as good as one that is paid for ; and, moreover, his outfit and dresses are generally, out of all comparison, better than those of the old hack actors who are usually to be found in such companies.

After a week's absence in Edinburgh, I returned to Threadham, in order to pack up my "traps," and then went on to Shippham to join the banner of Mr Watkins as a regular member of his establishment.

The company was much the same as the one we had at the former place, only it had been arranged to have a regular succession of stars—C. D. Pitt, Macready, the African Roscius, and Miss Helen Faucit, having been all announced.    At the time I joined, Mr Pitt was there, and the following brief entry from my note-book gives full particulars of my second advent on the boards :—

"Made my second appearance on any stage at the Theatre-Royal, Shippham, as first countryman in the 'Twa Drovers,' and one of the citizens in 'Virginius,' Mr C. D. Pitt playing the Roman hero."

"Oh, what a falling off was there, my countrymen !" what a yawning gulf to leap, from the graceful *Hamlet* to a clown in the "Twa Drovers."    I never could have dreamed of such a change a short month before.    Then there was to be no falling off—it was mount, mount, higher and higher then ; but now I had got to the lowest step of the ladder, and had to begin at the beginning, and climb from the countryman upward ; and, after all, that is the true way of getting on.    Many a man has risen to eminence by pursuing a single course.

In descending to the utilities of the drama, I, of course,

became so obscure as to be quite beneath notice or criticism; but one of my leading ideas had been to do away with some of the conventionalities of the stage. The reader, then, may judge of my annoyance at being constantly told by one or other of my compeers not to turn my back on the audience, and not to turn round as I made my exit. My leading idea when I resolved upon adopting the stage as a profession, was entirely to disregard the audience, in fact, to comport myself just as if there were no audience in the house. The old stagers, however, with whom I was associated could not stand this; there were certain rules and conventionalities, which, according to them, must be observed. It was in vain that I pointed out, among other things, how absurd it was for a young lady to interrupt the action of a play by coming always forward to sing incidental songs over the orchestra to the audience, which ought to be sung to the company on the stage; some of them admitted the absurdity, but said there was no remedy.

When I sobered down a little to my new way of life, and had seen the absurdity of my high-flown views, I came to the conclusion that the advice which my friend *Polonius* had given me was correct, and that comedy—low comedy—was unquestionably the line of business in which I was destined to shine, and to rival Liston was now the summit of my ambition; but how I succeeded in this high resolve the reader will find out by a careful perusal of the remainder of these " *Confessions.*" Some of my friends have told me that " adventures " would be a more striking word on my title-page ; but as there is not much to relate in the way of incident, and as, strictly speaking, what I have to tell is all in the way of confession, I prefer taking my own way, and hope that my candour will be duly appreciated, and that my experiences will act as a beacon to keep others from striking upon the same rock as myself.

# CHAPTER IV.

THEATRICAL aspirants may take my word for it, that the actor's, life, especially at the outset, is dull and miserable  It is one of the most annoying routine,—real, hard, disagreeable work.  Up betimes in the morning to study, if you have been so fortunate as to secure "the book," for in a country theatre there is no such personage as a copyist,—no nicely-written-out "parts" to study from.  There is in general only "the book,"—*i. e.,* a printed copy of the play; and as "the leading man," and "the leading lady," and "the heavy man," and "the low comedian," and "the light comedian," and "the chamber-maid," may all have to study their parts, there is little chance of the "utility" people getting a sight of it.  Rehearsal from about ten till four, with three parts incubating perhaps during its course, and in which you are expected to be "up" at night to a letter.  Home to dinner, (if, by any unexpected piece of good luck, you have such a meal to take,) which you eat with a well-thumbed playbook in your hand, swallowing your part and your bread and cheese at one and the same moment. A short interval here intervenes, which must be devoted to study, in order to get letter-perfect in your parts. Very "old stagers," who are studied in everything, devote this hour to the public-house. The public-house is, of course, next door to the playhouse, and the chances are, that half the members of the company are drinking at this hour of the day, not however, as the reader may suppose, at their own expense,—no, no, they usually find a simpleton or two to "stand sam" for them.

This drinking system is the curse of the theatrical profession, and degrades both the actor and his art. As has been mentioned, those old stagers who have little to learn are always tippling; and young men in large theatres, when there is little to do in the way of rehearsal, in consequence of a piece having a long run, are much given to frequent public-houses. There are always to be found "admirers of the drama," and silly young men, ambitious of knowing the actors, who, having more money than brains, are delighted to "stand" any amount of either beer or brandy. The conversation indulged in is usually of a very fourth-rate kind—stale anecdotes of second-class actors, and so forth—and the young men of the stage, instead of giving up their leisure time to hard study by way of perfecting themselves in their art, devote themselves to the worship of Bacchus with a zeal which, if devoted to their profession, would make them great men.

After laying in as much drink as can be obtained for

nothing, you then pack up in some old bag, such things as may be necessary for the night, and take them with you to your dressing-room. As none of an actor's private properties are ever left in a country theatre, all the company do the same; and at about half-past six o'clock, one after the other, the shabby-looking people may be seen to drop in at the stage-door, looking very like thimblers—for one of which fraternity I was at one time apprehended.

Acting begins at seven; and it was not uncommon for me to change my dress and make up my face seven times in a night. Hard work enough that of itself. You glance at the *caste* as you go out at midnight, and grin to find yourself in for five nice little parts in the three pieces put up for to-morrow night. To make this all the more delightful, you find on inquiry that the books are all engaged, and so you must learn your part in the best way you can. When you get home you are asleep in a moment; if you sit down in a vain attempt to collect your scattered thoughts, all becomes a whirl of confusion—a whirl of *Hamlets, First Actors, Second Gravediggers,* and "A rat, a rat behind the arras, dead for a ducat!"—or other similar exclamations. You go to bed, but not to sleep, for in your mind's eye you again and again go through the scenes of the night, and wake next morning to repeat the same routine.

As a lesson to novices, I will here go over what I had to do in one night—not that the amount of "study" was too much for me, but simply that the number of characters I had to personate on the same evening was confounding. The actor must write out, by way of facilitating his "study," the whole of the words he has to speak, and a sufficient number of the words to be spoken by the actor who precedes him, to obtain a *cue*, or idea when to begin speaking himself, as follows :—

### FRANCISCO.

#### HAMLET,—ACT I., SCENE 1.

(Discovered—enter Bernado.)

WHO'S THERE?

Nay, answer me ; stand, and unfold yourself !

LONG LIVE THE KING !

Bernardo?

HE.

You come most carefully upon your hour.

—GET THEE TO BED, FRANCISCO.

For this relief, much thanks ; 'tis bitter cold, and I am sick at heart.

—HAD QUIET GUARD?

Not a mouse stirring.

—BID THEM MAKE HASTE.

　　　　*Enter* HORATIO *and* MARCELLUS.

I think I hear them. Stand ! who is there ?

—AND LIEGEMEN TO THE DANE.

Give you good night.

—WHO HATH RELIEV'D YOU?

Bernardo hath my place. Give you good night.　　　　*[Exit.*

As soon as I was off the stage, I had to run to the dressing-room and take off, so to speak, my out-of-doors dress, and then take my place as a "lord" in the second scene. My *rôle* as a lord extended through several scenes ; but in the second act I appeared as the second actor, and in the play scene I had to speak the prologue :—

　　　" For us and for our tragedy,
　　　　Here stooping to your clemency,
　　　　We beg your hearing patiently."

　　　　　　　　　　　　　　　　　　　*[Exit.*

Again, I had to come on as "one Lucianus, nephew to the king," both my speeches, as my reader is no doubt aware, being in the play scene. I had after this to change once again to the "lord;" and, finally, to dress and "make up" for one of the clowns, or second grave-digger, as it is technically called. So much for the tragedy. In the after-piece, I had also to play one or two little parts, and the frequent changes of dress are thoroughly annoying to a novice. It takes a few minutes' reflection for him to find out who he is each time.

The ladies of the profession who belong to these small country theatres go through the same course, with, in addition to their share of the study, a good deal of washing and ironing work—doing up of muslin skirts, pinking of "tights," changing and darning of lace, and other such work. I must say that the greatest care is taken of all these "properties." It is often very difficult to procure the necessary dresses and ornaments out of the scanty salary obtained at a country theatre; hence each article of attire is rigorously looked after, and most carefully laid away after being used. Pieces of lace, gloves, and old satin shoes, are kept as if they were of fabulous value. Perhaps the young lady who does "the juvenile business" will be found busy after breakfast manipulating a pair of white satin shoes, or satin shoes which once were white, with crumbs of bread—great need to make them decent —in these same white satin slippers she has to go mad at night as the broken-hearted *Ophelia*, singing—

> " He is dead and gone, lady,
> He is dead and gone ;

> At his head a grass-green turf,
>   At his heels a stone."

In fact, the following moral, which I picked up in an old periodical, is apropos :—

> " Ye youths who velvet paths descry
>   In the home of a scenic king,
>   For a sight of the back of the picture try;—
>   To judge of a player is 'all my eye,'
>   Unless you have rubb'd the wing!"

Married ladies, who are in the profession along with their families, are generally great drudges, having not only to play the mother and the mistress at home, but to perform their part on the stage as well—having to attend rehearsal and the broth-pot at the same time. I was exceedingly sorry for one poor lady, who, along with a son and two daughters, was a member of the company at Shippham. Maternal ambition prompted her to aid in forwarding her children in the profession, and she sacrificed her own desires to their interest, and frequently got well abused by the manager for her pains. She has since died, poor woman, and so has one of the daughters in question, but her son, I observe, is getting on well, and is now in a good position in one of the first-class provincial theatres of England.

Seeing what this poor lady had to endure, I have often wondered, when I read fine criticisms in the newspapers cutting up Mrs So-and-so for her poor conceptions and bad acting, how it was possible for that lady to act at all. She had three young children to nurse and attend to, and the united salaries of herself and husband were exactly

thirty-seven shillings a-week — a little daughter being
thrown in as a sort of makeweight. She could have no
soul for art—she could have nothing but anxiety, poor
woman; what with lodgings to pay for, stage properties
to provide, and money to lay away for the next journey,
which might, for all she knew, be from Dundee to Dud-
ley, she could have but a poor time of it. The very
circumstance of the child thrown in to make up the salary
was an annoyance, because she must have clean skirts,
and would have occasionally to wear satin shoes. Why
stay in a profession where there is so much misery? I
think I hear my readers say, "But what can the So-and-
so's do? She was born in the profession, so to speak;
and he, what could he do but strut on the stage?" True,
his ambition is some day to start a tavern; that is apparently all his art does for him—makes him long to
change Shakspeare and the stage for the bar — of a
public-house.

I have somewhere read of a great *actor* who made up
a most lugubrious catalogue of the ills he had fallen heir
to, even after he had worked his way to the top of his
profession, and had become a famous London *actor;* and
one of his grievances I remember was, that there was in
the green-room only one glass out of which he had to
drink in common with all the members of the theatre.
Poor fellow! Had he never wandered over the country
with his unprotected toes peeping out of a pair of stage
boots, and with a "property" vest aiding to shield him
from the cold, and glad to beg a drink of beer or milk
to keep up the steam as he journeyed along? We sup-

pose not, or in the luxurious enjoyment of his fift pounds a week he had perhaps forgotten those days; but I am much mistaken if, like most of the members of the theatre at Shippham, he had not passed years of his life without having the privilege of drinking out of a glass of any kind. Few of the small country theatres have a green-room, and Shippham was no exception. As I have already mentioned, we assembled in a corner behind the scenes, all huddled together over a small spark of fire; and I never saw a glass there at all, except when a few of us might join for a bottle of ale, and borrow such a vessel to drink it out of, which we all did in common. I very shrewdly suspect the great actor in question had many a time to do the same thing.

Great actors have occasionally had wonderful endur-ances of poverty, and the miseries incidental thereto, to put up with; and strolling players were too long thought to be only so many blackguards. In a work which I have lately seen, the subject is thus alluded to :—" What recompence is position and emolument for the suffering, and frequently the dishonour, of such an early life? Who but an enthusiast would encounter such a trial? Who but one haunted by a restless burning desire for dramatic distinction would welcome years of poverty, privation, sickness of soul and body, a constant sense of self-im-posed beggary, and an internal reproach for frequent acts of meanness not to be avoided, and even dishonesty, which may not be shunned? We do not desire that persons starting in the great race for distinction should

have the innumerable difficulties which lie in their path
carefully cleared away for them, that the thorns and
briers should be lopped off and hid out of sight, and the
way strewn with roses; certainly not,—an acquaintance
with difficulties hardens and exalts their character, braces
their nerves, gives them readiness and power, and also
teaches them the great lessons of self-reliance and self-
respect. Let them struggle; it is well that they should do
so; trials and obstacles are the surest schools for genius:
we repeat, let them struggle—but let them not sink. Let
them be familiar with difficulty, but save them from dishonour; do not make the actor an outcast and a pariah;
do not drive him to a reckless indifference of right and
wrong, and crush in him the feeling that he has a noble
spirit within, which should shrink instinctively from
moral degradation."

Any person who wishes to test the truth of these remarks may easily do so by wading through a few of our
dramatic biographies. I recommend to the study of all
"would-be actors" the life of Edmund Kean, whose
privations and sufferings in pursuit of his goal are more
like romance than reality. He was compelled to pander
to the public for the mere sake of gaining his daily bread.
For years he tramped about the country, his sword over
his shoulder, and upon it slung a slender bundle, containing his scanty wardrobe, gaining a livelihood by pub-
lichouse exhibitions, teaching dancing, fencing, &c., &c.
Even the great John Kemble himself had his periods of
poverty and his days of starvation. Once upon a time

he was unable to pay his laundress a shilling for dressing his linen, and she refused in consequence to give him up his shirts.

An eminent London manager of the present day has more than once publicly alluded to his early struggles. On one occasion he mentioned that he had performed a walking journey of seventy-two miles with only fourpence-halfpenny in his pocket. He also at one time made a penniless passage from Folkstone to London in a coasting vessel, as part of a cargo of leather. His first engagement was to play walking gentlemen, and be useful, at ten shillings per week; and on being deserted by his manager, he made money by making out the Christmas accounts of the country tradesmen. This manager's name is Buckstone !

A few members of the company at Shippham usually took a stroll on the Sunday forenoons. It was generally the "painter," the "heavy man," and myself—when they retailed stories of their wondrous adventures and stage experiences. We had only one incident to talk about personal to the company, and it was really a laughable one. Walls the prompter, who was useful on the stage, happened one evening to play the *Duke* in the tragedy of "Othello," having previously given directions to a girl of all-work who attended on the wardrobe to bring him a gill of the best whisky. Not wishing to go out, as the evening was wet, the girl employed a little boy, who happened to be standing about, to execute the commission, and the little fellow, (no person being present to stop him,) without considering the impropriety of such

an act, coolly walked on to the stage, and delivered his
message—the state of affairs at this ridiculous juncture
being exactly as follows:—The senate was assembled,
and the speaker was—

> "*Brabantio.* So did I yours: Good, your grace, pardon me;
> Neither my place, nor aught I heard of business,
> Hath raised me from my bed; nor doth the general care
> Take hold of me; for my particular grief
> Is of so floodgate and o'erbearing nature,
> That it engluts and swallows other sorrows,
> And is still itself
>     "*Duke.*          Why, what's the matter?"

*Here the little boy walked on to the stage, with a
pewter gill-stoup, and thus delivered himself:*—"It's
jist the whusky, Mr Walls; and I coudna get ony at
fourpence, so yer awn the landlord a penny; and he says
it's time you was payin' what's doon i' the book."

The roars of laughter which followed are indescribable;
and, I daresay, the scene will long remain stereotyped in
the recollection of all who witnessed it.

As time went on, the town gave signs of being exhausted, and then commenced the "benefits," that sure
sign of a speedy winding up of the theatrical season. The
fag-end of a season is always a marked period in a country
theatre. Old Ducrow, in one of his conversations, gives
an inimitable description of it—too long, however, to
quote here; but it may be found in Alfred Bunn's work,
"Before and Behind the Curtain." Some of the company,
who have obtained better engagements, make no ceremony
about going—they go at once. Others who, like myself,
had no moneyed inducement—those for whom "the ghost

walk'd" in vain—soon get tired of the hard study consequent on heavy benefits, and under the pretence of being insulted, leave the company. The "study" at such periods is quite awful; in fact, so awful as to preclude any chance of its being accomplished. As for *acting* a part, there is no time to learn how to do that. Some actors think nothing at all, upon the occasion of their "ben," of putting up four plays or so; and as the same thing may be done for a week running, it is no joke, I can honestly say.

I never myself took a benefit, but I cannot help saying that I think the benefit system a bad one; it quite destroys an actor's independence; and the taking of a benefit is one of the great causes of an actor being so frequently seen in the public-houses—it is in these places he "makes" his ben. He is obsequiously civil to all whom he sees, and appears profoundly grateful when any one takes a pit ticket from him; in fact, he has to sink his independence in order to sell his tickets. Then he torments all his friends to sell for him; if he is slightly in debt to his baker or butcher, these unfortunate tradesmen are at once saddled with a score of pit, a dozen of stall, and fifty gallery cards. He must sell most of them, it is the best chance he will have of obtaining payment of his little debt. If the *bénéficiaire* be a freemason, he attends the free-and-easies of the lodge, and sings, and otherwise tumbles, in the hope of a patronage. A patronage is the grand hope of the actor, as an occasional bespeak is to the country manager. No stone is left unturned to obtain the colonel and officers of a regiment, if it be a garrison town; even a volunteer band is a godsend; and in this way a few pounds may be sometimes added to the actor's precarious income. Often enough the actor only works for the manager, the receipts not being enough to divide.

Considering the terrible work which is necessary in a country theatre at the benefit-time, it is no wonder the company sometimes breaks up rather suddenly. It did so on the occasion to which I allude. One slunk away after another in double-quick time, till all who were going had departed. The manager was left nearly *solus*— monarch of all he surveyed—viz., three men and two women, who were removing with him to Dundee. Seeing this, I began also to think of removing; and as I was not indebted in any way to the manager, I did so as soon as it suited my own convenience, having made up my mind to turn my back on Scotland, and try to woo fortune in the theatres of "merry England."

So ended my two months' novitiate at Shippham; and if it learned me nothing else, it at least taught me that to become an actor it is quite as necessary to begin at the beginning as when you learn any other profession. A man cannot become a surgeon and perform a difficult operation all at once. He must serve the necessary apprenticeship; therefore, why expect great success if you begin at *Hamlet* instead of *Bernardo?* All who seriously wish to adopt the stage as a way of living should recollect this, and "serve their time" to it in a regular way.

# CHAPTER V.

ENGLAND was naturally fixed upon as the goal of my
ambition. I had long resolved to try the theatres of
England, considering them the best field for a young
actor, both on account of their being so numerous, and
because the press takes more notice of theatrical doings
there, and so brings one's name more prominently before
the public. Besides, the player's head-quarters may
naturally be considered to be in London. It is always to
the great metropolis that country managers resort to fill
up or strengthen their companies; hence the employer,
and those seeking employment, consider the best common
meeting-place to be London. Many English actors, however, think Scotland the better field of the two; and say
that the Scottish people are more frequent in their
attendance at the theatre than the English, from their
being a more intellectual and a better-educated class.
Perhaps the real cause consists in the English people's
having a far greater variety of amusements than the more
staid people who live north of the Tweed. The English-
man has his cricket-field, his singing-saloon, his shooting
matches, his tea-gardens, and his skittle-ground, and John

Bull makes the greatest possible use of the whole range of the sporting world; but the Scotchman has not these resources, and is even restricted now in the number of hours in which he drinks his beer—and hence, when the opportunity offers itself, he runs to the theatre if the bill be at all attractive; in fact, it is " merry " England, and consequently, as I thought, certain to be a better field for the poor player. I naturally thought, also, that as it was greatly larger than Scotland, and contained a far greater number of large towns densely populated, that there would be more money to spend on theatrical entertainments than there could possibly be in the little fourth-rate towns which dot the " land of the mountain and the flood."

Before finally starting for England, I was prevailed upon by our scene-painter, and one or two other members of the company, to join a "gagging" expedition to a few of the small towns of Ayrshire.

Nothing is so common with actors whc may be engaged in a large market-town at the close of a season, as, in the interregnum which generally occurs before the manager is ready to open the next theatre on the circuit, for the company to divide and start in little . knots to the surrounding villages in order to enliven the rustic inhabitants with all kinds of entertainment. Dancing, spouting, posturing, magic-lanterns, dissolving views, and many other varieties of the means of amusing, are called into active requisition. A successful little tour is sometimes the result, but more frequently the affair is a miserable failure, and ends in debt and disgust.

Ours was a sickly expedition, and never throve, notwith-

standing our having a magic-lantern and three performing dogs, which were the property of the scene-painter.
We mostly played in the largest room of the best-fre-
quented public-house ; and our receipts were poor indeed,
generally averaging from 6s. to 16s. per night, out of
which travelling expenses, printing expenses, living expenses, and theatrical expenses had all to be paid.  The
result was the usual one in such cases—everybody that
would give " tick " was applied to, and after we had got
all out of them that could be got, we departed, as quietly
as possible of course, and left the deluded ones to get
their cash as best they could.   So it occurred that we left
the stench of the strolling player behind us in some half-
dozen villages.    This stench is debt — universal debt.
The reader, I daresay, will be able, by the use of a little
arithmetic, to see that our receipts could do no more
than keep us alive, and that only in a kind of miserable,
half-existing mode of life, anything but agreeable to those
who had not been seasoned to it, by being well-initiated into the mysteries of a stroller's existence, or able to sponge
on admirers for small treats of bread and cheese, or
thoroughly up to the art of borrowing an occasional half-
crown from a green acquaintance.   Many of the strollers
are adepts in this kind of business.   I knew one person
who boasted that he had never paid a penny for drink
since he entered the profession.   For myself I lived on
my capital—that is, I dipped pretty freely into my own
private purse—and it was lucky for me, that with my
notions of comfort, I had such a good *dernier ressort,* for
it was greatly needed.

Our receipts for a week's work, with two performances on Saturday, were generally as follows :—

| | |
|---|---|
| Monday, . . . . . . . | 8s. |
| Wednesday, . . . . . . | 5s. |
| Thursday, . . . . . . | 4s. 6d. |
| Saturday, . . . . . . . | 20s. |
| Making a grand total of | 37s. 6d. |

And when this was divided among five people, after deducting a necessary and paid expenditure of half-a-crown for candles, &c., it left us just seven shillings each to live upon, which any reader, not actually destitute of arithmetical perception, will find is exactly one shilling per day ; and it may safely be left to economists, both social and political, to say how this money should be expended, in order to extract from it the greatest amount of food, raiment, and the other etceteras essential to animal life.

What kind of pieces did you play? the reader very naturally asks.

Oh, all kinds, is my reply. We were adepts, as strollers usually are, in drawing bills. We stuck at nothing, whether possible or impossible ; and we took particular care to put a good face on all matters appertaining to the company and our resources.

We usually managed to hide our poverty pretty well ; and, as I was considered the best-dressed man of the *corps*, it generally fell to my lot to be sent forward in advance to prime the next village that we had selected as our scene of operation. Of course, I made up the best story possible, embellishing my narrative with appropriate quotations from the great bard, in order to shew my learning. The landlord of the hall or barn where we expected to pitch our tent was sure to be inquisitive, and would likely ask, "What players are they?"

My answer in such cases was pat—"Even those you were wont to take such delight in; the tragedians of the city."

Then, of course, came, "How chances it they travel?"

"Oh, it's our interregnum at present," would be my reply. "The season has just closed at Shippham, and we do not open at Dundee for a week or ten days yet."

"What kind of bill do you put out?" was, in all probability, the next question.

This was just what I wanted to be asked, as it afforded me scope to describe, in a rather imaginative way, I must confess, what we could do; or rather, to be honest, what we would attempt to do.

"We shall open, sir, with Tobin's admired comedy of 'The Honeymoon;' after which, the Learned Dogs will represent a little pantomime; this will be followed by an Exhibition of the Magic-Lantern, with movable figures; then we will give a *mélange* of singing and dancing, and a solo on the accordion; the whole to conclude with the grand new farce of 'Polkamania.'"

"Well, you have quantity enough at any rate; we shall see what your quality is when you come. You seem a decent-like fellow, and if the rest are like you, you can have my room; but the last lot who had it never paid me a copper for it, the swindling scoundrels! I hope you won't come that dodge, and leave me in the lurch as they did."

Such was generally the termination of my mission ; and in due time, the company would arrive, generally under the cloud of night, so as to escape observation—as the player's seedy coat dislikes the glare of the great orb of day ; and, besides, each member of the company had to carry a portion of the scenery, and, under the circumstances attendant on such carriership, we greatly disliked publicity. Stealing into the village, then, in this manner, we took possession of the place, and had it fitted up before the landlord had any idea that the "things," as he called them, had been brought upon the scene of action.

This system was repeated till the company broke up. which was, I think, in about three weeks.

# CHAPTER VI.

## "ALEXANDER THE GREAT."

NOTHING of very peculiar interest, or at least of sufficient interest to relate, occurred during my sojourn with these " gaggers."

Feeling, however, that it was lost time to wander about the country in this state of downright vagabondism—for such our mode of life undoubtedly was, although we made great professions in the bills about the high moral teaching of a well-regulated stage—I resolved at once to give up the gagging department, and endeavour to obtain a respectable situation and—a salary, which, at the outset of an actor's career, is generally a rather difficult matter to accomplish. With the view, therefore, of achieving this desirable change in the best and speediest manner, I wrote out a neat circular, stating my qualifications and aspirations, and sent it to as many managers as I could recollect the names of ; and, among others, I sent one to the late Mr Alexander, "sole proprietor of the then Theatre-Royal, Glasgow." But "Alick's" house has since been burned down, and a new theatre has been erected on the same site by Mrs Glover.

To my great astonishment, "Alick," as he was familiarly called by his townsmen, sent me, Frederick George Capelton, (that was my theatrical name,) an offer to come to "his *theature.*" The salary was very small—only fourteen shillings a-week—but then "the *Ghost* walked" regularly, and that was a great temptation to a young man who had never yet enjoyed the pleasure of entering the treasury of a theatre on the official errand of salary-drawing.

In due time my arrival was announced at the temple of the drama in Dunlop Street, and I was ushered into the sanctum of the great man.

"Ah, Mr ——, what's your name? How do you do," said he; "and what is your business with me?"

"My name is Capelton, and this is a note I received from you to join your company," was my reply.

"Yes, young man, I recollect; and no doubt you think, like other young stagers, that you are fit to play all the great characters of the drama—eh?"

"Once I thought that, sir, but I have been tamed down a little."

"What's your line of business?" said "Alick."

"I do not think I am capable yet of sustaining a line of business; but I think of studying low comedy chiefly."

"Can you sing?"

"Yes, and play the violin a little as well; but I have never yet sung on the stage, except in a chorus."

"Oh, well, you seem to have some modesty, which is commendable in a young man, and a scarce commodity among actors; but no doubt you have already done great things. Did you ever try *Hamlet?*"

I saw at once that he had heard of my adventure at

Threadham, so I laughingly replied "That I did at one time attempt that character, and "—

"Failed in it," said he; "and served you right, sir. Do as I did; work your way from before the mast, and get on by degrees—that is the certain way to success— and you may consider yourself fortunate in having me to help you. Look at me, sir; I have created this great establishment—this 'theature'—out of nothing, and I am proud of the fact, sir. It's the finest 'theature' out of London. You must work hard, Mr Capelton, and play all kinds of parts, and you will get on. Don't be above doing anything you can get to do; that is the road to success, sir, in every profession."

I could not do less than thank Mr Alexander for his advice; and that gentleman calling his stage-manager, said to him, "This is Mr Capelton, for the second utility. You can give him the *Second Actor, Bernardo,* and the *Second Gravedigger* for to-morrow night, and he can come on in the mobs. Sir, I am not above doing that myself, although I am manager here, and proprietor as well. Good-morning, sir;" and stroking his long chin, the great man "booed" me out of his presence.

Such was my introduction to "Alexander the Great," as some of his friends called him, from the fact of his having fought and gained so many theatrical campaigns. As to the "business" which was allotted to my share, the reader may picture my astonishment! three parts in one piece, and in the Glasgow Theatre-Royal, too; but it was part of Alexander's system to do with as few people as he could; and it is often related that he has gone through " Rob Roy" with five men and three women.

I did not get much to do with Mr Alexander—so far as parts of importance were concerned. This paucity of leading characters was amply made up, however, by the multiplicity of "little bits" in each play that fell to my share; and my having often to change was so confusing, that it frequently puzzled me to find out who I was. Such characters were called by the prompter "wing parts"—*i.e.*, parts that could be studied at the wing just before going on the stage. The weather was not more variable than I was—professionally. At one time I was a clansman of *Rob Roy;* next, a soldier in pursuit of him; after that, a person siding with virtue under the direst oppression; then again changed in a few minutes into one of the tools of the dread tyrant, who, with a heel of iron, was doing the oppressive; then I became a gallant, bowing admiration to the satin slipper (very dirty, by the way, and much in need of a good bread-crumbing) of some signora of high degree; being again transformed in half-an-hour (and after having partaken, at my own expense of course, of half-a-pint of ale and a sandwich) into a low spy in the interest and pay of her jealous-minded lord. A few brief weeks, indeed, saw me enjoying a taste of all conditions of society—kings, lords, and commoners; Spaniards, Cockneys, Irishmen, or Yankees, are all the same to the man who plays the second "utility." In short, that versatile gentleman is like a kaleidoscope, ever-changing, and, like the chameleon, he

must also reflect whatever character is laid upon him ;
and all this must be done, observe, you ladies and gentlemen of the public, at the extremely moderate charge of
fourteen shillings per week, for which sum you have likewise to find your own boots and shoes, collars, hats,
feathers, swords, &c.

I remained with "Alick" till the conclusion of his season, but no event of the slightest interest occurred to
render the period at all remarkable. Poor Alexander is
in his grave, and all the money he earned by his hard industry was swallowed up in the maelstrom of the Western
Bank of Scotland !

He was a very extraordinary man, and although he had
his foibles and eccentricities, there have been few like
him. His energy was great, and his perseverance inex-
haustible—the leading point in his character seemed to
be to make his theatre pay ; but, indeed, that is properly
enough the leading point with all managers. It has been
said that Alexander was narrow-minded, mean in money
matters, and gave small salaries; but to me he appeared
a true type of the thorough Scotchman. He had known
what it was to be in want, and when by hard work and
energetic pushing he had secured a competency, he did
right to take care of it. He had done everything that
could be done in his line—he had bearded and fought
the patentees of both Edinburgh and Glasgow. When
the stage of the Theatre-Royal in Glasgow was blazing
out with blue fire, "Alick" was engaged at penny prices
in setting off red fire in the cellars below it ; and what
with the firing of guns in the upper house, and the clash

of sabres in the lower one, the public felt no lack of excitement.

John Henry Alexander had unequalled powers, and combined a strong intellect with inimitable tact; and if there have been managers who have excelled him in acting, there have been none who evinced a loftier sense of integrity; and those who have called in question his small salaries ought to bear in mind that they were always paid, and—I speak with the authority of experience—it is much better to engage for twelve shillings a-week and get it, than to be promised double the amount and be paid with nothing. Poor "Alick," let his name be honoured among the votaries of Thespis for the energy of character which built him up a noble fortune. There is greatness even in this; and when his hand now rests from its labour, and his fertile and busy mind has sunk into its leaden sleep, we must not allow our recollections of him to be blotted out all at once, for he was a warm and leal friend to many, and ever ready to sympathise with the child of misfortune; and let us therefore bear in mind that "charity covereth a multitude of sins."

The following brief sketch embodies the principal points in Alexander's rather eventful career; of course, a much longer biography might be given were this the place for it:—

John Henry Alexander was born at Dunbar, in July 1796, of somewhat obscure but respectable parents. His boyhood was distinguished by the same resolute and persevering qualities that characterised his riper years. Early exhibiting great powers of memory, possessing a good voice and a handsome person, he was finally, after many amateur performances, launched upon the stage, under the auspices of the celebrated Harry Johnstone, and made his first appearance as a legitimate member of the profession at Ayr. His personal advantages and great industry soon made him a favourite, and after a short but successful season, he was engaged for the Queen's Theatre at Glasgow, then under the management of the elder Macready, father of the present eminent tragedian of that name. From thence he proceeded to Newcastle, where he had an opportunity of performing with the celebrated Mrs Jordan. His reputation attracted at this time the attention of Mr W. H. Murray of Edinburgh, with whom he shortly after contracted an engagement. Mr Alexander was only twenty years of age when he became a member of the theatrical company at Edinburgh, a fact which, of itself, speaks highly for his reputation. There is no doubt that, during the ten years he performed with Mr Murray, he obtained immense success with the Edinburgh critics of the period. The characters in which he excelled at that time were, *Dandie Dinmont* in "Guy Mannering," and *Ratcliffe* in the "Heart of Midlothian;" and as the Waverley dramas were in extraordinary repute, he was all but indispensable to the success of these and similar pieces. His powerful mind, free from the cares of management, enabled him to perform an extensive range of characters with great ability; but what contributed as much as any other element to his success was, an excellent taste in dress, and invariable correctness in reading. These are points frequently neglected by young actors, but never so with impunity. After having established his character as an actor in Edinburgh, and by judicious economy saved some money, he assumed the management of the Carlisle and Dumfries theatres, where he first gave an example of his unequalled powers of making a theatre pay. In the year 1822, Mr Alexander commenced his career as a Glasgow manager in Dunlop Street, which, as a minor house, infringed on the patent of the Royal Theatre in Queen Street. During the following seven years he carried on, through every kind of opposition, not only the Glasgow house, but also the provincial theatres at Carlisle and Dumfries, along with the Adelphi at Edinburgh. His successful management of these various enterprises developed his extraordinary power of labour, and indefatigable courage and perseverance. In 1829, he became the possessor of the patent for Glasgow, built a magnificent theatre, and continued from that period until within a few months of his death a course of profitable management, which enabled him to leave his family in a position of comparative affluence.

Were it the author's cue merely to retail anecdotes of "Alick," this little book might be filled with them. Of course there is not sufficient space at his command to admit of this, and the following are only given as samples of the general stock which is floating about in the " profession," heartily at the service of any collector of "ana" who will take the trouble to book them :—

### ALICK AND "AULD CLOCKY."*

Some of my readers will doubtless remember a queer-looking old man, who for many years took the money at the gallery door of "Alick's" theatre. He rejoiced in the euphonious cognomen of "Auld Clocky," and was, in his way, nearly as great an original as his master. One night, so many boys went out between the play and the farce that "Auld Clocky" was compelled to resort to the singular expedient of chalking their backs, his checks being all given away. The loungers outside were not long in ascertaining the circumstance, and lo, in a short time, lots of little boys crowded past "Auld Clocky," each one bearing on his back the white cross of St Andrew. On finding that more were coming up than went down, he seized upon a little boy at random and turned him down stairs, after appropriating his bonnet. The boy, who had really paid his sixpence, immediately went home and complained to his father, a tailor named Weir, who lived opposite the theatre. This person determined to appeal to Mr Alexander for redress of his son's wrongs, and, with that object, forthwith proceeded to the stage door of the theatre and asked for the manager, who quickly made his appearance, dressed as a sailor, with a drawn cutlass in his hand and pistols in his belt.

"Well, sir, what is it?" he inquired in no gentle tones.

"The old man at the gallery stairs has taken my son's

---

* The above anecdote appeared during the lifetime of Mr Alexander, but a feeling of delicacy prevented the author from mentioning that "Auld Clocky" was no other than the manager's father.

bonnet, and turned him out of the theatre," said the snip in a tremulous voice, evidently not a little awed by the warlike figure before him.

" Taken your son's bonnet, and turned him out of the theatre," repeated " Alick;" " just go up to the gallery door, sir, and I'll be with you directly." Obedient to this direction, the tailor reached the post of " Auld Clocky " just as the manager, still armed to the teeth, made his appearance from another quarter.

" So, sir, you have been stealing the boys' bonnets," said he, eyeing the culprit with the look of a hyena, " and chalking their backs ; gracious G—d, that accounts for the two tons of chalk that have gone amissing from the painting room. Give the boy back his bonnet, ' ye hoary-headed old villain,' or (and hereupon he flourished the cutlass in a manner that indicated a desire to bring the career of the aged ' Clocky' to an immediate termination) I will cut you into minced collops."

It is almost needless to say that this command was quickly obeyed, and that the tailor's son was re-admitted to the gallery to witness the remainder of the evening's entertainment.

## " DOON WI' THE DOO !"

I recollect being present in the Dunlop Street Theatre one night, about twenty years ago, when a ludicrous circumstance occurred. The manager personated a hunter in a piece the name of which I have forgotten. In the course of its action he had to discharge his gun at a bird, a stuffed effigy of which *should* have been dropped from the flats. But no bird was forthcoming, and terrible was the rage of "Alick" thereat. Shaking his fist at the property-man above, he ground out between his clenched teeth, "Doon wi' the doo, and be ——, ye ——." The words were perfectly audible to the people in front of the pit, and a roar of laughter accompanied the descent of the "doo,"—*i.e.*, pigeon.

## "ALICK" AND HIS OWN ORANGE-PEEL.

Mr Alexander had at one time a dispute with a neighbour of his about the contents of an ash-pit situated near the theatre. "Alick" asserted his claim to the whole deposit, every ounce of which he said came from his establishment,—adding that "he knew d—d well the colour of his own sawdust and his own orange-peel."

## THE ADVANTAGES OF BEING IN THE ORCHESTRA.

One or two seasons before his retirement, one of Mr Alexander's musicians asked him for an increase of salary, "Raise your salary," said the astonished manager ; "oh no, sir, I cannot afford to do that. All the people are leaving this beautiful theatre and going to that d—d bandbox above Walker's stables, (the Prince's.) And besides, sir, I think your position in my establishment is not to be sneezed at; you have a seat in the pit every night, and you pay nothing, either on ordinary occasions or when stars are performing."

## WATER *versus* FIRE.

When Messrs Byrne and Seymour took the Dunlop

Street house " over Alick's head," he made the expression literal by sub-renting the premises beneath, which were then occupied as a store. This cavernous-looking place he fitted up as a theatre, which he called " The Dominion of Fancy," a most appropriate name, as almost everything that should appertain to a theatre was left to that faculty of the mind. As may be imagined, no good-will existed between the rival houses. Byrne and Seymour were denounced by Alexander, in long harangues from the stage, as monopolists and enemies to the drama, while their followers, to square accounts, resorted to every scheme they could think of to annoy Alexander. Their most successful performance in this way was boring holes in the floor, and pouring down water on the heads of the denizens of " The Dominion of Fancy." " Alick" was not disposed to submit tamely to this treatment. He produced a piece, which he called " The Battle of Waterloo," with " new and startling military effects never before attempted in any theatre ;" and startling enough they were to the audience in the place above, for the company of soldiers whom " Alick " had engaged for the occasion kept up such a tremendous fusilade, that the voice of Stentor himself (had that ancient chanced to belong to Byrne and Seymour's company) would have been entirely inaudible. By this and other expedients " Alick " at length succeeded in dislodging his enemies from their stronghold, which he took possession of with flying colours.

# CHAPTER VII.

## "WILLIAM THE CONQUEROR."

FROM the metropolis of the west, and its gigantic temples of commerce, to the capital of the east, and its temples of learning and of law, is now, by means of the railway, but a step; that is, in point of time, and it is by time that distance must be measured in these days of railways and electric telegraphs. In the west I served under the banner of "Alexander the Great," and, by the merest accident, I came to lend a little assistance to another great man,—viz., William Henry Murray, manager of the Theatre-Royal, Edinburgh, or, as I used to designate him, "William the Conqueror," from the struggles he had had to make his position.

The Theatre-Royal, Glasgow, was about to close on account of the Sacramental preachings, and I was preparing to take my departure for Liverpool, when our stage-manager told me that Mr Murray had written through to secure the services of one or two of our utility people, as one of his folks had met with an accident, and another had left. "Mr Capelton, this will be a capital chance for you; you have some good properties, and are pretty well rigged out, and you know it is easier to get a situation out of the Edinburgh theatre than out of any other. You ought to go at once; the 'sal.' is £1 a-week, and you may be engaged for the summer." Such was the information and advice tendered to me on the occasion by my friend the stage-manager, over a little cold whisky and water mixed up with sugar, at the tavern opposite the Theatre-Royal, Dunlop Street—of course at my expense. I was pleased at being selected as one of the two, and thinking the being able to say in England that I had been on the Edinburgh stage an advantage, I at once jumped at the offer, and next day I was in the green-room at Shakspeare Square.

I am much surprised that no literary man has thought of writing the life and times of Mr Murray. Could any gentleman gain access to his papers and correspondence and obtain the confidence of his family, and also a knowledge of the progress of the theatre in Edinburgh for the last half century, it would make a most amusing and entertaining volume.

Mr Murray, it is well known, was highly respected; and in the days of Sir Walter Scott he mixed in the literary and artistic society of Edinburgh on terms of equality with the Great Wizard of the North, meeting at his table Lockhart, Moore, Hogg, Wilson, Jeffrey, and Ballantyne, and others who then ruled the roast in all matters of art and taste in Auld Reekie.

As I was only a few weeks connected with the Edinburgh company, I shall not venture to say much about it. I found Mr Murray always polite and kind, so far as a "nod" was concerned; but I do not think he ever addressed me half-a-dozen times during my short stay in his company. He was a singularly reticent man among his actors, but most honourable in all his transactions; the treasury was always open, and the business of the theatre went on like clock-work. No man ever left Mr Murray's theatre on a Saturday without his week's salary in his pocket.

The principal members of his company at this time were—Mr Glover, Mr Mackay, (better known as *Bailie Nicol Jarvie,*) Mr Howard, Mr Lloyd, Miss Nicol, &c., all of them well known in the profession. The work at Edinburgh was not so intolerable as I found it in Mr Alexander's "theature." Some nights I was not required at all, and in general I never had to appear in more than one character in the same play, and often enough only in one piece per evening. This was pleasant, and I enjoyed it exceedingly, except for the fact that I did not get on fast enough.

As nearly every person given to theatricals is aware, Mr Murray was famous for what were called in Edinburgh his "Farewell Addresses." By this term was meant the address usually given to the audience at the end of each season, and I cannot do better than lay before my readers the one which I heard delivered at the close of that season during which I was a member of his company. It was as follows:—

> " When last we brought our winter to a close
> A sober sadness murmur'd through our prose;
> And when the curtain on our summer fell,
> The playbills in my absence said, ' Farewell.'
> Dark were our prospects then, subdued our tone,
> ' *And melancholy mark'd us for her own.*'
> Hence some supposed I *sulk'd,* or lack'd the fire

Which in more youthful days essay'd the lyre.
*Sulks* I deny; although I will not swear
I'm not, like other men, the worse for wear;
'Tis one-and-forty years since I began
The acting trade, and that tries any man;
While thirty-seven of those forty-one
Have in your service, gentle masters, run;
But brass corrodes, and iron rusts with age,
Can, then, the mimic children of the stage
Hope to elude the tyrant? We may writhe
And struggle, but cannot 'scape the scythe:
Although 'tis wonderful what renovation
Is oft the product of your approbation!
You frown—the aged actor droops—but when
Your smiles return, '*Richard's himself again;*'
Applauding hands his former fires renew,
And, like the veteran that Goldsmith drew,
He once more, ere his lessening sands be run,
'*Shoulders his crutch, and shews how fields were won.*'
So I to-night, embolden'd by success,
And brighter prospects, sport a new '*address.*'
'*Errors excepted,*' our accounts give reason
To calculate a profit on the season,
And no mistake, no error of summation,
No phrenological creation;
'*No coinage of the heat-oppressed brain,*'
At which the manager may snatch in vain;
But a *de-facto* balance, plain and clear,
And this, I'm sure, you will be glad to hear.
Yes, friends, I'm certain, from your kind applause,
You fully share the happiness you cause;
And though my management may blunders show,
Yet with Jack Falstaff you'll exclaim, I know,
'*We're very glad you've got the money, though.*'
One time I own, we thought the die was cast,
And that this season was indeed our last;
For, from the schedule, we had little doubt
That '*the North British*' meant to turn us out.
In Fancy's ear we heard their engines roar
Where *human locomotives* had before;
In Fancy's eye we saw the parting day

> Which tore us from our Theatre away—
> When Lloyd and Howard, every pleasure past,
> Pack'd up their wigs, and fondly look'd their last—
> When Glover left these scenes and sought relief
> In all the silent tragedy of grief;
> And Murray, poor Murray, counting all his store,
> Stood bathed in tears to think he 'd make no more.
> But let us hope our anxious fears are vain,
> And that in Shakspeare Square may long remain
> Glover and Lloyd, and all our ' *first-class train,*'
> Both male and female, tragic, light, and heavy,
> With General Murray to lead on the bevy,
> To toll of many seasons yet the knell,
> Offer his grateful thanks, and say, Farewell ! "

As I have given a brief sketch of the career of " Alexander the Great," I shall here subjoin a companion account of " William the Conqueror;" only premising that it was written at the period of that gentleman's retirement from the stage, on the 22d of October 1851, at which time I had " cut" the boards, and was essaying a literary line of business :—

Mr W. H. Murray is a grandson of Sir John Murray of Broughton, Prince Charles Edward's secretary during the rebellion of 1745. At a very early age theatrical necessity gave him to the stage, on which he made his first appearance, when only two years old, as *Puck*. The place where this occurred was Bath,—where his father was lessee of the theatre, and a much-esteemed actor of the period. He afterwards removed to London, where he was engaged at one of the national theatres. Mr W. H. Murray had now entered on the profession, and his first steps were guided by a Siddons and a Kemble. After receiving lessons in his art from Mr Charles Far-

ley, with whom he was a favourite, he came to Scotland,
and found fortune and a home among the citizens of
Edinburgh. Mr Murray made his *début* in the same
theatre (the *Adelphi*) in which he now takes his farewell benefit. At first he was not a favourite among the
"canny Scotch;" but time, faith, and energy, brought
about a revolution in public opinion, and after a certain
period of probation he nightly grew in favour as an actor,
his efforts gaining him the admiration of the town and
the applause of all who saw him.

Mr Henry Siddons, Murray's brother-in-law, had in
1809 purchased, for the large sum of £42,000, the right
to the patent of the Theatre-Royal of Edinburgh, and
the company, including Murray, removed to Shakspeare
Square. This heavy burden weighed down the energies
of poor Siddons, who, after struggling for a few years,
bade adieu to the world and its vanities, leaving the concern in debt, and his wife and children almost totally
unprovided for. It was now that Murray's great energies
were called into requisition. The whole weight of management and retrievement fell upon his shoulders, and he
worked like a very giant to sustain the stability of the
house that was to give food to his widowed sister and her
fatherless little ones. Edmund Kean was engaged, Miss
O'Neil was brought down, and the illustrious John
Kemble gave his assistance; but the grand panacea
which saved the theatre was the melo-dramatic opera of
" Rob Roy," which ran for a long number of nights, and
produced a sum of £3000. Indeed, the Waverley dramas,
both before and after this period, (1819,) were almost the

stock-in-trade of the Edinburgh theatres. It was here, from various concurring fortunate circumstances, that they had the strongest hold on the public; and although they put money in the purse of almost every manager in the kingdom, in Edinburgh they rained fortune in golden showers into the dramatic treasury. There was also at this period a first-rate resident company for the perfect carrying out of such plays, and not the least worthy of mention among the number were Mrs Henry Siddons— a clever and graceful actress, and the inimitable *Bailie Jarvie*—Mr Mackay.

It would require too much of our space, nor is it necessary, to enumerate all the stars brought to bear with triumphant success on the fortunes of the theatre— suffice it to say, that under the spirited management now adopted, the house was speedily relieved from all its difficulties. The establishment in 1819 of the Edinburgh Theatrical Fund, and the visit of George IV. to see "Rob Roy" at the Theatre-Royal, are well-known occurrences, in all of which Mr Murray took a prominent and efficient part, and up till 1830, when he secured the patent on his own account, there is little in the unvarying round of his fortunes worth relating.

In the same year he also became joint-lessee with Mr Yates, of London, of the Adelphi, which, after a time, was left entirely under his own management, and conducted as a summer theatre. At the end of 1844, Mr Murray lost his accomplished sister, who, for a quarter of a century, was a distinguished member of the Edinburgh theatre. This was a severe blow to him, and he felt it so much that he retired for a time from all active duty in the establishment. From that time to this, death has been busy among his early friends, and many of those who had supported and encouraged him in his early struggles are gathered to the grave. The death of Sir William Allan, two years ago, and the retirement from permanent duty of Mr Mackay, seem to have determined Mr Murray to seek repose, and retire from the toils and cares of management, while yet almost as able as ever to delight and instruct the public with his inimitable personations.

Mr Murray, during his long sojourn in Edinburgh, has been honoured with the friendship and approbation of some of our most celebrated citizens. Sir Walter Scott was one of his warmest patrons, and often took occasion to speak of "honest Will. Murray" with warm commendation and respect; and during the period of his brilliant run of fortune, the great novelist frequently graced the theatre with his presence, the leader of a gay bevy of the intellectual and the honoured of the city. There in his company might at times be seen Joanna Baillie, Moore, Wilson, Jeffrey, Lockhart, Mackenzie, Dugald Stewart, the Ettrick Shepherd, the Ballantynes, and numerous others whose names and genius were wont to cast a halo over the length and breadth of the land. These, too, were the days when the Edinburgh stage could boast of its occasional visits from Kemble, Kean, Liston, the elder Matthews, Emery, Munden, and O'Neil. At the present day these are but names. John Kemble is in his grave— the fiery Kean is hushed in death—the charming O'Neil graces another sphere—Munden, Liston, and nearly all their contemporaries, have flitted from the scene, and the boards of the present day are trod by a new race of performers.

To offer, in the brief limits of such a sketch as the present, any detailed critique on the genius for delineation possessed by Mr Murray, would be almost impossible. We could fill some of our pages with a description of his achievements as an actor. His *Falstaff*—his *Osric* —his *Tony Lumpkin*—his *Mock Duke*—his *Dominique* —his *Grandfather Whitehead,* pass before us, as in a mirror, followed by a long procession of other parts, all of them equally excellent. Every character sustained by Mr Murray was a portrait painted by an artist—full of excellence—a living, walking personation of the character, no matter what it might be. A foppish footman, an eccentric citizen, a jealous husband, a doting father, or an old worn-out *roué,* all came alike to Murray. The flash of his genius vivified and lighted up the part, and placed it before his audience a breathing type of what such an actor was capable of realising.

The painter retires from his easel, and his fame is perpetuated on the canvas—the sculptor leaves behind him the enduring block of marble, which for ages tells the tale of his labours—the warrior retires, and his battles are pictured in the pages of history—the statesman is ousted from the scene of his triumphs, but his sayings are preserved—his deeds endure for ages; but the actor!—is his history not written in water and dried up by the next day's sun? He exists but for the time—he amuses us with his merry humours, sends us laughing home, pleased with ourselves and all the world besides. Truly, he lives but in the memory of his contemporaries—for a brief period some garrulous old play-goer may prattle of his achievements—then his fame dies out, "leaving not a wrack behind."

Whilst engaged with Mr Murray, I had an opportunity one day of taking a peep at an old cash-book of the Theatre-Royal, from which I obtained a few notes of the salaries and expenses of that establishment during the year 1835, during which Mr C. Kean played one of his most successful engagements, and when the stock company was of unusual excellence. Thinking that these notes might be interesting to my readers, I have taken the trouble to transcribe some of them here.

As the pantomime is now the *piece de resistance* of the Edinburgh theatre, and enjoys a long run, although the critics, I see, usually cut it up as a bit of literary trash, it will be interesting to state that the pantomime of 1835 was played only for twenty nights, and was backed up for its last week by the engagement of Mr Wilson, the great vocalist. The prices in those days were much higher than now,—the upper gallery being one shilling, and the other places of the house in proportion. The money taken on the first night of the pantomime (Friday, 26th December 1834) was £87, upwards of £45 of which was received at half-price. On the last night of the pantomime, for the benefit of the pantomimist, the takings were £50. Now-a-days, our pantomimes will run fifty or sixty nights, and yield a gross receipt of perhaps £3000, with a sixpenny gallery and a shilling pit.

The salary list of Saturday 24th January 1835 included Mr Ball, five guineas; Mr Murray, (as actor,) four pounds; Mackay, three guineas; Stanley, the same; Lloyd, two guineas; and a good number of people at a guinea and a half. The chief lady's salary was four pounds, paid to Miss Coveney, whilst Misses Novello and Fairbrother had three guineas each. The company in those days embraced thirty-six performers—viz., twenty-two gentlemen and fourteen ladies; and there was a band of fifteen, led by Mr Wilkinson, at a salary of three guineas. The total amount paid for salaries to actors and musicians was £98, 13s. for the week I have named; and the total expenses of the week, exclusive of rent and manager's salary, were £158, 1s. 7½d.

Mr C. Kean commenced a very successful engagement on the 9th of March 1835, playing to a fifty pound house, receiving half after £30, and a half-clear benefit. On his fourth night the drawings were £80, 19s.; on his twelfth night, the receipts were £92; and on his benefit night, £154.

Benefits in those days were *benefits*. I give a few of them only; but there were more than a dozen actors about that period who could draw money to the house on their benefit night :—

| | | | | | | |
|---|---|---|---|---|---|---|
| Mr Baker's night, | | . | . | . | £102 | 7 | 0 |
| Mr Wilkinson's, | . | . | . | . | 105 | 17 | 6 |
| Miss Novello's, | . | . | . | . | 76 | 3 | 0 |

| Mr Mackay's, | . | . | . | . | 118 | 0 | 0 |
|---|---|---|---|---|---|---|---|
| Miss Newton's, | . | . | . | . | 67 | 5 | 6 |
| Montague Stanley's, | | . | . | . | 95 | 0 | 0 |
| Mr Lloyd's, | . | . | . | . | 105 | 16 | 0 |
| Mr Murray's, | . | . | . | . | 152 | 13 | 0 |

I could give other interesting information about the £ s. d. of Murray's time, but think it would be invidious, as my information would be a reflection on theatrical enterprise as exhibited in Edinburgh at the present day.

Mr Murray left a considerable sum of money for the benefit of his widow and family; but the greater portion of it, as in the case of Mr Alexander, of Glasgow, was swallowed up by the Western Bank calamity.

# CHAPTER VIII.

DISCOURSES OF BAILIE NICOL JARVIE, AND HIS " WORTHY FAITHER THE DEACON AFORE HIM. MY CONSCIENCE !"

IN addition to " Alexander the Great" and " William the Conquerer," there is another name which once bulked largely in the eyes of the play-goers of Scotland. I allude to Mr Mackay, the famed personator of *Bailie Nicol Jarvie*, who, like his two friends, Murray and Alexander, is now numbered with those who, háving played out their brief part in this life, have been called away to the regions of " dusty death." Yes ! " the living Nicol Jarvie—conceited, pragmatical, cautious, generous,"—is dead ! Having attained to man's allotted span of three-score years and ten, he received his final " call" on Monday forenoon, the 2d of November 1857, when he made his " exit" from this earthly stage. This gentleman's name had been, along with those of Murray and Alexander, for the forty years, preceding, a " household word" throughout all broad Scotland ; and although he had been dead to the stage for the last twelve years of his life, the people of Scotland felt as if he had just been summoned direct from the boards. There are now no old, familiar faces left in the Edinburgh company to carry us back to the palmy days of the drama in Edinburgh—the days when the theatre was the fashion—when Scott led the *literati* of Modern Athens to Shakspeare Square ; and when these men of intellect carried along with them the rank, beauty, and wealth of the city, to foster and encourage the dramatic art; and when the Edinburgh theatre, as a consequence of this was, considered one of the best schools of acting in the three kingdoms, and sent out more good actors than any other establishment. The theatre itself even is no more—on its site there has been erected a post-office ; and the laying of its foundation-stone was one of the last public acts of the lamented Prince Albert.

The principal characters in the " Waverley " dramas afforded Mr Mackay the means of firmly establishing himself as one of the most popular Scottish comedians. The drama of " Rob Roy," in which he gained such reputation as the *Bailie*, was played in Edinburgh for forty-one successive nights—having been produced with great care in February 1819—and of all the performers in the original cast Mr Mackay was the last survivor. It was also selected for performance on the visit of George IV. to the Theatre-Royal in 1822 ; and altogether, it has been acted at least four or five hundred times in Edinburgh alone ; and even within the last few years, " Rob " could always be depended on to draw a fifty or a sixty pound house. During the first season of the play, Mr Murray netted by it no less a sum than £3000 ; and more than once (as that gentleman was not slow to acknowledge) it has redeemed the fortunes of a losing season ; and at the time of its production—a time of general depression, when the treasury was almost bankrupt—its success saved the theatre. The drama of "The Heart of Midlothian"—celebrated by Mackay's personation of *Dumbiedykes*, his best part, in my opinion—was produced in Edinburgh early in 1820. From the scenery and associations being entirely local, as well as, perhaps, from the tragic interest of the story, it became very popular. In the same year, "The Antiquary" was first performed in Edinburgh—the part of *Edie Ochiltree*, with its caustic humour and gleams of feeling, being represented by Mr Mackay. Neither in these new parts, however, nor as *Ritchie Moniplies* in "The Fortunes of Nigel," or *Peter Peebles* in "Redgauntlet," or *Jock Howison* in "Cramond Brig," and others of the same type, did he achieve such success as in his, according to the popular idea, great part of *Bailie Nicol Jarvie*. In the interlude of "St Ronan's Well," however, (first performed at the Edinburgh theatre in 1825,) he also obtained, as *Meg Dods*, the encomiums of Sir W. Scott. My own opinion is, that his *Dumbiedykes*, *Dominie Sampson*, and *Peter Peebles*, were his best parts; his *Dumbiedykes* was a perfect masterpiece.

If I am not misinformed, Mr Mackay had been playing in Aberdeen before he was invited to Edinburgh, even in the character he afterwards made so celebrated—the *Bailie;* the play of "Rob Roy" having been first produced in the Granite City, where, and all over the north of Scotland, it had quite a "tremendous success"—Mr Corbet Ryder being the original, and by far the best, delineator of the bold outlaw. As has been already stated, Mr Mackay was, for a period of upwards of twenty years, a regular member of the Edinburgh theatrical *corps.* He relinquished his permanent engagement in 1841, and in April 25, 1848, he had made up his mind to bid a final adieu to the boards, playing on that occasion the *Bailie* and *Jock Howieson.* On the evening of his farewell, the house was indeed brilliant, and it has been only on the most rare occasions that we have seen so much enthusiasm displayed. The night, too, was rendered remarkable by the appearance of the late Mr John Wilson Scotland's best vocalist, who kindly gave his services in honour of the event. In the course of the evening Mr Wilson, in the name of the dramatic company presented the eminent performer with an elegant cup, suitably inscribed. In his farewell address, the veteran actor, warned by the infirmity of his years, said :—" Many of my friends ask, Why should you leave the stage while yet your personation of the Scottish character is as vigorous as ever? Alas! they know not the effort it costs me to appear so. Surely my kind friends would rather let me secure my retreat from the stage than behold me linger thereon when declining years and mental weakness would but remind them that the *Bailie* was now become the shadow of his former self."

Although Mr Mackay found in the Waverley dramas his principal stock of characters, there were many other plays in which he performed. He delineated, with rare success, some of the more comic personages of the legitimate drama.; and in a wide range of parts—embracing such characters as *Rolamo* in "Clari," *Old Dornton* in the "Road to Ruin," &c.—he exhibited a power and pathos which many an audience has been compelled to acknowledge. Even in his later years, and long after he had established his fame as a first-rate comedian, he was found making a " first appearance " in a new part. During one of his later visits to the Edinburgh stage, a considerable time after he had retired, he essayed the part of *Sir Pertinax Macsycophant*, in " The Man of the World." It was during an accustomed visit to an old friend in Kincardineshire, that, being a good deal confined within doors by a festering toe, he found a copy of " The Man of the World" in the library, and set about studying the character with the greatest interest—in fact, the book was seldom out of his hand or his pocket during the remainder of his stay; and that he made himself master of the part, his admirable performance of it was sufficient proof. Nor, during the twenty-two years in which he was a resident member of the Edinburgh company, was his fame confined to his native city, for in Liverpool, Newcastle, and other towns in the sister kingdom, where Scotsmen are to be found in numbers, he was quite as popular as he was in Edinburgh.

The incidents in an actor's life are usually very few. I am not aware that Mr Mackay, although I understand he had once been a soldier, ever experienced any of those moving incidents by flood or field which afford a " show-off" to the biographer. In addition to being a professional star of the first magnitude throughout all broad Scotland, he made a visit to London, where he appeared in some of his best characters; but his metropolitan appearances were comparative failures, Liston's *Dominie Sampson* carrying the day with the Cockneys. Sir

Walter Scott was a constant patron of "the Bailie's," and on this said visit to London he took occasion to introduce him to such of his influential friends as were resident in the great metropolis. For instance, the author of "Waverley" wrote in this strain to Mrs Joanna Baillie regarding his appearance in "Rob Roy:"—"He is completely the personage of the drama—the purse-proud, consequential magistrate, humane and irritable in the same moment, and the true Scotsman in every turn of thought and action. In short, I never saw a part better sustained." "The English," he also wrote to Lord Montagu, "will not enjoy it, for it is not broad enough, or sufficiently caricatured for their apprehensions, but to a Scotsman it is inimitable." And again, to his friend Terry, Scott wrote—"The man who played the *Bailie* made a piece of acting equal to whatever has been seen in the profession. For my own part, I was actually electrified by the truth, spirit, and humour which he threw into the part; it was the living *Nicol Jarvie*—conceited, pragmatical, cautious, generous, proud of his connexion with *Rob Roy*, frightened for him at the same time, and yet extremely desirous to interfere with him as an adviser. The tone in which he seemed to give him up for a lost man, after having provoked him into some burst of Highland violence — 'Ah! Rab! Rab!'—was quite inimitable. I do assure you I never saw a thing better played."

It has required several actors to "succeed" Mr Mackay —not any one artist being able to impersonate the variety of characters which he included in his line of business.

# CHAPTER IX.

## IN WHICH, MELANCHOLY TO RELATE, HAMLET LANDS IN A BOOTH.

As my readers are already aware, I was bent on going to England, and although strongly recommended to " write in" to the Edinburgh manager for an engagement for the summer season, I did not do so, even though I felt confident that my application would have been successful had I done as advised; for notwithstanding that Mr Murray never commended any little part intrusted to me, he once or twice looked his approbation, and that was much from him. To get on quickly was at that time my one idea, as it generally is that of ambitious fledglings in a newly-adopted profession. I had quite settled in my own mind that I could not get on fast enough in Scotland, and, therefore, when the season closed in Edinburgh, with me it was, Southward, ho! Returning, then, to Glasgow, and bidding adieu to various friends, I started off in search of fortune, determined that I should yet be heard of.

Taking the railway to Greenock, I embarked at once on board that beautiful steamer, the *Princess Alice,* and although I had a comfortable little sum of money in my purse, I resolved upon this occasion to be as economical as possible—and with this view, I chose a deck passage, and bargained with a sailor for the use of his berth for a few hours. This is the way a number of actors are forced to travel, as they are seldom blessed with such a full purse as to enable them, like the members of any other profession, to engage a cabin. Indeed, it is a sort of rule in England, as well as in continental countries, for railway and steamboat managers to make a considerable reduction from the usual fares in the case of travelling "professionals." The steward, with whom I at once cultivated friendship, gave me a capital dinner for a sixpence, and for a similar coin I washed down the roast beef with a bottle of first-rate Dublin porter. The weather was fine, and the voyage remarkably pleasant, and not without a diversity of little incidents ; chief of which was the captain's mode of treating some Irishmen who had smuggled themselves on board, and remained in hiding in order to escape payment of the fare. After the unfortunate Paddies had been all routed out from their hiding-places, and it was found that they were quite destitute of anything in the shape of bullion, they were packed like so many cattle into a large wicker-basket, and then, in despite of all their united remonstrances, they were hoisted by means of convenient tackle into mid-air, there to be kept, like Mohammed's coffin, suspended, not between heaven and earth certainly, but between the cross-trees and the deck, exposed to the cold and biting breeze of an autumn night. In due time we arrived in safety at the great seaport, when the unfortunate Patlanders were allowed to take their departure without further punishment.

Even with a good few guineas in my purse I could not

resist an overpowering feeling of loneliness as I wandered about the streets of Liverpool—I knew not a human being in that vast wilderness of people. I was alone in a strange city, with no person to look on me with one kindly smile—a unit among millions, whose loss would never have been felt. It was a season, too, of plague and sickness—of exodus from Ireland, and emigration to the fair land of promise across the Atlantic. The angel of death, brandishing with a terrible strength around their heads his awful sword, was among the people, and they fell down on all sides like new-mown corn. Nothing but the sights and sounds of death met the view or burst upon the ear. Lamentation and mourning were in the looks of all, and there were almost none to bury the dead of the poor stranger. These sights of death were intensely affecting; and the thought of the tinsel and mockery of the stage at such a time jarred painfully on my feelings. Crossing a street one night, I saw two poor creatures—a common sight—hurrying along to the nearest cemetery, bearing, in a rough black-painted deal-box, (the parish coffin, grudgingly bestowed,) the remains of some loved one who had died of famine or the plague among the strangers of Liverpool—the heavy coffin sustained only by a thin cord, which cut into the hands of those who bore it—a truly heart-rending sight, and well fitted to chill the spirit of a passing stranger. Such scenes, however they might affect me, were too common to excite the attention of the residents in the town, and so the tide of business rolled on as usual, conveying prosperity to some and ruin to others.

But of course the plague and the famine affected the "business" of the playhouse. The audiences were scanty, and the managers consequently dispirited, and accordingly when I applied for an engagement, and offered my services at every theatre in the town, it was without success. I had mistaken the time—all were full—not a single vacancy remained. This was disheartening enough; but still I hoped, and hoped, alas! in vain, for no encouraging offer came to cheer me.

I naturally went to the tavern in Liverpool where actors most did congregate, in order to obtain news of opening or closing houses; and here I was soundly rated by one or two actors for being so foolish as to come to England without having a greater knowledge of the profession.

" Why, you see, my boy, you are nothing but a novice," one would say.

" Yes, and your Scotch is so d——d broad, my boy, it won't do here at all."

" And, besides," added a third, " you can't jump into a line of business all at once, as you want to do."

" No, no, managers put all novices into the spoony parts—lovers, and that sort of thing—and, excuse me, but I see you don't look that line of business at all."

" Take a friend's advice, my son," another would say, as he took a pull at his beer and a puff at his pipe, " and hook it. The sooner you cut this bloody profession the better; the theatre in this country is going to the dogs, sir, it is. Why, let me see, I've been nine-and-thirty years in the profession, and here I am, you see, glad to

play 'utility' at five-and-twenty bob a week. It's another
case of second childhood; I began at that, and have played
through the whole range of the British drama, and here
I am again, God help me, glad of the salary."

"Ay, Jem, that's the case with many more of us as
well as yourself; Capelton should take warning and get
out of the mess in time."

"If you wait till about Christmas you may get something to do in the pantomime," was another remark.

"Try the sawdust at the *Amphi*—Copeland will give
you a job to hold the garters," sneered a would-be wit.

"I suppose you began there," I retorted; "and, from
all I can judge, ought to be there still."

This remark told—I had hit the mark unawares; and
so I left the room in the flush of victory.

Such were the remarks which I had daily to listen to.
I neglected this good advice, however, which I have no
doubt now was honest and well meant, but which I then
looked upon as sinister and made up. I still hoped on,
therefore, and applied to various managers for an opening, but the answer was invariably the same:—"Not in
want of a novice at present."

After ten days of fretting, I was almost beginning to
lose heart, when it occurred to me to try the then rising
town of Birkenhead, and see if any opening could be
found there. This was a fortunate step. Hendry's booth
was nearly the first object that presented itself, and I
mounted up the steps filled with a buoyancy that gave
me hope. Fortune smiled at last. The booth was a

sharing affair, and I, the ambitious *Hamlet* of a few weeks before, who would at one time have spurned the idea of becoming a boother, was, after a brief conversation with the manager, offered a place in it, which I thankfully accepted.

# CHAPTER X.

HAMLET BEING, LIKE JONAH, A DISCONTENTED CHARACTER,
LANDS IN THE WHALE'S BELLY, "ALIAS" THE BOOTH.

THIS boothing business was a new life to me. The company was a numerous one for a booth, and the various actors, old stagers most of them, quite able to perform their business; and "business" in a booth is quite different from "business" in a theatre, because it is necessary in a booth that plays should go off with the rapidity of lightning. Richard runs his wicked career, offers his kingdom for a horse, has his "go in" at Richmond, and gets killed off-hand in twenty minutes. A piece follows, with all those striking varieties of scene and character that so delight a mixed audience. This is succeeded by a "screaming farce," and the performances, after an hour's hard work, are over for a time.

In this way, especially on a Saturday night, and more particularly in densely-populated manufacturing towns, is audience after audience entertained, until, tired with their great exertions, the wearied company, after pocketing their share of the receipts, depart to their several lodgings —the king of the night perhaps to enjoy his hot tripe, and the queen to indulge in a bottle of mulled porter, with an accompaniment of fried sausages. Professionals do love a hot supper. During my stay I fell heir to a tolerable share of the *bawbees*. It was, as I have said in the previous chapter, a sharing company ; and the price of admission being a moderate sum—I may as well confess that on Saturday nights the back-seats were a penny —we had no lack of spectators, and the receipts sometimes averaged as much as eight or nine pounds, which were divided into portions as follow :—

        1 share for H. as manager,
        1    „      „   as actor,
        2    „      „   as proprietor,
        1    „      „   for tear and wear,
        1    „      „   for properties.

Being six shares for granting the use of the affair and its appurtenances, as it were. Then the remainder was allocated as follows :—

        4 shares for ladies,
        6    „    for gents.,
        3    „    for band,
        1    „    for supers.,
        1    „    for 2 horses.

Making a total of twenty-one shares—the general average of which was about eight shillings a-head. I may state that, during the weeks I was engaged in the booth, my salary was never less than thirty shillings, which afforded me a comfortable living, and helped me also to add to my stock of "properties"—and good "properties," let me tell the uninitiated, are a principal feature in a country manager's eyes.

The "boothers" are pretty nearly a distinct class of

the "profession;" and in a great number of instances
the booth is hereditary, and is handed down from father
to son for generations together. In a good booth like
Hendry's—or, as I christened it, from the way in which
it was built, "The Whale's Belly"—the dresses, scenery,
and properties are very fine and costly, having been
(originally) got up "quite regardless of expense." The
performers in these companies are generally composed, in
addition to the hereditary members of the booth, of some
of the broken-down actors of the regular theatres—men
who have taken to the bottle, or lost their situations from
some other cause. As the boothers make a point of
attending all the fairs, they are in general able to divide
large sums of money among them, and so they live in
capital style, and seldom want a good meal or a Sunday's
dinner, composed of all the delicacies of the season.
There are but few rehearsals required in such places—
the pieces being all well-known ones; and as it is ever
the same round of plays in each town, the actors are
well up in their parts. "Blue Beard," "Richard III.,"
the "Castle Spectre," and that class of dramas are the
greatest favourites, and draw the largest audiences; and
these pieces are in general supplemented by a good farce,
such as "Robin Roughhead; or, the Ploughman turned
Lord;" and very often a pantomime is got up without
waiting for the Christmas holidays.

The day's work is nearly as follows :—We get up, perhaps, at ten o'clock—there is nothing to study; and some
of us have most likely agreed upon taking a stroll for an
hour or two before dinner. We dine about three, and

during our walk we have told each other what we are to have; we drink a cup of tea, or a glass of beer, about six o'clock, and then we start for the booth. A portmanteau, with a couple of pairs of tights, a pair of boots, shoes, &c., is carried along with us to the stage, and we then proceed to make our toilet in order to be in time for "parade." This is usually done in that picturesque style which has been immortalised by the genius of Hogarth, ladies and gentlemen mixing pretty freely together. As we each get the adornment of our outer man completed, we mount to the outside, and strut about for perhaps half-an-hour or so, sometimes having a dance to the music of our select band, the low comedian all the while (sometimes dressed as a pantomime clown) making as much fun as he possibly can, by "mugging," or otherwise. Usually, all are dressed in a most exaggerated style, especially "the comedy chaps," in order to raise a laugh. After the parade, and after various speeches have been delivered to the people outside, with the view of obtaining their patronage, we proceed round to the stage, when the curtain draws up, and the "grand performances" of the evening commence in earnest. The play and farce are repeated as often as the place fills, the time occupied by the performance varying from three quarters of an hour to an hour and a-half, so that by the time we have entertained three audiences, or on Saturday night six, and then counted up and received our shares, we are pretty tired, and in a glorious mood for that nice little bit of hot supper which constitutes an elysium to the poor actor; after which, echoing *Lady Macbeth*, the cry is, "To bed, to bed," and so ends the uneventful day.

As I have already stated, the pieces acted in the booth can either be played at full length, which they very seldom are, however, or they can be curtailed to any extent to suit the exigences of the evening. Thus, on the Saturday nights in a manufacturing town, or during visits to the fairs in the country, the audiences get the "Castle Spectre" in the shape of an essence, which may be swallowed up in twelve or thirteen minutes; whilst in a regular play-house it would take nearly three hours to play it. The best way to give the reader an idea of how this is managed will be to quote the last scene of the play in question, (Scene III. Act V.,) as it ought to be acted, and then to give, in parallel columns, the same scene as it is gone through in a booth at a fair :—

| THE CASTLE SPECTRE. | THE CASTLE SPECTRE. |
|---|---|
| ACT V., SCENE III. | ACT V., SCENE III. |
| AS USUALLY PERFORMED IN THE THEATRES-ROYAL. | AS PERFORMED IN A BOOTH ON A BUSY EVENING. |
| SCENE—*A gloomy subterraneous dungeon, wide and lofty; the upper part of it has in several places fallen in, and left large chasms. On one side are various passages leading to other caverns: on the other is an iron door with steps leading to it, and a wicket in the middle.* REGINALD, *pale and emaciated, in coarse garments, his hair hanging wildly about his face, and a chain bound round his body, lies sleeping on a bed of straw. A lamp, a small basket, and a pitcher,* | SCENE—*A dungeon, pure and simple, without the appurtenances required in the larger theatres, there being no space on the stage of a booth for the "various passages leading to other caverns." The lamp, the small basket, and the pitcher, are supposed to be somewhere at the side of the stage, and must be imagined by the audience.*<br><br>*Manager.* [*Behind.*] Now, then, do go a-head; don't you hear the mob outside. Cut out |

*are placed near him. After a few moments he awakes and extends his arms. The stage nearly dark.*

*Reg.* My child! My Evelina!— Oh! fly me not, lovely forms!— They are gone, and once more I live to misery. Thou wert kind to me, sleep! Even now, methought I sat in my castle-hall: a maid, lovely as the queen of fairies, hung on my knees, and hailed me by that sweet name, "Father!" Yes, I was happy! Yet frown not on me, therefore, darkness! I am thine again my gloomy bride!—Be not incensed, despair, that I left thee for a moment; I have passed with thee sixteen years! Ah! how many have I still to pass?—Yet, fly not my bosom quite, sweet hope! Still speak to me of liberty, of light! Whisper, that once more I shall see the morn break, that again shall my fevered lips drink the pure gale of evening! God, thou knowest that I have borne my sufferings meekly: I have wept for myself, but never cursed my foes; I have sorrowed for thy anger, but never murmured at thy will. Patient have I been; oh! then reward me; let me once again press my daughter in my arms; let me, for one instant, feel again that I clasp to my heart a being who loves me. Speed thou to heaven, prayer of a captive!

[*He sinks upon a stone, with his hands clasped, and his eyes bent steadfastly upon the flame of the lamp.*

Reginald's first speech, can't you.

*Reg.* Oh! come; dem it, you know that's the best of it.

*Man.* Go to blazes; don't you hear the people outside, as many as will fill us three times yet. Get on, can't you; let us make hay whilst the sun shines. [*N.B. It is nine o'clock.*]

[*First speech cut out accordingly.*

*Man.* Now, then, Angela and Father Philip, do cut it short. Never mind the words; here, go on, go on; there you are; that's the cue.

Angela *and* Father Philip *are
seen through the chasms above, passing slowly along, from* R. *to* L.

*Ang.* Be cautious, father!—Feel
you not how the ground trembles
beneath us?

*F. Phil.* Perfectly well; and would
give my best Breviary to find myself
once more on *terra firma.* But the
outlet cannot be far off: let us proceed.

*Ang.* Look down upon us, blessed
angels! Aid us! Protect us!

*F. Phil.* Amen, fair daughter!
[*They disappear.*

*Reg.* [*After a pause.*] How wastes
my lamp! The hour of Kenric's
visit must long be past, and still he
comes not. How if death's hand
hath struck him suddenly? My existence unknown—away from my
fancy, dreadful idea! [*Rising, and
taking the lamp.*] The breaking of
my chain permits me to wander at
large through the wide precincts of
my prison. Haply the late storm,
whose pealing thunders were heard
e'en in this abyss, may have rent
some friendly chasm: haply some
nook yet unexplored—Ah! no, no,
no! My hopes are vain, my search
will be fruitless. Despair in these
dungeons reigns despotic; she mocks
my complaints, rejects my prayers,
and when I sue for freedom, bids
me seek it in the grave!—Death!
O death! how welcome wilt thou
be to me! [*Exit* R. S. E.
[*The noise is heard of a heavy bar
falling; the door opens.* L. U. E.

*Reg.* Death! O death! how welcome wilt thou be to me!
[*Exit* R. S. E.
[*In the booth "noise" is not heard, for
in the hurry it is quite forgotten.*

*Enter* FATHER PHILIP *and* ANGELA,
L. U. E.

*F. Phil.* How's this? A door!

*Ang.* It was barred on the outside.

*F. Phil.* That we'll forgive, as it wasn't bolted on the in. But I don't recollect—surely I've not—

*Ang.* What's the matter?

*F. Phil.* By my faith, daughter, I suspect that I've missed my way.

*Ang.* Heaven forbid!

*F. Phil.* Nay, if 'tis so, I shan't be the first man who of two ways has preferred the wrong.

*Ang.* Provoking! And did I not tell you to choose the right-hand passage?

*F. Phil.* Truly did you: and that was the very thing which made me choose the left. Whenever I am in doubt myself, I generally ask a woman's advice. When she's of one way of thinking, I've always found that reason's on the other. In this instance, perhaps, I have been mistaken: but wait here for one moment, and the fact shall be ascertained. [*Exit* R. S. E.

*Ang.* How thick and infectious is the air of this cavern! Yet perhaps for sixteen years has my poor father breathed none purer. Hark! Steps are quick advancing! The friar comes, but why in such confusion?

*Re-enter* FATHER PHILIP, *running,*
R. S. E.

*F. Phil.* Help! help! it follows me!

*Enter* FATHER PHILIP *and* ANGELA,
L. U. E.

*F. Phil.* How's this? A door!

*Ang.* It was barred on the outside.

*F. Phil.* That we'll forgive, as it wasn't bolted on the in. But I don't recollect—surely I've not—

*Ang.* What's the matter?

*F. Phil.* By my faith, daughter, I suspect that I've missed my way.

*Ang.* Heaven forbid!

*F. Phil.* Nay, if 'tis so, I shan't be the first man who of two ways has preferred the wrong.

*Ang.* Provoking! And did I not tell you to choose the right-hand passage?

*F. Phil.* Truly did you. But wait here for one moment, and the fact shall be ascertained. [*Exit* R. S. E.

*Ang.* How thick is the air of this cavern! Yet perhaps for sixteen years has my poor father breathed none purer. Hark! Steps are advancing! The friar comes, but why in such confusion?

*Re-enter* FATHER PHILIP, *running,*
R. S. E.

*F. Phil.* Help! help! it follows me!

*Ang.* [*Detaining him.*] What alarms you? Speak!

*F. Phil.* His ghost! his ghost!— Let me go!—let me go!—let me go!

[*Struggling to escape from Angela, he falls and extinguishes the torch; then hastily rises, and rushes up the staircase, closing the door after him,* L. U. E.

*Ang.* Father! Father! Stay, for Heaven's sake!—He's gone! I cannot find the door!—Hark! 'Twas the clank of chains!—A light, too! It comes yet nearer!—Save me, ye powers!—What dreadful form! 'Tis here! I faint with terror!

[*Sinks almost lifeless against the dungeon's side.*

*Re-enter* REGINALD, *with a lamp,* R. S. E.

*Reg.* [*Placing his lamp upon a pile of stones.*] Why did Kenric enter my prison? Haply, when he heard not my groans at the dungeon door he thought that my woes were relieved by death! Oh, when will that thought be verified!

*Ang.* Each sound of his hollow plaintive voice strikes to my heart. Dare I accost him?—yet perhaps a maniac—no matter; he suffers, and the accents of pity will sound sweetly in my ears!

*Reg.* Thou art dead and at rest, my wife! Safe in yon skies, no thought of me molests thy quiet. Yet sure I wrong thee! At the

---

*Ang.* [*Detaining him.*] What alarms you? Speak!

*F. Phil.* His ghost! his ghost! Let me go!—let me go!—let me go!

[*Struggling to escape from Angela, he falls and extinguishes the torch; then hastily rises, and rushes off, (there is no staircase in the booth,)* L. U. E.

*Ang.* Father! Father! Stay, for Heaven's sake!—He's gone! I cannot find the door!—Hark!— A light, too! It comes!—Save me, ye powers!—What dreadful form! 'Tis here! I faint with terror!

[*Sinks almost lifeless against the dungeon's side, and has a little beer handed to her.*

*Re-enter* REGINALD, *with a candle in his hand,* R. S. E.

*Reg.* [*Placing his candle upon what is supposed to be a pile of stones, but is in reality a table.*] Why did Kenric enter my prison? Haply, when he heard not my groans at the dungeon door he thought that my woes were relieved by death! Oh, when will that thought be verified!

hour of death thy spirit shall stand beside me, shall close mine eyes gently, and murmur, " Die, Reginald, and be at peace ! "

*Ang.* (L.) Hark! Heard I not ——Pardon, good stranger—

*Reg.* (R.) [*Starting wildly from his seat.*] 'Tis she! She comes for me! Is the hour at hand, fair vision? Spirit of Evelina, lead on, I follow thee!

[*He extends his arms towards her, staggers a few paces forward, then sinks exhausted on the ground.*

*Ang.* He faints! perhaps expires! Still, still! See, he revives!

*Reg.* 'Tis gone! Once more the sport of my bewildered brain! [*Starting up.*] Powers of bliss! Look where it moves again! Oh! say, what art thou? If Evelina, speak, oh! speak.

*Ang.* Ha! Named he not Evelina? That look! This dungeon, too! The emotions which his voice —It is, it must be! Father! O Father! Father!

[*Falling upon his bosom.*

*Reg.* Said you? Meant you? My daughter—my infant whom I left—Oh! yes it must be true! My heart, which springs towards you, acknowledges my child! [*Embracing her.*] But say how gained you entrance? Has Osmond—

*Ang.* (L.) Hark! Heard I not ——Pardon, good stranger—

*Reg.* (R.) [*Starting wildly from his seat.*] 'Tis she! She comes for me! Is the hour at hand, fair vision? Spirit of Evelina lead on, I follow thee!

[*He extends his arms towards her, staggers a few paces forward, then sinks exhausted on the ground.*

*Ang.* He faints! perhaps expires! Still, still! See, he revives!

*Reg.* 'Tis gone! [*Starting up.*] Powers of bliss! Look! Oh! say, what art thou? If Evelina, speak, oh! speak.

*Ang.* Ha! Named he not Evelina? That look! This dungeon! The emotions—It is! Father! O Father! Father!

[*Falling upon his bosom.*

*Reg.* Said you? Meant you? My daughter—my infant whom I left —Oh! yes! My heart acknowledges my child! [*Embracing her.*] But say how gained you entrance? Has Osmond—

*Man.* [*In a perfect fume.*] Do cut it short—the business I mean. — [*Aloud.*] "John Orderly" * there.

* "John Orderly" is a phrase used by showmen to expedite the business.

*Reg.* [*Aside.*] Stuff, man ; won't those who are in tell those who are out, that we do it stunning ?

*Man.* [*With force.*] Yes, but be quick as well.

*Ang.* Oh ! that name recalls my terrors ! Alas ! you see in me a fugitive from his violence, guided by a friendly monk, whom your approach has frightened from me. I was endeavouring to escape : we missed our way, and chance guided us to this dungeon. But this is not a time for explanation. Answer me ! Know you the subterraneous passages belonging to this castle ?

*Reg.* Whose entrance is without the walls ? I do.

*Ang.* Then we may yet be saved ! Father, we must fly this moment. Percy, the pride of our English youth, waits for me at the Conway's side. Come, then, oh ! come ! Stay not one moment longer.

[*As she approaches the door lights appear above,* R. U. E.

*Reg.* Look ! look, my child ! The beams of distant torches flash through the gloom !

*Osm.* [*Above.*] Hassan, guard you the door. Follow me, friends.

[*The lights disappear.*

*Ang.* Osmond's voice ! Undone !

---

*Ang.* Oh ! that name recalls my terrors ! I was endeavouring to escape ; chance guided me to this dungeon. But this is not a time for explanation. Answer me ! Know you the subterraneous passages belonging to this castle ?

*Reg.* Whose entrance is without the walls ? I do.

*Ang.* Then we may yet be saved ! Father, we must fly this moment. Percy, the pride of our English youth, waits for me at the Conway's side. Come, then, oh ! come ! Stay not one moment longer.

[*As she approaches the door lights don't appear above, simply because they can't, there being no above,* R. U. E.

*Reg.* Look ! look, my child ! The beams of distant torches flash through the gloom !

*Osm.* [*Above.*] Hassan, guard you the door. Follow me, friends.

[*The lights do not disappear, because, of course, they were never there.*

*Ang.* Osmond's voice ! Undone !

Undone! Oh! my father! he comes to seek you, perhaps to—Oh! 'tis a word too dreadful for a daughter's lips!—

*Reg.* Hark! they come! The gloom of yonder cavern may a while conceal you : fly to it—hide yourself —stir not, I charge you.

*Ang.* What, leave you? Oh! no, no!

*Reg.* Dearest, I entreat, I conjure you, fly! Fear not for me.

*Ang.* Father! Oh! father!

*Reg.* Farewell! perhaps for ever! [*He forces Angela into the cavern, then returns hastily, and throws himself on the bed of straw.*] Now, then, to hear my doom!

*Enter* OSMOND, L. U. E., *followed by* MULEY *and* ALARIC *with torches.*

*Osm.* The door unbarred! Softly, my fears were false! Wake, Reginald, and arise!

*Reg.* You here, Osmond! What brings you to this scene of sorrow? Alas! hope flies while I gaze upon your frowning eye! Have I read its language aright, Osmond?

*Osm.* Aright if you have read my hatred.

*Reg.* Have I deserved that hate? See, my brother, the once proud Reginald lies at your feet, for his pride has been humbled by suffering! Hear him adjure you by her ashes within whose bosom we both have lain, not to stain your hands with the blood of your brother!

---

Undone! Oh! my father! he comes to seek you, perhaps to—Oh! 'tis a word too dreadful for a daughter's lips :——Father! Oh! father!

*Reg.* Farewell! perhaps for ever! [*He forces Angela into the cavern, then returns hastily, and throws himself on the supposed bed of straw, but there is in reality none.*] Now, then, to hear my doom!

*Enter* OSMOND, L. U. E., *followed by* MULEY *and* ALARIC *with torches.*

*Osm.* The door unbarred! Softly, my fears were false! Wake, Reginald, and arise!

*Reg.* You here, Osmond! What brings you to this scene of sorrow? Alas! hope flies while I gaze upon your frowning eye! Have I read its language aright, Osmond?

*Osm.* Aright, if you have read my hatred.

*Osm.* He melts me in my own despite.

*Reg.* Kenric has told me that my daughter lives ! Restore me to her arms; permit us in obscurity to pass our days together ! Then shall my last sigh implore upon your head Heaven's forgiveness, and Evelina's.

*Osm.* It shall be so. Rise, Reginald, and hear me ! You mentioned even now your daughter; know, she is in my power; know, also, that I love her !

*Reg.* How !

*Osm.* She rejects my offers. Your authority can oblige her to accept them. Swear to use it, and this instant will I lead you to her arms. Say, will you give the demanded oath ?

*Reg.* I cannot dissemble. Osmond, I never will.

*Osm.* How !—Reflect that your life—

*Reg.* Would be valueless, if purchased by my daughter's tears— would be loathsome, if embittered by my daughter's misery. Osmond, I will not take the oath.

*Osm.* [*Almost choked with passion.*] 'Tis enough. [*To the Africans.*] You know your duty ! Drag him to yonder cavern ! Let me not see him die !

*Reg.* [*Holding by a fragment of the wall, from which the Africans strive to force him.*] Brother, for pity's sake ! for your soul's happiness !

*Osm.* Obey me, slaves ! Away !

*Reg.* Kenric has told me that my daughter lives ! Restore me to her arms ! Then shall my last sigh implore upon your head Heaven's forgiveness.

*Osm.* It shall be so. Rise, Reginald, and hear me ! Your daughter is in my power; know, also, that I love her !

*Reg.* How !

*Osm.* She rejects my offers. Your authority can oblige her to accept them. Swear to use it, and this instant will I lead you to her arms. Say, will you give the demanded oath ?

*Reg.* I cannot dissemble. Osmond, I never will.

*Osm.* How !—Reflect that your life—

*Reg.* Would be valueless, if purchased by my daughter's tears. Osmond, I will not take the oath.

*Osm.* [*Almost choked with passion.*] 'Tis enough. [*To the Africans.*] You know your duty ! Drag him to yonder cavern ! Let me not see him die !

*Reg.* [*Holding by a fragment of the wall, from which the Africans strive to force him; not, however, before it was time, as the wall shook consumedly.*] Brother, for pity's sake ! for your soul's happiness !

*Osm.* Obey me, slaves ! Away !

*Man.* [*Behind.*] Now, dem ït, this is too bad; why the blazes don't you cut out more of the infernal rubbish?

*Reg.* [*Aside.*] See you blowed first, spoiling my business in this way; I shan't play it again.

*Man.* Now, then, where is that woman? Where is Angela? My eye, Miss Steggs, (that was her name,) don't you see the stage is waiting?

*Ang.* Yes; but my slipper has come off, and I can't go till I put it right.

*Man.* Confound your slipper; go on [*shoves her on.*]

[ANGELA *rushes in wildly from the cavern.*

[ANGELA *rushes in wildly from the cavern, minus the slipper in question, which omission is speedily detected by the intelligent British audience assembled on the occasion, as is also the fact, that the lovely Angela's stocking is not quite so perfect as it ought to be in the circumstances.*

*Ang.* Hold off!—hurt him not! he is my father!

*Osm.* Angela here!

*Reg.* Daughter, what means—

*Ang.* [*Embracing him.*] You shall live, father! I will sacrifice all to preserve you. Here is my hand, Osmond. Osmond, release my father, and solemnly I swear—

*Reg.* Hold, girl, and first hear me! [*Kneeling.*] God of nature, to thee I call! If e'er on Osmond's bosom a child of mine rests  if e'er she

*Ang.* Hold off!—hurt him not! he is my father!

*Osm.* Angela here!

*Reg.* Daughter, what means—

*Ang.* [*Embracing him.*] You shall live, father! I will sacrifice all. Here is my hand, Osmond. Osmond, release my father!

*Reg.* Hold, girl, and first hear me! [*Kneeling.*] God of nature, to thee I call! If e'er on Osmond's bosom a child of mine rests; if e'er call him husband who pierced her hapless mother's heart, that moment shall a wound, by my own hand inflicted—

*Ang.* Hold! Oh! hold—end not your oath!

*Reg.* Swear never to be Osmond's!

*Ang.* I swear!

*Reg.* Be repaid by this embrace.
                    [*They embrace.*

*Osm.* Be it your last! Tear them asunder! Ha! what noise?

*Enter* HASSAN, *hastily,* L. U. E.

*Has.* My lord, all is lost! Percy has surprised the castle, and speeds this way!

*Osm.* Confusion! Then I must be sudden. Aid me, Hassan!

[*Hassan and Osmond force Angela from her father, who suddenly disengages himself from Muley and Alaric. Osmond, drawing his sword, rushes upon Reginald, who is disarmed, and beaten upon his knees; when at the moment that Osmond lifts his arm to stab him, Evelina's ghost throws herself between them : Osmond starts back, and drops his sword.*

she call him husband who pierced her hapless mother's heart, that moment shall a wound, by my own hand inflicted—

*Man.* [*Fuming behind.*] Cut it short; why the blazes don't you cut it short?

*Ang.* Hold! Oh! hold—end not your oath!

*Reg.* Swear never to be Osmond's!

*Ang.* I swear!

*Reg.* Be repaid by this embrace.
                    [*They embrace.*

*Osm.* Be it your last! Tear them asunder! Ha! what noise?

*Enter* HASSAN, *hastily,* L. U. E.

*Has.* My lord, all is lost! Percy has surprised the castle, and speeds this way!

*Osm.* Confusion! Then I must be sudden. Aid me, Hassan!

[*Hassan and Osmond force Angela from her father, who suddenly disengages himself from Muley and Alaric. Osmond, drawing his sword, rushes upon Reginald, who is disarmed, and beaten upon his knees; when at the moment that Osmond lifts his arm to stab him, Evelina's ghost throws herself between them : Osmond starts back, and drops his sword.*

N.B.—This ought to be the "business;" but in the hurry and bustle of a booth it is frequently passed over altogether, or so bungled as not to be understood by the audience. It is generally thought to be quite sufficient if the bleeding ghost of Evelina manages the stabbing correctly.

*Osm.* Horror! What form is this?

*Ang.* Die. [*Disengages herself from Hassan, springs suddenly forward and plunges her dagger in Osmond's bosom, who falls with a loud groan, and faints. The ghost vanishes: Angela and Reginald rush into each other's arms.*

*Man.* Now, then, down with the curtain—down with the curtain!

[*Down it comes accordingly.*

*Reg.* I say, Hendry, this is too bad.

*Man.* Oh! humbug; out you go to the "parade," and announce three more performances. Come, Bill, why don't you ring the bell? As I say, let us make money whilst the sun shines.

*Enter* PERCY, SAIB, HAROLD, &c., L. U. E., *pursuing* OSMOND'S *party.*

[*They all stop on seeing him bleeding upon the ground.*

*Per.* Hold, my brave friends! See where lies the object of our search.

*Ang.* Percy! Dearest Percy!

*Per.* [*Flying to her.*] Dearest Angela!

*Ang.* My friend, my guardian angel! Come, Percy, come! embrace my father! Father, embrace the protector of your child!

*Per.* Do I, then, behold Earl Reginald!

*Reg.* [*Embracing him.*] The same, brave Percy! Welcome to my heart! Live ever next it.

*Ang.* Oh! moment that o'erpay my sufferings! And yet—Percy, that wretched man—He perished by my hand!

*Muley.* Hark! he sighs! There is life still in him.

*Ang.* Life! then save him! save him! Bear him to his chamber! Look to his wound! Heal it, if possible! At least give him time to repent his crimes and errors!

[*Osmond is conveyed away; servants enter with torches, and the stage becomes light.*

*Per.* Though ill deserved by his guilt, your generous pity still is amiable. But say, fair Angela, what have I to hope? Is my love approved by your noble father? Will he—

*Reg.* Percy, this is no time to talk of love. Let me hasten to my expiring brother, and soften with forgiveness the pangs of death!

*Per.* Can you forget your sufferings?

*Reg.* Ah! youth, has he had none? Oh! in his stately chambers, far greater must have been his pangs than mine in this gloomy dungeon; for what gave me comfort was his terror, what gave me hope was his despair. I knew that I was guiltless—knew, that though I suffered in this world, my lot would be happy in that to come.

[*Exeunt.*

I could give, were it necessary, another version of the "Castle Spectre," still more abridged—indeed, the booth people seem to have a special faculty for cutting down; but from this specimen the reader will be able to realise in his mind's eye the manner of performance usual in a booth. The version of the last scene of the "Castle Spectre," now given, is an accidental one, not arranged for among the company, but rendered necessary by the overflow of visitors upon the particular night we have alluded to, when there was a more than ordinary demand for places in the booth. The reader will probably suppose that, with the bustle and swearing behind the scenes, which I have given in its mildest form, and the time wasted in direction by the manager, the abridged version was very nearly as long as the author's one. If the reader supposes this, and it would merely be giving him credit for very ordinary 'cuteness if he did, I can only say that he is as nearly right as possible.

It need hardly be said, that the farce of "Fortune's Frolic" was gone through with equal rapidity—of course, all the "points" were carefully given, "cartfuls of beefsteaks and bucketfuls of gravy" especially. The whole play, indeed, which takes up twenty pages of "Cumberland's British Theatre," and is in two acts, seldom lasts above eight minutes—*Robin Roughhead, Snacks, Rattle,* and *Mr Frank* being quite able to get through the business in the short time I have mentioned. The whole affair, as performed in the booth, is done in one act—a change of scene being the only requisite.

There are many dramas which are never acted now

except in booths; indeed, there are some acted regularly
in these places which I do not so much as know the name
of. Many of those who perform in them are also ignorant
of their titles, if they ever had any. They are known
as "That double-ghost piece," or as "That dog affair," or
by such other name as will sufficiently designate them.
One of these I performed in myself—it was all about a
usurper baron, and a young chieftain who was falsely
kept out of his estates. Of course, the young man had
an innocent but faithful servant, who, by a ludicrous mistake, brought everything right in the end. There was a
highly sentimental young lady, with a pert chambermaid,
and two villains, who supported the usurper. The last
scene was nearly as follows :—

*Enter two* Villains, *dragging on* Rightful Heir *to be tried by the*
Usurper.

*Usurper.* Ha, minion; how now!

*Rightful Heir.* I despise thee, and am no minion of thine.

*Countryman.* Now for it—tooraladdy, tooraladdy ! 　　*[Dances.*

*Enter* ELVIRA, *the supposed* Daughter *of the* Usurper.

*Usurper.* Away with him to the dungeons of the castle, there to
await my vengeance.

*Elvira.* 'Old, I say,—he shall not be taken 'ence—I love 'im.

*Usurper.* Confusion ! Darest thou love a villain ?

*Countryman.* Go it, my covey; your time will be but short. [*Dances.*

*Usurper.* I will have the villain—

*Old Woman.* [*Who has entered quietly.*] Villain yourself; Baron, he
is no villain, but the rightful heir of these broad lands. I was his
nurse, and he has a cross on his right arm, [*Seizes the member in question*]—Behold !

*Rightful Heir.* Great heavens !

*Countryman.* Tooraladdy, tooraladdy—its's all right. Read that;
it's a will. Tooraladdy, tooraladdy. 　　　　　　　　　　*[Dances.*

*Usurper.* What say you, hell-hound? Never; no, never!—perish the thought!—the cross is a forgery!

*Old Woman.* If it is, then it is a forgery of Heaven—it has been ever there since the day he was born.

*Countryman.* [*Dancing with great vengeance*]—Tooraladdy, tooraladdy!

*Enter* Old Priest.

*Priest.* Benedicite! It is so; Athelbert is the rightful heir; and Elvira is——

*Elvira.* 'is wife! yes, before man and 'eaven, *'is wife!*

*Countryman.* Tooraladdy, tooraladdy!                    [*Dances.*

GRAND TABLEAU!—CURTAIN.

# CHAPTER XI.

I ENDEAVOUR TO FOLLOW OUT THAT ADAGE OF THE
IMMORTAL BARD'S, WHICH TEACHES US THAT "ONE
MAN IN HIS TIME PLAYS MANY PARTS," BY TAKING
UPON MYSELF THE CHARACTER OF CLOWN IN A
CIRCUS.

No sooner did I get comfortably initiated into the manners and customs of the boothers, and to the kind of
acting required, than my vanity began to whisper to me
that I ought to have a soul above "the parade;" and
therefore I became quite discontented at my position,
and my teeth watered again for the honours and conventionalities of the regular drama. Efforts in a booth
seemed to me a loss of time—a stoppage on the pathway
of fame—so at all hazards I resolved to say good-bye to
my kind-hearted friends at Hendry's ; and, indeed, it is
but justice to say of them that they were as agreeable a
lot as I ever met. The concern, too, was in all respects
remarkably well appointed. The scenery, in particular,
was beautiful, and had been painted by an artist of note
specially for its present owner. The receipts were regularly divided every night, and the engagement was exceedingly pleasant ; but being bent upon a change, I took
my leave, amid the kind wishes of the whole company,
some of whom, no doubt, said—" Well, he is a precious

greenhorn, to leave the comforts of a booth like this for the miserable and uncertain chances of a regular theatre."

My next place of sojourn was Birmingham.

The reason for my going there was as follows :—I had gone back from Birkenhead to Liverpool, and from thence by railway to Manchester, from which cotton metropolis I was tramping much at random, not caring greatly whither I went, when chance directed me to the town of Littleton, and, according to my usual rule at the time, having a few sovereigns in my pocket, I made for one of the best hotels in the town, in which to rest my wearied bones. It was during the week of the assizes, and every hotel, good, bad, or indifferent, was crammed either with witnesses, barristers, attorneys, or barristers' clerks, and accommodation was at a premium. By chance there was one bed to let in the "Bull and Mouth," the name of the hotel I had chosen, and which was appropriately situated in the cattle-market. The landlord, with many apologies, informed me that I would have to share my sitting-room with Mr George Chirper, the manager of a well-known travelling circus. This rather jumped with my grain than otherwise, for it occurred to me that through Mr Chirper I might learn where to procure an engagement. In fact, it was a lucky chance for poor Roscius. Chirper made himself vastly agreeable, and his countenance got illuminated as the brandy and water and the joke passed between us. Of course, I at once started upon the subject nearest my heart—an engagement. I told him who I was, whence I had come, what I had done, and what my aspirations were. After thinking for a little, and taking a few whiffs at his pipe, he seemed from his manner to have hit upon an idea favourable to my wishes.

"Gadzooks, my dear fellow," exclaimed the manager, "if I were an educated cove like you, I could make my fortune in a few years."

"Ah! how?" said I, anxious to obtain information from one who had the reputation of knowing a thing or two.

"Why, by turning clown, to be sure," was the answer. "Join my circus; we open at Birmingham in a week. I have just come from Newcastle, where I have been with Bella, my black mare, and am now in search of novelties. You are just the man I require. I will give you thirty bob a week to start with; and if *we* hit it, and *you* hit the audience, why, in a couple of months I will double it. What do you say?"

"What do I say? Done at once. But," said I, after a short pause of reflection, "will there not be some difficulty in my all at once turning clown without having served something like an apprenticeship?"

"Bah!" said Chirper; "never, while you live, talk of difficulties—the man who invented that word was a curse to society, and ought to have been hanged, and hung in chains as a warning, with the word painted on a label and tied over his breast. I never see a difficulty, now, and never could see one all my life. Why, man, if they wanted a professor of Hebrew at Oxford, I could take the job on a couple of days' notice—ay, and give satisfaction, too. I know what difficulties are—but always conquer.

Rely upon it, turning clown is the easiest thing in the world; you will, with the exertion of a little of your Scottish tact, appear to the manner born."

"Good," said I. "But how about the jokes? You can't expect me to be 'up' in them all at once: I mean intuitively, or to be able to turn out a dozen of new ones every night, like a practised hand?"

"Oh! as for the jokes, never fear, man. The ring-master has all the old standard ones ready cut and dry; and as for a new supply, there is no danger. You can soon get up a few by reading *Punch* or the *Family Herald*, so we will trust to the chapter of accidents on that score."

"I'll endeavour to do my very best," said I.

"In course you will; the great thing now-a-days is to give parodies from Shakspeare—burlesques of 'To be, or not to be,' &c. Shakspearian clowns are all the go."

"Oh! I see; pretend, for instance, to have toothache, and after making a few good 'mugs,' commence, 'To draw, or not to draw, that is the question?' Eh?"

"Yes, that's the style," said Chirper; "such as these, with a few witty sayings, and lots of all sorts of chaff, are the very things we want. You'll do, I can see."

"I have a great store of witty sayings, but will perhaps feel awkward as to how to introduce them properly."

"Oh, that is easy enough—a clever man will make his opportunities. For instance, you have thin legs; you can, therefore, start with the old story about them. Here's the style—suppose a scene between you and Childers, my ring-master:—

" ' *Clown.* Oh ! Mr Childers—oh, dear ! oh, dear !

" ' *Childers.* Why, what 's the matter, you great fool ?

" ' *Clown.* Oh ! matter enough, matter enough, I can tell you.

" ' *Childers.* Well, then, what is it ?

" ' *Clown.* Oh ! my precious legs ! oh, dear !

" ' *Childers.* Legs ! why, what on earth is wrong with 'em ? They are there all right, ain't they ?

" ' *Clown.* No, sir ; oh ! dear no, they ain't all right at all, sir. Don't you see they are gone to a shadow ?—two drumsticks, sir ; and yet they 're not strong enough to be played with, I can tell you.

" ' *Childers.* Come, come, sir ; jump about, sir, and no capers, sir ; a British audience expects every man to do his duty, sir. (Flourishing his whip.)

" ' *Clown.* What, sir ? it 's quite impossible to jump without capers, sir ; but my legs won't jump at all now, for they have no strength.

" ' *Childers.* How does that come about, sir ? Let us hear how they lost their strength, will you ?

" ' *Clown.* Why, you see, sir, it 's a melancholy story, but won't take long to tell ; my father, being a very economical man, had our shoes always made for our growth, and to keep them on our feet we stuffed them with hay ; and oh ! sir, my calves came down one day to have a feed upon the hay, and they forgot to go up again, sir ! and that 's all, sir—a melancholy tale, isn't it, sir ? '

" You know you can give them lots of gag in telling it, and no fear of its success. Then, you know, you could follow it up with the porter business. Childers will ask you to bring a pint of stout. Of course you do so. He objects to its being in pewter, and tells you to be genteel, and bring it in a *tumbler*. There is a good hit; for, stepping aside, you drink the stout, and then, when he is in a great passion, you quietly ask him if he didn't tell you to bring it in a tumbler, and if you are not a *tumbler*, and so on."

This "gag" is a great commodity in the circus—and even on the stage it is useful. I have seen on the Edinburgh stage a whole scene "gagged," by Murray, Mackay, and Lloyd, and capital fun it was. In a circus, and by clowns and ring-masters, "gag" is ever in demand. "Oh, just gag it," is a common saying, and by a little physical exertion an immense deal of fun may be made out of nothing. A good clown knows how to keep the ball rolling and the audience in good humour.

Here, then, at last, was something like a stroke of fortune. No need for the present to encroach further on my rapidly-diminishing stock of bright sovereigns. Thirty shillings a-week, and a good prospect of a speedy increase, was more than a tolerable piece of good luck to fall to a stroller who, in as many months, had been in five theatres-rural. After a written memorandum of our engagement had passed between us, (for Chirper was a good man of business,) I left Littleton for Birmingham, partly by coach, and partly by rail, and also partly on foot, which, to my taste, is by far the most pleasant mode of travelling.

Without accident or adventure of any kind, either by flood or field, I arrived at my destination with a light heart and a fierce appetite. My first business was to find out a lodging. I liked to be housed in a neat and tidy place, however humble it might be; and this was soon found in a street near the outskirts of the town— and yet, as I would have said when I was a clerk, not very far away from my " place of business," *i.e.*, the circus —in the house of a Mrs M'Allister, a widow lady of respectability, whose husband had been a Scotchman, and, as the saying is, her heart "warmed to the tartan" at once; or rather, in my case, it warmed to a good Scotch tongue, which is much the same thing. I was soon made quite at home by my hospitable landlady, and after refreshing my inward man, I made my way to the circus.

# CHAPTER XII.

IN WHICH I SMELL THE SAWDUST; AND HAPPILY IN-
CREASE MY FAME AND MY SALARY BY WRITING A
HORSE PLAY.

THE change to the interior of a circus, even from the smoke
and soot of dusky Birmingham, was striking indeed. The
building was large, built partly of wood and partly of
brick, with a double tarpaulin roof. It was vast and dim,
and the sunlight endeavoured almost in vain to peep
through. Everything had a dull and tarnished appearance. The gilded parts were covered with cloth, and any
portion of the paint and gilt work that was visible to the
naked eye was coarse and dauby-like. The place smelt
dreadfully of sawdust, decayed orange-peel, and stable
manure, which, coupled with a large escape of gas, formed
anything but an odoriferous compound. Rehearsal had
just commenced, and I was at once introduced to the
company by the manager as "Mr Capelton from Edinburgh, the eminent Scottish comedian." The sneers usual
on these occasions of introducing new members to an
organised company were not wanting; and several
pointed *asides*, of course loud enough for me to hear, at
once gave indication that I was not remarkably welcome.
Not one had ever heard the name before; and one rather
impudent fellow, with a prominent nose, asked what I

was "eminent" for ; but I at once settled him by answer-
ing that I was rather celebrated for pulling noses—would
he like a specimen of my abilities ?

Luckily for me I at once fell into a most fortunate
position. A "grand" new piece had just been prominently
announced, entitled, "The Revolt of the Eunuchs," and
by some chance the book or books of the *spectacle* had
not arrived from London. The head man, the late well-
known Broadfoot, "the great swearer," at one time stage-
manager to that prince of riders and managers, Ducrow,
was wringing his hands in despair, and no one knew how
this terrible emergency was to be got over. The town
was pining for novelty, the Brums. had been satiated with
all the old circus pieces, and something new was decidedly
wanted. This circumstance formed the talk at the rehearsal, and various opinions were given as to what should
be done. I heard quietly all that was said, and then,
thinking that here was a chance to get on a little, in as
great a spirit of modesty as I could command, I offered
to contrive a piece to supply the *hiatus*. After some talk
about what kind of thing it ought to be—half *spectacle*
and half drama, with all the stud introduced, was the sort
of piece that was wanted—my offer was accepted. I got
to work, and next morning brought to the circus the result of my midnight reflections,—a well-written-out copy
of a piece, to which I gave the title of "The Abduction of
Selina ; or, The Revolt of the Eunuchs : a Tale of India."
I read it over to the assembled company, and, with joyous
acclaim, it was voted by them "a regular stunner." There
was all the variety of character in it necessary for a large

company—that is, there was a tyrant Sultan, a heroic eunuch, a virtuous slave, a sailor Irishman, and a capital Scotchman for myself. I took good care of "number one;" and it was rather a rich idea to have a "Sawney" disguised in a black face as an attendant in the harem. He was dumb when on duty, but, as was to be expected, had a capital tongue of his own when he had an opportunity of letting it loose. All were pleased. Even the dissipated-looking youth, in the plaid vest and ragged shirt, with the exuberantly-scanty front and the indescribable air—who played all the sentimental parts—allowed that the "gag" was sure to be swallowed. As there was little *study*—*i.e.*, but a small quantity of matter to commit to memory—the piece was copied and cut up, and we got at once into rehearsal.

Extraordinary as it may appear, some of the members of the company could not read manuscript, and had to be instructed in their parts as we progressed in the rehearsal. This is not an uncommon circumstance at all; there have been *many* instances of good actors who could neither read nor write, and who had to be taught their parts by friends who were kind enough to take that trouble. However, such a circumstance delayed and muddled the rehearsal. It was a confused affair altogether, especially at the outset, a perfect tumult of shouting, screaming, swearing, yelling, falling into confusion, doing things over again, dressing the stage, forming tableaux, fighting terrific combats, dancing hornpipes and Highland flings, &c., &c., &c., and I was really very glad when it was well over.

At three o'clock we had a grand parade in honour of

the new production; that is, we all went out in couples
to ride through some of the principal streets of the town
to show off the extent of the stud and the number of the
company. This occupied about an hour and a half. We
then returned to the circus, and I at length got home,
wearied enough with my day's exertions as a sawdust
author.

I did not make my *debut* till the first night of my own
piece—a Saturday night; and on going for the first time
in the evening to the circus, I was quite startled at the
change. Writing out the parts—studying some new
scenes that were suggested—and getting "up" in my own
character, had so completely occupied all my evenings as
to prevent my seeing the place during the time of performance. Now the scene was quite brilliant and striking.
The dark, dirty circus was transformed indeed. Innumerable jets of gas lighted up the place till it was in a perfect
glory of brightness. The coarse appearance of the paint
was softened down, and all was gay and radiant. The
boxes were crowded with ladies, and the house generally
was full to the ceiling.

The new piece wound up the evening's amusement, its
reception being all that could be desired; and, without
boasting, I may state that it was certainly as good as the
general run of sawdust plays, if not better, having what
I conceived to be a good plot, and also an attempt at the
delineation of "character," which is more, I think, than
can be said of the greater portion of the pieces which are
written for the use of the circus. My own *debut* as clown,
as also my appearance in the "drama," as I had called it

in the bills, was most successful; and the announcement made by Chirper at the close of the performance, of
my being the author, was the signal for a great burst
of applause. I was "called," and had to appear before the
curtain, when the audience made a renewed ovation. Although all this took place in a circus, I was as proud and
happy as if it had been at Drury Lane, and my "drama"
a successful tragedy; and when, next morning at rehearsal,
the manager took me aside and complimented me, and
said that I might have three guineas a week in future
I thought I was blessed indeed.

# CHAPTER XIII.

IN WHICH I DETAIL MY EXPERIENCES OF LIFE IN A
  CIRCUS, AND LET MY READERS UP TO "A THING
  OR TWO" IN THE ART OF HORSEMANSHIP.

I WILL in this and the following chapter* take it upon
me to detail in full my experiences of life in "a horsemanship," because I think I can enlighten the public, who are
said to delight in obtaining a glimpse behind the scenes,
about the ground and lofty tumbling, and the other extraordinary novelties which are to be seen in that wonderful
institution, "The Imperial British Hippodrome," as the bills
now call the circus.    Clever tumblers, professors of the
single and double trapeze, riders of trick acts, exhibitors of
trained ponies, Shakspearian jesters, and champion vault-
ers of the world ; the glittering paraphernalia incidental to
the gorgeous spectacle of " The Camp of the Cloth of Gold,"
or " The Sprites of the Silver Shower ; " or the tortuous
pyramidal feats of the dusky children of the desert ; have
not been invented quite at a moment's notice, but have
grown to perfection by slow degrees and by means of incessant practice on the sawdust.    The circus is so entirely
changed from what it was some thirty or forty years ago,
as to be almost a new institution to those who recollect

* Which appeared originally in *All the Year Round.* and are reprinted by permission of Mr Dickens.

the little mountebank parties that used to pay an annual visit to the village green, and delight the rustic sightseers of agricultural districts by giving away an occasional fat pig.

There was nothing in those times to be compared to CHIRPER'S CIRCUS, in which I was a clown. The huge travelling circus of our day, such a one as that of the Brothers Chirper, may be looked upon as a colony, and the capital requisite to carry on a profitable business may be guessed from the fact, that about sixty horses are required to work a large concern, besides a den of lions, a brace of camels, and a tumbling elephant or two, to say nothing of half-a-dozen ostriches, a performing mule, a dancing bull, and a real live deer with movable horns. Then, in addition to a corps of about thirty male and female performers, including of course the inevitable lion king or queen, and no end of acrobats, voltigeurs, and amazons, there must be a stud-groom, or "master of the horse," (circus people delight in fine language,) and under him a score of stablemen. Then, there must be a tent-master and tenters, besides the agent in advance, the members of the brass band, the pair of bill-stickers, and the many other wonderfully-nondescript hangers-on, who contrive to extract a living out of the concern. While out "tenting," as it is called, some ambitious showmen, not contented with the usual slow style of getting on, and to obtain additional notoriety, indulge now in a locomotive to drag them from town to town: thus making their grand *entrée*, preceded by what they term a real fiery dragon.

The Messrs Chirper were, so to speak, born showmen, as they came into the world at Greenwich Fair, and started in life with an exhibition of white mice. They travelled the country with all kinds of shows, growing from small to large, until now they are wealthy men, with a bank account, and the largest circus on the road. Their "Magic Ring," as they have christened it, is on a gigantic scale, having all sorts of clever people attached, to minister to the amusement of its patrons, and it dispenses daily bread and butter to a party of one hundred and thirty-seven men, women, and children—if the young of show-folks ever are children—who are dependent on it. The Brothers Chirper, like most showmen, are pleasant fellows, not overburdened with the learning of the schools, but crammed to repletion with the sterner acquirements of dear-bought experience of men and manners. Like all their class, the brothers are fond of diamonds—one of them, showman-like, wears a hoop of brilliants that cost three hundred pounds. Why is it, I have often wondered, that all showmen are fond of diamonds? The show-folk are altogether a peculiar race, and, like the fishermen of our sea-coasts, are not prone to intermarry with other classes. I could not help noting that, in our circus company, thirty-two of the persons engaged were related by blood or marriage to the brothers.

The behind the scenes of circus-dom is a quaint enough region, and of course a contrast to the "front." There is always a *soupçon* of that very peculiar zoological aroma indicative of the king of the forest. A great fire of coke burns brightly in a large iron funnel, placed in the centre of the vacant space, (the extempore green-room ;) at the curtained door, where the company enter the ring, and round it, there loiter a crowd of performers, grooms, &c. Some of them have just made their exit from the sawdust; others are making ready to enter. The fire is of great use for ventilating purposes, for there is always uppermost a strong perfume of damp sawdust, wet litter, and horse-breath, with a faint indication of bad drainage and other miseries. The scene at the fire is motley enough. The lazy black servant, habited in the gorgeous oriental robe, is attentively chalking the pumps of Mademoiselle Aurelia, the tight-rope dancer and " ascensionist," who is adjusting her pink skirts preparatory to taking her 'turn." A medical student is making hot love to Madame Francatelli, the lady-devil rider, who, as the bills tell us, " has been clothed with fame in all the capitals of Europe and Russia." The funny gentleman with the nodding queue, or tail-piece, as he calls it, looking waggishly over his whitened scalp, his nose buried in a pint of half-and-half, is one of the seven great clowns of the establishment—indeed, he is our leader—and motley is certainly his only wear, or, to borrow again from the bill, the gent in question is "that oracle of pungent satire, Mr Henry White, surnamed the Modern Touchstone." One can easily surmise that Mr White must have just given birth to something new in the joke line, and, in apt confirmation of my opinion, he offers the ring-master (that grand-looking personage, elaborately got up as a field-marshal, who is of course in the confidence of the clown) the reversion of the pewter pot. All round the fiery furnace, in concentric rings, "the strength of the establishment" crowd for warmth, and are only at intervals disturbed in their banter by the manager's warning bell, or the more than ordinary bursts of laughter evoked by myself or some other clown. There is usually lots of chaff about Tommy Griffins's "toe-rags," (*i.e.*, stockings much torn in the feet,) or any other slang subject that may be uppermost. Griffins being one of our clowns, and not over particular about the feet of his tights, a little out-of-the-way circumstance of any kind affords a great deal of food for merriment or grief. In front, all is ablaze with light and gaudy calico, and each acrobat and horseman seems to excel his neighbour in his leaps and bounds. The three hours of performance fly rapidly away, as artist after artist bounds into the ring. Trick acts, feats on the trapeze, revolving corkscrews, descending Mercuries, in short, all the varied and puzzling acts of contortion incidental to the modern circus are exhibited with a grace and dexterity, and with a firmness of nerve, which never fail to astonish.

All is *couleur de rose* at night—an applauding audience and smiling performers make the work go off with spirit. In the daytime, the circus is dark, cold, and miserable; the fiery furnace has been carried into the centre of the ring, and most of the corps are again at work, practising; for it is only by hard practice that the agility of the acrobats and horsemen can be kept up. Miss Caroline Crockett (name in the bill, Mdlle. Salvadori de Medici) is being put through a new act by her uncle. She is dressed in a short ballet skirt, and has on a pair of light canvas shoes. She takes the various leaps with wonderful precision, and only once does she miss her "tip." For a long hour, until both horse and lady shew signs of great fatigue, she is kept at her lesson ; and at night the policy of this rehearsal is apparent, for none of the company are rewarded with louder plaudits than Mdlle. de Medici. In various quiet places of the ring, little boys are trying hard to twist themselves into the most fantastic shapes ; their fathers, or the persons to whom they are apprenticed, superintending their tumbling, and sometimes joining in it. In another siding, Professor de Bondirini is practising his three sons for their drawing-room entertainment. One of them is only four years of age ; he is the little fellow that comes on as a clown, and has so many oranges and sixpences thrown him. Already, he can tumble like a ten-year old ; he made his *debut* two years ago as Tom Thumb, and has performed all sorts of business—from Cora's child, to being baked in a pie for the clown's dinner.

In the acrobatic profession culture and practice will achieve anything, if the artist can only manage to live through his trials, he may ultimately manage to defy the principle of gravity itself. Some circus children can walk better on their hands than on their feet ; indeed, at a certain age, while in training they are like to be oftener on the one than the other. By means of the kind of training they undergo, their sense of danger becomes blunted, or rather, as danger is to them a normal condition, it is ultimately disregarded. It is just by sheer physical training that some men can come down from the summit of a long pole with the most graceful air when they reverse the order of nature and descend head foremost. As a born acrobat—one of a family of tumblers—once said to me, "It's all in the practice, sir; you can train up the young 'uns to stand on their heads as easy as you could teach them to set up types."

Most people know by this time, from seeing so many entertainments *à la Risley,* that acrobats begin to work and earn money almost before they can speak. I have seen younkers twenty months old, and at that age full of knowledge of the world, dressed in spangled tights, and with cheeks brightened by rouge, assisting their parents to gain a livelihood, or "living," as we professionals call it. I need not describe how they are kicked up like balls into the air, and then tossed about from one foot to the other by their anxious parent or tutor—the practice is patent to all who visit the circus or the alhambra. Some of these children serve an apprenticeship of fourteen, or even twenty-one years ; and during that long period they have the rudiments of tumbling well flogged into them. Hard work in daily practice for many hours, by both adults and juveniles, is the price paid for the smiles and applause of the evening; old and young, indeed, must "keep at it;" and the apprentices, in some instances, have, in addition to their hard work, hard fare as well, and in many instances, cruel treatment besides. Many circuses are, in a great degree, supported by the male and female apprentices, whom the proprietor has agreed to .teach their business—the terms being their services, in return for which are given board, lodging, and instruction. Many of these bargains turn out very profitable, yielding a handsome return to the contractor, who holds the power of hiring out any pupil that may be likely to turn the penny to a handsome tune. I have known in my time one or two accomplished equestrians and acrobats who have been worth as good as twenty pounds a week to their master; and now-a-days I am told such sums are greatly exceeded, especially in the case of handsome and clever young women, as much as forty pounds a week having been given for a clever female apprentice. There is, of course, this per contra to the bright side of the account, that many apprentices turn out to be worth nothing at all, and never in the whole course of their lives achieve any reputation, or earn more than will suffice to feed and clothe them; they certainly never become what would now be called "sensation" tumblers, i.e., Blondins, or Léotards.

The preparations for the tumbling campaign which is fought in the saw-dusted arena at night, extend over the greater portion of the day. Many of the scenes at rehearsal are exceedingly picturesque. The activity of a circus corps is, so to speak, quite violent; and there is usually a large group assembled to see what is going on, or to assist in the various feats that are being got up. Ladies are there in demi-toilette practising their leaps; gentlemen in soiled tights and pilot-coats, indulging in beer, or drawing fragrant wreaths from a short "cutty," in the intervals of rehearsal, and cheered in their labours by the strains of a loud brass band, are there also; and there may likewise be seen a numerous congregation of

those nondescript supernumeraries who are always found
loafing about a circus. If there be a star performing in
some particular line of business, either equestrian or acrobatic, all the youngsters are sure to be "a-imitating of
'im ;" if the bounding youth be swinging to and fro on
the flying trapeze, the chances are that some of the
budding acrobats will try and do likewise.

How knowingly Tom Hughes glides down that rope,
descending in slow time, whirling round and round. He
is an ugly-looking fellow just now—"pock-pitted," and
badly dressed ; but at night, with his 'air plastered with
grease, and his clean white tights and close-fitting jacket,
he will look graceful enough, appearing in the bills as
the descending Mercury. Now is the time to find out
the secrets of the prison-house ; the face of that pale-
looking youth in the rather fast tweed suit haunts you,
no doubt—no wonder; that is *the lady* who has been
creating all the winter a great sensation. This wonderful
feat of a man's passing for many years as a handsome
woman, although a great fact of circus life, has never yet
been publicly known. Neither is it publicly known that
most of our best equestrians are Irishmen ; all the great
names familiar to the ring are Milesian in their sound,
and the manners and speech of their possessors smack of
the Emerald Isle. My own friend, the German Hercules,
Herr Strasburg, is a Connemara man, and was picked up
originally by a travelling circus proprietor, who saw his
great strength, and knew what, by a little *finesse,* could be
made of it.

Let me now speak of the art of getting up "wheezes,"

as the clown's jokes are called. It is a very simple affair, although I was rather nervous about it, when I was first spoken to about turning clown. In the scenes in which I act as clown, I arrange my little patter with the ring-master. If I go in with Miss Caroline, I tell him first that I will do the names of the streets; he takes his cue from that, and asks me some trifling questions which brings out the names of all the principal streets in the town. Thus, I say a desponding person ought to live in *Hope* Street, sir; a thief should have his house in *Steel's* Place; a lady who is fond of flowers should live in *Rose* Street; a humorist in *Merrilies* Court, and so on. A good portion of what is said, however, is arranged on the spur of the moment; the clown gives the ring-master his cue as they walk round following the horse, and at the next pause—there are at least two pauses in an act of horse-manship, for each scene, allow me to say, is divided into an exordium, an argument, and a peroration—the clown flies off in a verse or two of poetry about

> " What are lovely woman's sparkling eyes
> Compared with Bagot's mutton-pies?"

or,

> " Scots wha hae wi' Wallace bled,
> Scots wham Bruce has often led;
> If you want to fit your head,
> Rush to Ross the hatter's."

At rehearsals there is usually a great consumption of beer, and any quantity of professional slang, with some talk about last Sunday's dinner, and speculation about roast-pork for next Sunday. As to Blondin, or Léotard, all the men in the place, according to their own idea, are quite equal to *him;* and it is generally true that our circus acrobats could walk on a tight-rope at any height if, as they say, they had the headpiece for it—it is all a matter of nerve. There have been far greater men in the profession than either Blondin or Léotard. The greatest I take to have been a pantomimist and acrobat—a professional of the far-back ancient time, who performed for love. The story is told by Herodotus. A certain king wishing to get his daughter married, several young princes disputed for the honour of her hand. One of them appeared to be a marvellous proficient in the pantomimic art. In his enthusiasm and desire to astonish the princess he outdid himself; for, after having represented all manner of passions with his hands, he stood upon his head, and expressed his tenderness and despair in the most affecting manner by the movement of his legs.

# CHAPTER XIV.

A THING OR TWO MORE, SHEWING THAT "IT IS PRACTICE
AS DOES IT" IN THE CIRCUS, AS THAT VIRTUE DOES
IT EVERYWHERE ELSE.

IT was lately mentioned at a "crowner's quest," that in
seven months there had been no fewer than seven violent
deaths among acrobatic performers in the three kingdoms.
But what of all that? The never-ending cry still resounds
from all the shows in the country, "Walk up, walk up,
ladies and gentlemen; this is the best booth in all the
fair!" And accordingly on all sides there is a crowd of
"talent" ready to feed the market; there is strong competition for employment even among acrobats and
mountebanks, One man will stand against a board and
allow a companion to surround him on all sides with
naked daggers flung from a distance. Has not Mr James
Cooke written to the *Era* that he has "performed the
astounding feat of throwing a somersault four times in
the air before reaching the ground;" and is it not the life
ambition of Signor Jerome Mascaroni to earn money by
imitating the ape? Another man will balance himself,
head downward, on a pole thirty feet high, and in that
position drain a bumper to the health of the audience.
Somehow the physical culture and nerve requisite for
such performances are more than ever abundant; for ten

shillings a night, plenty of men can be had who will risk their lives ten times.

Many young and old folks imagine that the clown who writhes so comically under the lash of the ring-master, and who dives without introduction among the people in the pit, and whose whole existence seems one round of jokes and heads-over-heels, and an occasional personal "turn," is a merry fellow, happy as the day is long. I know better. I know one circus clown yet living, and not yet an old man, whose countenance could, and still does, set the audience and the actors, down to the very sawdust-raker, in a roar. Poor fellow! Once upon a time, when his duties called him to the circus, his only son, a lad of seven, was lying on his death-bed. He was left in charge of his sister, a girl of ten. Before his first entry into the ring for the evening, he came to me in tears: "Oh, Capelton, I 've got to be funny to-night, and my boy, my dear Willy, dying all the while! And yet I must go in." While we talked, the bell rang for his entry, and in he went, amid the roars of a crowded house. After a short interval he had again to appear ; but in that interval the servant of the lodging-house brought word that Willy was dead. My poor friend was nearly distracted ; yet the inevitable bell rang again, and he went in once more. The newspapers next day said that he had excelled himself. So he had.

There is one remarkable point of circus economy worth thinking of. How is it that we never find in the bills of the National Hippodrome such announcements as we find frequently in the bills of the theatres? For instance

we never find that the Courier of St Petersburg is to be
performed by " a young gentleman, his first appearance
on horseback ;" or that " Miss Cora Montressor will make
her *debut* on the *corde élastique*." No. circus people
never make " first appearances," in the common sense of
the term ; they are indigenous to the sawdust, as their
fathers and mothers were before them. They must be
all bred to the work. The artistes of the circus, in most
instances, fulfil a long bondage of gratuitous labour—
fourteen years generally, and in some cases twenty-one.
Their fathers and mothers being in " the profession"
before them, they commence their studies at perhaps two
years of age. I have seen a score or two of tiny tumblers
hard at work at that tender period of existence. There
is no going into the circus without preparation. On the
stage of a theatre, an ignorant pretender, who knows
nothing of the passions, may pretend to embody them,
every one, for me, (though I know better,) without hurting
himself. Let him make as free with a horse as with
King Lear, and he will find his collar-bone the worse for it.

Consequently, all circus people must work hard and
long. How hard they work to be sure ! But then, as an
old acrobat once said to me, " It is practice as does it ;
once at it, they daren't stop, but must go on till the end."
And so the child becomes father to the man, and the
infant Romeo in due time swells into the great Professor
Montague de Capulet, who, as a matter of course, exhibits
his glittering spangles before all the crowned heads of
Europe. The acrobatic child is quick to learn, for all
his faculties are preternaturally sharpened by rubbing

against those about him. When the children of society
are at school, he is drawing money to " the concern," and
can pick up pins with the corners of his eyes, as he
bends back and over, and can throw fore springs, head
springs, and lion leaps ; can, in short, do a hundred odd
things to earn applause and money. It is no joke to re-
hearse with bodily hard work all day, and then work at
night. I have had to change my clothes thirteen times in
the course of a night, because, when not otherwise engaged, I had to dress in a smart uniform and stand at the
entrance-way, to be ready to hold balloons, garters, poles,
and whatever else was required. All who enter a circus
are engaged for " general utility."

Circus business is now greatly changed, and is worked
entirely on the sensation plan, as indeed is fitting for all
kinds of showmanship. Indeed, a show is got up for the
very purpose of creating a sensation.

Even the old-fashioned travelling menagery has been
forced, by the exigencies of the times, the thirst of the
public for novelty, to go into the sensation line ; performing lions and tumbling elephants having now to be provided for the delectation of the public ; so that, instead of
the old invitation to " Walk up, and view the huntamed
hanimals of the great Hafrican desert, including the great
Rhineosirious," we are politely invited to view the dancing
elephant and the performing lions. Van Amburgh introduced this style of things to us, and at present there is
scarcely a paltry travelling menagery in which there is
not a lion-tamer or a lion queen. I once asked Miss
Helen Chapman (now Mrs George Sangers) what her

sensations were whilst whipping a den of lions through their performance, her answer was that she had no feeling about it ; she was so accustomed to it as to have no idea of the feat being a dangerous one. I feel astonished that the old lion and dog-fight which took place in Wombwell's menagery at Warwick has not been revived in this era of sensation shows ; but perhaps the taste of the present age is too refined for such a spectacle.

The pulse of the tumbling market can be felt weekly through the columns of the *Era*, a London journal devoted to the wants and wishes of all kinds of "professionals," and about which I shall have more to say in another portion of this narrative. Whatever novelties may be in the market, from a performing monkey to a declaiming tragedian, are sure to be announced in the first page of that newspaper. Thus, in a recent number, an enterprising *entrepreneur* offers a lot of "startling novelties," as, for instance, young Gunerius, (Ecuyer Norwegian,) "the original artiste on 'le passage du pont;'" Leonardo, the Danish boneless youth, "the wonder of creation ;" Felice Napoli, "the modern Hercules ;" Les Touareg, a new tribe of wild Arabs from the Atlas Mountains, bordering on the great and trackless desert of Sahara ! In the *Era* we ascertain all about Mdlle. Genevieve, the celebrated rope-dancer and ascensionist —the French Blondin, who surpasses all other artistes for grace and skill. There are a great number of other novelties besides these in the market, as "John Doe," "the Star Wizard," a great circus troupe of dogs, and "Joe Holbrook ;" and it is pleasing to note that all have

a chance of employment, as *artistes* in all branches of
the profession are wanted by more than one enterprising
manager, none, we are politely informed in most circumstances, but "first-class talent" need apply.  In the same
journal we find that while Shakspeare won't draw a house
in a provincial theatre, "Jack Sheppard" will; and generally
in all the theatres we gather that high art is at a discount,
and that sensation shows are the order of the day.

The "profession," as it is now called, had no organ in
my young days.  The news travelled quite at leisure, as
indeed did the circus, from town to town, and from village
to village.  Many a long mile I have travelled through
forest and glen in the good old circus waggon.  It was
delightful, in the fine summer mornings, to smell the
blossom of the bean or other native perfumes ; the birds
were singing their finest tunes ; and the fresh breeze,
scent-laden, struck with a sweet violence on our cheek, as
we strolled merrily along to our performing station, helped
on our path by sundry quarts of wholesome home-brewed ;
and it was equally delightful to see the happy crowd
assembled on the village green to gaze at the wonderful
show-folk ; a man riding at full gallop on a bare-backed
steed, being sensation enough for all the rustics of the
country round.  Then, in the midst of the performances,
there was the lucky bag, with the very few prizes and the
immense number of blanks.  The fun of getting a pig or
a painted tea-tray, and the roars of laughter which
saluted the clown, as he presented the rustic gamblers
with their prizes, is really beyond description.  While, to
conclude, there was the grand private wind-up of sharing

among the company the proceeds of the performance, for such companies at the time I speak of were generally conducted on the principle of a commonwealth, so many shares being allotted to the capitalists, who found the horses and wardrobe, and so many being divided among the company, according to their experience or ability.

All this sensation business, which has now become the rage, has been gradually introduced. I can remember how great a man he was thought who could turn off the spring-board ten consecutive somersaults; but now there is an acrobat (I have seen him do it in Sanger's Circus) who can turn seventy without once pausing to look over his shoulder. Surely that is thoroughly sensational! To throw a somersault on horseback, aided, as the performer is, by the velocity of the horse, is comparatively easy; but to turn heads over heels seventy or eighty times from a common spring-board, and in about as many seconds, is a feat that must have taken a long time to achieve. I once asked Mr Barnes as to this, and he told me that for a long time he could only do from twenty to thirty, but that, by constant practice and hard work, he eventually one day contrived to make out the fifty, and he does not despair of some day accomplishing the hundred! The first time that a man ventured to turn a somersault on horseback, with the animal progressing at full speed, was thought a wonderful epoch in the annals of horsemanship; but only lately I saw young Hubert Meers, on a flying animal, turn upwards of a score in succession, and think nothing of the feat. Several deaths have resulted from acrobats turning somersaults in the air. There was a man killed a year or two ago at Dublin, while endeavouring to accomplish a quadruple turn ; and I shall never forget the death of " the man from the far west." Poor fellow ! as an attraction for his benefit, he had " put up," in the hope of drawing a large audience, that he would turn three consecutive somersaults in the air ! He accomplished the feat at rehearsal, but at night—it was a sensation I shall never forget—he only turned two and a-half times, alighting on his head. We carried him to his lodgings on the vaulting board, and in a few hours he was a dead man ! He was an American, far away from home or kindred—a stranger in this country, and so he met his death.

# CHAPTER XV.

IN the summer-time we go "a-tenting." That is the word
now in use among circus people to describe their mode
of doing business in the country. It is an improvement on the old mountebanking system. Tenting continues from about April to October, and it involves a
large amount of travelling—the whole process partaking
more or less (especially when business is good) of a holiday character; but it is not, of course, all play even to the
curious nomadic race who are engaged in it, and who are
undoubtedly its most successful professors.

The system of working is very simple. A large tent,
generally about a hundred and twenty feet in diameter,
having been procured, and the various officials being well
trained in their business, the work of the summer can at
once begin. During the winter, a route, which will
occupy a month or two to travel, has been mapped out,
and about a fortnight before the town season has been
brought to a close, "the agent in advance," or *go-a-head*,
as he is now called—a gentleman whose salary and expenses for travelling will cost "the concern" about twelve

pounds a week—accompanied by a bill-sticker, starts off
in advance of the troupe. His duties are to engage suitable ground for the encampment, stalls for the horses, and
to " wake up " the *natives* with a display of gaudy bills
stuck up at all the points of vantage along the route. It
is also part of the business of this functionary to talk the
concern he represents into notoriety; he must bounce at
the various taverns at which he stops about the magnitude
of the stud, the beauty of the animals, the ability of the
company, and the immense " business " they have always
done on their tenting tours.

The company and circus " traps "—*i.e.*, properties of
all kinds fixed up in a score of huge waggons—start, perhaps, about six o'clock in the morning, according to the
distance to be gone over, which, on the average of the
season, may be twelve miles a day. Waggon after waggon
defiles from the ground, till all are gone : the band-car-
riage, gaudily decorated, containing the musicians; the
great cage, with its lions ; the black servant follows with
his herd of camels ; then come the handsome living-car-
riages of the "propœrietors," the wife or daughter preparing breakfast as they trot over the ground. The acting
manager dashes along, last of all, in a Chinese pavilion,
drawn by a pair of dwarf horses ; and all along the route
there are congregated groups of the discerning public,
who stare, open-mouthed, and wonder at the new-created
phantasmagoria.

Arrived at their destination, the performers start off to
procure lodgings and obtain breakfast. This is not so
easy a matter as may be supposed; many good people

having very hearty prejudices against the show-folk.
Breakfast being satisfactorily accomplished, it is time for
the company to get themselves "made up" for the grand
parade, which is generally fixed for one o'clock, when the
corps of performers, and all the auxiliaries that can be
pressed into service, in their gayest character-dresses,
preceded by the band, and accompanied by the den of
lions and other zoological phenomena, march in procession
through the town and its neighbourhood. The period
occupied by the procession allows the tent-master to have
the tent put up, to superintend the placing of seats and
the hanging of lamps, so that, by two o'clock, the place
may be ready for the reception of company. Red-tapists
would stare in horror at the celerity with which a circus
tent rises on the village green. The place is no sooner
fixed upon than two or three nondescript-looking men—
those odd men one always finds so plentiful about a
circus, who can do anything, from looking the part of
Bluebeard in a pantomime to shoeing a horse—rush with
pick and hammer, and drive a short central stake into the
ground, to which is affixed one end of a long measuring
tape, and round and round the ground this tape is carried,
the man at the outer end leaving a stake at certain distances; another man gets these stakes hammered into the
ground to serve as staples for the canvas, whilst nearer
the ring another row of pillars arise to support the roof.
In the grand centre stands the great pole, and round it is
cut out of the turf the magic ring, or arena, for the combined army of acrobats, horsemen, ascensionists, lion-
tamers, clowns, &c. All is got ready in little more than

an hour : performing tent, dressing tent, money tent, and every other accessary.

On the return of the company from parade, escorted by those who are to form the spectators, the performance at once begins, and is carried on with great rapidity for an hour and a-half. After the company have been dismissed, the performers have time to dine and take tea—a most welcome refreshment, for at seven o'clock all hands must again muster for the evening's performance, which is longer and more elaborate than that given in the morning. So soon as the last chords of " God save the Queen " have died away, the tent is " struck " and packed up ready for another day's march, and the lingering crowd having gradually dispersed, all is quiet. After work is over the manager and his chief aides will have their pint of beer and their pipe at the inn. The acting manager settles up all the bills—for ground money, for board and lodging, for the horses, and for all sundries supplied to the concern. Some of the tradesmen of the place will join the group, and there is no end of gossip and tobacco reek in the best parlour of the Cock and Trumpet. This pleasant dissipation is but of brief duration, however : the showman's motto must be, " Early to bed and early to rise," for next morning's journey must be duly accomplished.

The " parade," or grand *entrée*, which always takes place in each town, is the cause of what may be called " a profound sensation," especially if the day be a genial one. Then the company shine out resplendent in tinsel and gold, and spangles and feathers, and glass and zinc diamonds. There are, besides, crowns and tiaras, and rich silk and satin dresses. In the grand *entrée,* as it is called, all is *couleur de rose ;* private woes or sorrows, general to the company, are hidden for the moment, and on blood chargers, curveting and prancing, decorated with magnificent trappings, may be seen the more prominent heroes and heroines of the heathen mythology. The parade may be described as the peroration advertisement, which puts the copestone on the gaudy bills that have hitherto served to whet curiosity.

In my young days the greatest sensation that a travelling circus could get up was a " lucky bag," from which the spectators drew occasional—very occasional—prizes of a fat pig or a thumping cheese. There was no flying trapeze then, the principal interest being centred in the horsemanship, or in a little innocent ground tumbling, neither of course was there a Léotard nor a Blondin ; we had not even a pair of bounding brothers, or an exhibitor on " La Perche." A champion of England, except at coronations, was unheard of ; and Tom Sayers, or any other boxer, would have been repudiated. We had Ireland's leaps, however, a vault from the naked sawdust, without a board or any assistance, clean over a dozen horses, or a pile of soldiers with their bayonets drawn ; and old Ord, of prayerful memory, a veteran circus manager and horseman, contrived to make a slight sensation in the course of " a scene act," by changing his dress about a dozen times. Now, even our smallest circuses travel in state, their very bills being got up to produce a sensation. The agent in advance orders these gaudy posters to be stuck up on the smithy door, and in the public-house par-

lour, where they are sure to be well seen by the rural population. Circus posters now-a-days are got up in the very
highest style of the lithographic art, whilst in former
times the best advertiser was the town-crier or village
bellman. The highly-coloured sensation bills of the present day shew the sensation performers of a sensation
circus at one view, elephants and other zoological assistants included. On a circumscribed field of pink or
azure are depicted ladies of ravishing beauty, robed in
scant apparel, poised on horseback in all kinds of impossible attitudes. Then there are acrobats of the true sensation kind, men who evidently never had a bone in any
part of their body; and in these bills there are god-like
children as well, with Jupiter brows, who appear to have
been carved out of lumps of India-rubber. I can scarcely
trust myself to speak of the charming ladies who just
condescend to touch with the tips of their "sandalled
shoon" the tightest of tight-ropes. Clumsy elephants in
the gay group reverse the order of gravity and stand on
their heads with an evident degree of pleasure; and I
never in my life saw such beautiful horses, except on the
placard of some other circus; and, as any and every person
may observe who studies these bills, they are attended by
grooms of faultless proportions, who are dressed in boots
and buckskins that must have been fastened on them at
birth, and so grown with their growth. Of course there are
also British Samsons, and *artistes* of "the corde volante,"
with the oiliest of hair—an unsparing use of the best
Macassar being a *sine quâ non* in all well-regulated
circuses; and in addition to all these there is an army of

clowns evidently bursting with wit, acrobats on poles that seem to kiss the clouds, and ladies flying over garters and through balloons, with the shortest of skirts, the pinkest of pink silk tights, and the whitest of white satin slippers, all of which must at once captivate the rustic mind, and so tend to crowd the circus or hippodrome, or whatever grand name it may be known by—perhaps Champion Circus, perhaps Magic Ring. In short, the bird's-eye view of the company, as presented to the natives in this highly-attractive lithograph, forms "a *tout ensemble* unsurpassed in the annals of the equestrian art,"—*vide* handbill. I am of the opinion of the gentleman who thought the newspaper placard would be a better bargain at a penny than the paper itself; the bill of the circus in fact is the best of it, the sensation inside not being quite so perceptible.

"If circus be so grand on peaper, what will 't not be in t' real tent, with all them fine animals, and with such real live pratty men and women?" ask the natives of the rural hamlets of each other, and eagerly pay their money to see the fun. The tent is crammed full, and our friend the rustic, who has never before been in a circus, gazes around him with all his senses open. Suddenly, while John Clodpole is staring about him, a bell rings, and almost simultaneously the horse and the rider appear in the circus, the latter floating gracefully into the ring like a pinky cloud. And then is summoned Mr Merryman, who announces the style and title of the lady, and, at once, all present know that she is "Mdlle. Hamletina de Rozencrantz, the floating zephyr rider." The lady being assisted to mount, the fun and wonder begin. Now is John Clodpole in a heaven of delight; wonder, mixed with a little dash of fear, is his prevailing expression. The horse, with arched neck and flashing eye, is flying round the ring at the rate of eight or ten miles an hour, and the nymph of the floating zephyr, standing upon his back, goes through her great "trick act" with a power, if not a grace, that evokes the thunder of the gods most liberally.

Next comes the "turn," as it is called, of Mr Merryman, who, after asking the ring-master in the gravest possible tones what he "can go for to bring for to fetch for to carry for him," straightway introduces some most interesting family reminiscences, by asking the audience if they knew his grandfather; upon the simple folks laughing at this, he then launches forth no end of stories about his different relatives, from his great-great-grandfather down to his nephew's wife's last twins. It is astonishing to see with what gusto everybody laughs at the old Joe Millers. No doubt they are quite new in Rusticshire, and circus clowns are not famed for their inventive powers.

The modern Touchstones might do better, though. The clowns of the circus might, if they liked, considerably elevate their art. Our clowns cling too rigidly to the old traditions of the ring. They ought to reform this altogether, and become more than they ever have been "the abstract and brief chronicles of the time," and so satirise the "living manners as they rise."

The clown having finished his "patter," or, in professional phrase, "cracked his wheeze," and the "star-rider of the world" having entered the ring with a humility quite wonderful for one so great, the natives begin to feel astonished indeed. To see "the favourite pupil of the great and mighty Andrew Ducrow, the *ne plus ultra* of British horsemen," sitting upon the extreme verge of the horse's hindquarters with neither bridle nor saddle, so lightly that he scarcely seems to touch the animal as it flies round the ring, almost makes the gazer giddy. Again, when he springs suddenly to his feet, and, with one foot on the horse's head and the other on his shoulder, sweeps round and round at redoubled speed, the horse and he both leaning into the ring at an angle which seems to threaten every moment to send them both whirling into the sawdust, the spectators cannot choose but breathe hard.

At this point I must beg leave to make a slight digression. " How is it, papa," I once heard a little boy say, " that the horse doesn't fall into the ring altogether? and how is it that the man doesn't fall to the ground when he is leaping on the horse's back?" Now, as some of my juvenile readers may be in want of similar information, I will tell them all about it. Know, then, my intelligent young friends, that there are two well-known mechanical forces—the centrifugal and the centripetal— the first being the tendency to fly from the centre, and the last the tendency to seek it. These two forces, acting upon each other, sustain bodies, such as the planets, in their revolutions round the centre. When a horse gallops round the ring of a circus it is compelled to incline inwards, and the faster it goes the greater must be the inclination ; but, however much or little, according to the varying speed, the inclination may be, it is one which the horse could not maintain for a moment if at rest. Were the horse to be suddenly brought to a standstill in its circular course, it would at the same instant fall inwards on the sawdust. Were it to maintain an upright position, and attempt to circle round the ring, its impetus would force it outside the barrier ; but the antagonism of the centrifugal and centripetal forces upholds it, although running round inclined many degrees beyond its own centre of gravity. As to the other portion of the question, it may be replied that the motion of the horse being communicated to the rider, he is sure to alight on the animal again, no matter how high he may leap. It is the same with the balls of the juggler : the motion which is communicated to them carries them forward, so that they are sure to alight in the cup, no matter how many paces the horse may have advanced.

In due time all the wonders of the travelling circus are accomplished, and the wearied performers are glad to rest. It is no easy task this tumbling, tight-roping, and equestrianising—changing dress perhaps three times in the course of the performance, and "going in" for five or six turns. Although the salaries sound large in the ears of people who do not earn more by their brain and pen, still it must be kept in mind that "mountebanking" is a wearing-out profession, and that a decrepit old age may be yet in store for the " bounding brothers " of the ring, or even for Herr Strongbeard, the "modern Samson," himself.

In the evening, again, perhaps under the smiling

beneficence of a grand patronage, there is a second performance, the patronage having most likely been obtained through the impudence ("cheek" it is called in the profession) of the acting manager. Unfortunately, there is also a dark side to the picture, and accordingly we sometimes find a manager, on the occasions of "bad business," compelled to leave a horse behind for hay, corn, and stabling.

The tenting system is now so well organised, that everything connected with it is conducted with effect and punctuality. Every now and then the "go-a-head" will hark back across the country to consult his employers as to change or prolongation of route. The acting manager of the circus holds an important position in such consultations, and is also of great use in "working the oracle," as it is called—that is, in obtaining patronage from the influential people of the neighbourhood ; and also in seeing the gentlemen of the press, because a good word from the local newspaper goes a great length with the country people. In this way the colony of show-folks passes over a large district of country, selecting with great tact and knowledge the best places at their best time—namely, when there is a fair or other *fête* in prospect—and hitting on popular watering and sea-bathing places when they are most resorted to. As may be supposed, a large sum of money is carried off from the various halting-places on the route—one hundred pounds a day being frequently taken in the pay-carriage of a travelling circus. But it is not all gold that glitters, and such sums are, of course, subjected to heavy deductions before they reach the bank account of the proprietor. The salaries and other charges, and the miscellaneous expenses of a large circus always on the road, are too multifarious to particularise ; but they frequently amount to fifty or sixty pounds a-day, and the occasional loss of a valuable horse, or the purchase of a couple of lions from Mr Gimrack, makes a large hole in the purse. Nevertheless, circus people do occasionally retire from business with fortunes.

# CHAPTER XVI.

CONTAINS MORE CURIOUS DETAILS OF CIRCUS INDUSTRY;
SHEWS HOW TO TRAIN PERFORMING HORSES; PUTS
THE READER UP TO THE BUSINESS OF "MAZEPPA;"
AND BRINGS RAREY DOWN TO THE LEVEL OF THE
SAWDUST.

MY readers have no doubt gleaned from what I have related of circus life in town and country that the persons
employed are required to lead a tolerably industrious life
—at any rate, a circus or a show is not exactly the idle
place that many have supposed. All hands have to lend
their aid in fitting up and taking down these places of entertainment; and on such occasions as the getting up of a
pantomime, as I will by and by relate, many of the acrobats and tumblers are exceedingly useful. One of the
many avocations of circus-men is the training and breaking-in of horses; and it will no doubt be interesting to
the general public to know how these curious feats of
horsemanship, which are seen in the modern circus, are
accomplished. As I make it a rule always to keep my
eyes open wherever I am located, I saw and noted down
how these animals were taught, and I will now relate
what I observed.

One of the favourite stage directions of a former well-
known lessee of Astley's amphitheatre was, to " cut the

dialogue, and come to the 'osses." This pet maxim was no doubt founded on an extensive knowledge of mankind, who, in the aggregate, are fond of animals of all kinds; and it is certain that, to the majority of the spectators, the "'osses," as Ducrow called them, are the chief attraction of a circus. The equestrian scenes give more delight than the contortions of the acrobats, which are apparently fraught with pain to the performer, and certainly alarm a large portion of those who witness them. The scene or trick acts of the circle, in which the horses are provided with a prominent *rôle*, are always greatly applauded, and have a quiet charm about them, which the more exciting feats of the well-trained but haggard-looking voltigeurs do not possess. The spotted horses employed in equestrian performances have long been considered by the uninitiated to be a hereditary breed, cultivated only for exhibition in the arena; but that is quite a mistake, and has doubtless arisen from the eccentric colours of the larger number of circus horses. This distinction, however, is rapidly passing away, animals of all colours being now indiscriminately used—the circus proprietor picking up a good horse, wherever he can find one at a suitable price, zealously and patiently training him for exhibition purposes, and so adding to his value. Some folks have even gone so far in their ignorance as to assert that circus horses are dyed or painted. This assertion is not true as a rule, although the rustic public, fastidious in their notions of colour, and not believing in a circus with horses of a common hue, have before now been gulled by necessitous mountebanks with painted steeds of the desert, which a pitiless shower of rain sometimes exposes, to the great discomfiture of the owners. The money power being granted, it is an easy matter to obtain all kinds of horses; and proprietors of circuses, or their agents, constantly travelling about, have every opportunity of picking up suitable animals; but whatever value these may have for ordinary equestrian purposes, they have a long training to endure before they can be publicly christened "the fiery steeds of the Ukraine," "the prancing coursers of the god of day," or such other sounding name as may look well in the phraseology of the bills.

The living horse which was introduced into Corneille's tragedy, in order to represent Pegasus, upon the revival of "Andromeda" in 1682, gives us a clue to the mode of training adopted in the modern circus. Means were taken in that tragedy to give the animal a warlike ardour. Before he was hoisted up in the air by machinery, he was kept fasting so long, that his appetite became extreme; and when he appeared, a groom behind the scenes stood shaking oats in a sieve. Pressed by hunger, and excited at seeing food, the horse neighed, pawed with his feet, and perfectly answered the end designed. By this stratagem, the piece had a great run, for everybody was eager to see the animal which performed to such perfection, and which pranced high in the air as well as he could have done on *terra firma*.

Picking up a handkerchief from the sawdust is one of the "trick" acts always taught to a circus horse; and the whole teaching is achieved by the aid of a little bit of carrot, or a handful of oats, seasoned with an amount of patience and good temper on the part of the teacher which is wonderful to contemplate, and which quite bears out the fundamental principles of Rarey's system of horse-taming—that the animal is so constituted that he will not offer resistance to any demand which he fully comprehends, if made in a way consistent with the laws of his nature; that a horse has no consciousness of his strength beyond his experience, and can be handled according to our will without force; and that we can take any object, however frightful, around, over, or on him, that does not inflict pain, without causing him to fear.

Apropos of Rarey and his manifestations, our showmen all maintain that he taught *them* nothing, his process of laying down a horse having been familiar in the arena for generations back, and in constant use for the breaking-in of "scene" or "trick" horses. All the merit assigned to Rarey by our circus horsemen is, that he has had the Yankee tact to make a mystery and a fortune out of their knowledge. A well-known equestrian, for instance, tells us that "to lay down a horse" can only seem extraordinary to those unacquainted with the equestrian profession; and that for his part he was always too modest to bring a horse before an audience till the animal was so thoroughly trained that he would lie down, as in the case of the horse in "Mazeppa," without the use of any strap or other coercive means. Kindness, indeed, is laid down as a cardinal point in the breaking-in and training of all horses. The modern system is founded on sympathy, and the ancient cruelties of whip and spur are almost entirely discarded. The process, therefore, of teaching circus horses is now a very simple one, and is more a matter of unceasing labour than the exercise of any particular art or charm on the part of the performer.

To return, now, to the handkerchief. A white cloth containing a considerable quantity of oats is spread out on the saw-dust, and the horse being led round the circle, and taken up to it, is suffered to partake of the corn. This is lesson the first; and it at once fixes on the mind of the animal a connexion between the cloth and his food: he knows that by putting his head down to the handkerchief he can obtain a mouthful of oats. This, it is needless to say, he is encouraged to do; and the march round the ring being once or twice repeated, the animal requires almost no further hint, but stops at the cloth as a matter of course—indeed, would almost require to be forced past the object of his love. "You see, sir," said a circus groom to me, in the progress of my inquiry, "it's the oats as does it; the animal *will* stop at them oats; and the reason is plain, sir—he's fond on 'em, and perhaps precious hungry as well, sir."

Hard practice for a week or two will teach the animal to stop at the white cloth as readily in a trot or a gallop as in a walk. We are all this time fancying our pupil to be a quiet, steady, well-behaved horse; but if, on the contrary, the animal be high-spirited, mettlesome, and inclining to kick away with contempt the corn and hand-kerchief, a different initiatory process must be adopted—a smart hour's gallop round the circle twice a day, and an occasional short allowance of oats, will soon effect a cure, and bring the most frolicsome Pegasus to his senses. Some horses are wonderfully acute   We have known a raw animal trained to perform the part of "White Surrey" in the space of four days. Other horses, again, take months to learn the most simple trick. Future lessons in the handkerchief business are very similar to the first one. The horse having been taught to know that where there is a white cloth he may expect to find a feed of corn, naturally enough assists greatly in his own teaching. After a time, the teacher doubles over the cloth, and fastens it in a knot—the horse shakes it, in order to find the grain, but not getting at it so readily as usual, he finishes this lesson by lifting the cloth from the ground, which is just the one thing required. After the animal has done this a few times, and finds that although there are no oats to be obtained from the cloth, he yet obtains a few handfuls by way of reward, he may be safely trusted to perform the trick in public. The next step is to persuade the horse to carry the cloth a little distance—to lift it up, and bring it to the ring-master. Now, as the horse of his own will holds the parcel till it is taken from him, a very little coaxing easily persuades him to walk a few paces across the ring, it being understood that he gets a reward in the shape of a little bit of carrot, or a handful of oats.

Circus horses are taught many other tricks besides picking up a handkerchief—such as standing in tableaux, dancing to waltz or quadrille time, forming parts of the royal arms, halting instantaneously at the sound of a drum, or falling exhausted after carrying Mazeppa over the wilds of the Ukraine. In a well-appointed circus, it is necessary for them to stand quiet under all kinds of excitement. They must hear the shrill clang of the cymbals, the noise of ordnance, and the shouts of the audience, without being tempted to move or become in any way alarmed ; but when a horse has learned to do one trick, it is much easier to teach him a second one. To teach a horse to make a sudden halt at beat of drum, an assistant must be provided ready to strike that instrument the moment the animal gets into a smart trot. "If he disobeys from fright, or from not understanding the signal, cause him to trot round the circle again in the same manner as before, for a few minutes, and then repeat the signal, but not so loud. Exercise him in this till he learns to halt in obedience to the signal, yourself assisting him with all your judgment. Should he express fear at the sound, endeavour as much as you can, by your caresses and management, to convince him that it is not meant to hurt or terrify him, but as a kind of language by which he is to understand your desires. In order to impress him the deeper and sooner with the meaning of this language, let it always be used as a signal for the end of his labour or exercises. The grand secret is invariably to use a soothing tone of voice, and to reward him with an apple, or other little condiment, when he obeys." Such is the opinion of the experienced Professor Pablo.

If a loaded pistol be attached to a post or other erection in the circus, a horse can be taught to fire it by means of a piece of white cloth attached to the trigger, which the horse seizes in his mouth, and tugs under the expectation of being rewarded for his trouble.

This principle seems to be thoroughly carried out in all circus training. For instance, while teaching the animal to stand quietly, with his fore feet on a platform, he is kept supplied with portions of some delicacy, such as a bit of apple or carrot; every day this platform is heightened, till the required elevation is obtained, and so long as the horse is "good," and is attentive to his lesson, he obtains some slight reward at its conclusion.

In what the bills describe as the "Gorgeous Equestrian Spectacle of the Wild Horse of the Ukraine," otherwise, the play of "Mazeppa," the direction given by the *Castellan* is this: "Bring forth the untamed steed. Now bind the traitor on his back; let scorching suns and piercing blasts, devouring hunger and parching thirst, with frequent bruises and ceaseless motion, rend the vile Tartar piece-meal." The stage direction here is: *"Music—Cassimir is now bound to the horse's back—the horse is released, and immediately rushes off."* In other words, he bounds from the ring at his very fiercest speed, and in a moment or two we see him careering over the rocks at the back of the stage, which are supposed to represent the moun-tainous boundary between Poland and Tartary, with the helpless victim firmly strapped upon his back—dashing him about at a sad rate. But the spectators need not be in the least alarmed, for while one horse is careering up the rocks, touched every here and there by unseen grooms, the real actor is quietly smoking his pipe in his dressing-room, a duplicate horse and a well got-up dummy-rider doing duty in the various ranges of hills which have to be crossed. By and by, Mazeppa, after having endured all sorts of horrors, narrowly escaped being torn to pieces by a pack of wolves, and many other kinds of death, again enters on the scene, having reached his native and beloved Tartary. Both horse and rider are supposed to be thoroughly exhausted, and it is the cue of the animal immediately to fall down. From the constrained position of Mazeppa, it is difficult for him to give the beast any aid or guidance; but so effective has been the training of the animal, that by means of a few pats on the fore leg with a morsel of twig, it falls to the ground, as if completely exhausted; it is needless to say, amid the hearty applause of the audience.

Merely to see a trick-horse perform this Mazeppa feat, or a *manége* horse do a little "passaging" (that is, dancing sideways) conveys no idea of the unpleasantness involved in teaching—days of patient and hard work on the damp saw-dust, amid the gloom of a cold and cheerless circus.

The mode of teaching a horse to dance, and keep time to the music, is to fasten the animal with two side-reins, between the posts or pillars which support the leaping bar. The teacher provides himself with a long whip, and, as the music plays, he gently touches him with it, using the well-known "jik, jik" of the groom as he goes on. Being securely fastened to the posts, the horse can neither go forward nor backward, but the teaching of his trainer induces him to lift his legs, and from that action he obtains the rudimentary movement of his lesson. After a time, the *manége* rider will mount on his back; the horse, however, being still fastened by the side-reins, and by means of these, just at the time he is to raise his leg, he gives a gentle tug at the proper side, and so aids the movement. The whip applied gently to the horse's hind-quarters teaches him to bring them gracefully under his body, and so adds considerably to the grace of the exhibition. After a time, the side-reins are loosened, and the horse is entirely guided by the delicate hands of the rider, and, if at all apt, in a few lessons he marks time perfectly—either quick or slow time, as may be desired—with no other guide than a gentle jerk of his bridle. The master can then dismount, and come before the horse, and teach him to dance, or keep time to the music, with a wave of the hand. This is achieved by simply giving the horse a pat on the foot which he is required to lift. An intelligent animal at once takes "the office," and in course of time comes to learn what is wanted, and, like a sensible creature, in order to save the rap on the shins, lifts the leg without the whip; the mere swaying of his master's body being sufficient to shew him what is required.

There are a great many other feats performed by the circus horse, such as unbuckling his own girths, taking off his master's hat, lifting a tea-kettle from the fire—now seldom introduced, as the fire injures the horse's sight—supping with the clown, &c., all of which are taught on the same principle. In all these tricks, the moving influence is the same ; to recur again to the practical philosophy of the stud-groom, "It's the oats as does it."

The performing pig is just another example of its being "the oats as does it." This wise animal will go round in

a circle and point out the letters of the alphabet or read
a sentence, the sole power of piggy's intelligence being
vested in a quick sense of smell; as, below the A or R
that it has to point out is placed some perfumed substance that naturally attracts the nose of the pig, which,
I have heard say, in addition to its being able to *see* the
wind, is imbued with great olfactory power; and the perfection with which this is accomplished creates a sense
of wonder, especially among rustic spectators, who, as a
general rule, are fond of all kinds of animals.

## CHAPTER XVII.

DURING the period of my engagement with the Brothers Chirper, a part of the company went out on a tenting excursion to a neighbouring fair, or "mop," as it is sometimes called. We filled our purses on this occasion pretty well, and all were satisfied with the affair. It is the custom, as I have already said, on these tours to parade the town in full costume; and, as clown, I had to ride and grin upon a donkey, on which despised animal I attracted more attention than all the rest of the company, as is usual with clowns, for they are universal favourites (when not too vulgar) with both high and low.

The humours of a country fair have been often described, and I do not think that I can say much that is new upon the subject; but as I came into very close contact with a great number of showmen and performers of various kinds, a few words about the world of shows, and the show-folk, may not prove uninteresting to my readers.

The country-fair is the great field on which the penny-showman fights his battle of life, industriously wandering from one fair to another, in many instances with the show on his back, and accompanied perhaps by his better-

half, carrying a child. At these places are usually congregated a multifarious crowd of exhibitions, swings,
merry-go-rounds, Punch-and-Judys, and living skeletons
—the general price of admission being limited to the coin
I have indicated. What a powerful cause of excitement
to the whole country round is that almost indescribable
scene, "the fair," where, as I used at one time to think,
all the wonders of the world were concentrated, where
under canvas roof, there was a heaven upon earth, since
the very angels could not be more beautiful than the
enchanting being who danced on the tight-rope in the
travelling circus. A whole street of shows, with the caravan of wild beasts, containing the great lion-king in the
centre of one side, the grand original Cirque Olympic being its *vis-à-vis;* and next door to these always a theatre,
with "Blue Beard," the "Castle Spectre," "Fortune's
Frolic," and a pantomime every twenty minutes. On either
side ranged booths of various sizes. One held the astonishing black brothers, Muley Sahib and Hassan, celebrated
for jumping down each other's throats, with lighted candles in their hands; another contained the only real yellow dwarf now travelling. In the immediate neighbourhood of these celebrities were located the great Hibernian
conjuror, the pig-faced lady, the spotted boy, the Norfolk
giant, the wonderful black giantess, the far-famed ventri-
loquial celebrity, the original theatre of arts, containing
the best storm at sea ever yet invented, the five-legged
sheep, and the sea-unicorn—these two in the same booth
—the learned pig, and a host of similar exhibitions. All
around was the busy hum of the show, the eternal itera-

tion of " Walk up, walk up, ladies and gentlemen ; " the grinning of clowns from the "parade " of the booths ; the tumbling of posturers ; the ceaseless whirl of the merry-go-round ; the popping of the pop-guns at the nut-stalls ; the shrill squeak of Punch ; the everlasting crack of the ring-master's whip in the Cirque Olympic ; the terrific growl of "the celebrated spotted hyena," or the cry of " the jackal, the lion's provider," in the neighbouring menagery ; the clash of cymbals, and the sound of the drum, as well as the terrific clangour of the gong, used by the actors in one of the theatrical booths to announce the awful doom of " The Bloody Usurper ; or, The Caledonian Bloodhound and the Hag of Cape Wrath," sounding every half-hour, or at the exact period "the doomed baron " was tossed into the "bloody foam," amid a magnificent display of fireworks—two squibs and a blue-light—all these sights and sounds were mingled with the sharp " Move on there " of the watchful policeman. And the myriad crowds of gaping rustics circulated up and down, wondering, no doubt, whether the giantess inside would really be as big as the one painted on the canvas outside ; or whether the great Hibernian conjuror could, in solemn earnest, eat fire, and bring out yards of ribbon from the innermost recesses of his intestinal canal, as he promised in his speech ; or what kind of a show "Hajax a defyin' of the litenin'" might be, and whether there was really any difference between the lion and the dog, in the renowned combat, except—the skin ; or whether the whole scene was not a mockery, a delusion, and a snare ; and whether it would not be better to spend their money at the ginger-bread stalls, than risk it upon the great sea-serpent—seeing that there were three of that genus in the fair—or the cobra-de-capella, or the albino lady, or any of the hundred other exhibitions that dotted the show-ground.

All this lasts, however, only for a day. The morrow comes, and the magic of the scene is over, the dregs of the excitement alone remain, and all who have taken part in the orgy are fatigued and *blasé*. The tents are speedily struck, and the show-folk are again on the move to their next place of rendezvous. The roads are covered with caravans; the great waggons containing the unequalled menagery of wild beasts move slowly along the dusty highway, closely followed by the circus and its "stud of 'ighly-trained hanimals," and the theatrical booth with its bloodthirsty dramatic paraphernalia. Following in the wake of these we have the clean little pigmy waggon, with its brass rails and polished knocker, which the showman calls his living waggon, and which is looked upon by the fraternity as an index of social condition. "It has always been considered a proof of the showman's improving circumstances when he adds the living waggon to his establishment." The road from the fair is but the road of life. We have the aristocrat of the "perfession," travelling comfortably in his gig, his wife and family settled, may be, in a pleasant farm in the country, from whence the food for the animals is obtained; the middle-class showman, again, rides in the waggon; the next class move on in their donkey-carts; while the lowest grade of all leave the fair as they came to it—on foot—the man with show on back, and wife and child trudging patiently by his side, happy in having collected two or three pounds' worth of penny-pieces by the preceding day's exertions.

So much for the general aspect of the country fair, I now come to the details as engaged in by myself.

We arrived at the town which we had fixed upon on the evening before the grand day, and on proceeding to the show-ground we found that a countless host of exhibitors of various kinds had arrived before us, and were proceeding to erect and fit up their places of exhibition. The shows were of the usual description—conjurors, theatrical booths, menageries, giants, dwarfs, pig-faced ladies, learned pigs, peep-shows, swings, hobby-horses, merry-go-rounds, performing-dogs, the horse with three tails, the sheep with five legs, the happy family, the industrious fleas, the performing canaries, and perhaps a score of others, even the names of which I cannot now remember. Of course, no performances can be given on the fitting-up day. All are busy, however, preparing for the morrow, and the show-ground is crowded by wondering rustics, anticipating with gleeful laugh the wonders of the shows.

At an early hour upon the day fixed for the fair or mop, the business commences. Little bands of rustics have been pouring in from all parts of the surrounding country, and the market town and its houses of entertainment speedily become crowded. In the early part of the day business goes on apace. Goods are bought and sold, and servants are hired with due despatch ; and about twelve o'clock the sounds of martial music are heard, and the crowds on the street divide to each side. " It's the show-folk ! it's the show-folk !" is now the cry, and onward we sweep in grand procession, headed by a band, the musicians sitting in an elegant carriage, or rather triumphal car, drawn by six splendid cream-coloured horses. The company followed in pairs, dressed like cavaliers and ladies of the olden time. Reader, your humble servant brought up the rear of the procession, dressed as clown, riding upon a gaily-caparisoned donkey ! If admiration of the show of horses and grandees greeted the first part of the procession, bursts of laughter waited upon the clown. The fool was the great feature of the scene, and there he sat, grave as a judge, with his face tailward, unmoved by the cries of " Oh, but look at the fool !" " Look at the fool !" "Here be the show-folk," &c. In country places, " the show-folk " is the universal name given to all persons connected with exhibitions, no matter whether they are exhibitions of wax-work, shows of wild beasts, or theatrical booths.

Our procession, or rather parade, was meant simply to be an advertisement, and it answered the purpose admirably. We were only out for about half-an-hour, during which we made the tour of the town, and were followed up and down by great crowds of people, most of whom followed us to the scene of performance, and witnessed our efforts. We had a very large tent, and, with the aid of additional canvas, fitted up a place that accommodated a thousand people ; and as it was choke full at each performance, and as we performed eight times at the prices of one shilling and sixpence, we reaped a golden harvest —not less, I should say, than two hundred and fifty pounds. Our manager worked the speculation with great tact. He brought nearly the whole stud of horses from Birmingham, in order to make a fine parade, but took good care to send most of them back, so as to be in time for the performances at home. The remainder was still more than was necessary; but it allowed the various performances to follow each other with greater rapidity, as the horses were only required for alternate exhibitions. Those of the company engaged at the fair were of course allowed extra pay.

A great deal of money is pocketed upon such occasions, and many exhibitions do nothing else but make the tour of the fairs. It pays them well to do this, and some of the more popular kind have made fortunes in the business. A few members of a circus often join together in the summer season, and go out to the country upon what are called mountebanking excursions, giving away presents in the way of lottery, and resorting to various devices to keep the steam up. The party, of perhaps six people, with three horses, &c., also attend the smaller fairs, and continue, as they say, to knock out a living by such means. They usually perform in the open air, just upon a common or in a grass field, and trust to the liberality of the company for their reward—or to the success of the lottery, where, as usual, the blanks greatly outnumber the prizes. These open-air exhibitions frequently give rise to circumstances of a ludicrous nature. I remember being told of a party who went out on an excursion of this kind with their horses; but these animals, not being of the usual piebald colours, failed to draw any spectators; the public would have nothing but horses of the right sort. There was no alternative left but to paint the horses the usual fantastic colour. "But the rain, sir," said my informant, "spoilt the thing entirely. A sudden shower came on one day while we were out, and muddled the whole thing, so that we were obliged to cut, amid the jeers and laughter of the people."

For showmen to deceive the spectators at a country fair is a very common thing; and this plan of painting a horse is just a type of the petty rogueries which are constantly taking place. Barnum has so effectually laid open the "Behind the Scenes" of showmanship, that there is nothing left for the poor gullible public but to doubt the evidence of their own senses, and never to believe that anything in the shape of a show is really what it is represented to be. Lady giants, for instance, are always humbugs; they have long dresses made to trail on the floor of the caravan, in order to hide the erection on which they are mounted,—viz., a pair of high sandals, with soles perhaps six or eight inches thick, on which they walk up and down the exhibition booth with great dignity; and with such aids it must be admitted that they do look rather tall. I remember even of a giantess who walked on short stilts; and on one of these going through a hole in the caravan, she bent forward in order to release it, and, to the great horror of the spectators, broke her leg; but it only ended in an *exposé* and a burst of laughter at the deception. As to exhibitions of mermaids, six-footed sheep, three-horned bulls, &c., I can honestly say, from personal experience, that most of them are shams. I knew of one show which was drawn from fair to fair by two oxen. It always arrived about midnight, so that nobody saw how it was propelled; and when I state that these very identical oxen, painted fantastically, one of them ornamented with an additional horn, and the other with an additional tail, formed the very prosperous and sole exhibition of the ingenious showman,—my readers will see how they can be gulled. Even as I correct these sheets for the press, a paragraph is " going the round," explaining how a cattle-dealer had cheated the judges at a prize cattle-show, by putting false horns upon one of the prize animals, and otherwise ingeniously cooking it up for the show. Farmers, however, have not one-half the ingenuity of showmen, who can make any man's eye the fool of his other senses.

This part of my subject naturally leads to a consideration of what has been called the showman's "mission;" touching which a grave political journal condescended, once upon a time, to leave off politics and discuss the social position of the "brutal showman," and his victim, "the show." The line of argument adopted was, that the pig-faced lady, the spotted boy, the yellow dwarf, and all similar exhibitions, were in the position of slaves, held captive against their will, in order that the showman might grind them into cash. Now, seeing that it is within my own knowledge that a pig-faced lady has been manufactured out of a shaved bear, I cannot help thinking that, in her ladyship's case, the best thing that could have happened, both for herself and the public, was her being strictly retained in slavery by the showman. Giants

and giantesses, again, may be presumed to be so well able
to take care of themselves as to be beyond the pale of our
sympathies; while the spotted boy, seeing that his spots
are amenable to the well-known action of soap and water,
may be considered one of the knowing ones himself.

And as to the "victims" of the showman in general, I beg
to inform all who may feel interested in the question, that
they are great adepts in the art of what is vulgarly called
taking care of "No. 1." In fact, to speak the truth, the
"show" is often more than a match for the showman; and
I once knew "a wild Ingian" who made little ceremony
about hiring a new master whenever he thought the old
one slow in his duty. I may say, in reference to the
show world, that a good show can be manufactured out of
very little. The Feejee mermaid, as will be seen in my
next chapter, is an example of this; and I knew a man
who made a deal of money by exhibiting a few coloured
views of Windsor Castle through a magnifying glass at a
penny per head. The shaved bear was the last remaining
inhabitant of a menagery. The proprietor saw that he
was used up in the wild beast line, and so he had his old
performing bear done up as a woman, clean shaved, and
tied into a chair, and then announcing her as the celebrated
pig-faced lady, recruited his finances, and so replenished
his menagery. In fact, there is no end to the trickery,
and barefaced, although amusing, robbery which are per-
petrated by showmen and exhibitors. In the right
hands, as I have indicated already, anything will make a
show. I have seen a more than ordinarily large egg (it
was cut out of chalk and deftly spotted) exhibited in an

English market town. I knew of an egg-hatching apparatus that was a swindle. Eggs at the point of bursting were procured and shewn to the wondering spectators as being hatched by steam. As my next chapter will initiate my readers into the working of the oracle as regards showmanship, I need say no more on these points.

# CHAPTER XVIII.

THE exhibition-world, and what it contains, and the singular people who are in most instances connected with it,
have ever been a pleasant source of wonder, especially to
the gullible portion of the public ; and a really good show
is one of those things which are certain to yield any number of fortunes.   It is no matter what it is ; it may con-
sist of but one thing, or it may be a museum containing
a thousand articles ; it may be either Tom Thumb, or
Wombwell's united collections of wild animals, the original
learned pig, or Richardson's dramatic booth—only let it
get properly afloat, under the charge of an enterprising
manager, and it becomes straightway a magnet drawing
to itself the superfluous cash of the country for miles
around.   Has any person ever calculated the enormous
amount of money annually expended on shows ?   Were
the receipts of all our exhibitions, stationary as well as
itinerant, added together, and the amount shewn, it would
appear fabulous.   Without including an occasional show
like the World's Fair of 1851, but taking into account all
established places of amusement, from such high-class
shows as her Majesty's Theatre, down to the humblest

exhibition at a country fair, we could easily shew, startling as it may seem, that the annual amount expended on
our various shows and exhibitions is greater than that
expended on books and periodicals. Mr Richardson, the
proprietor of the well-known dramatic booth, or "Richardson's show," as it was called, died, we are assured, worth
£50,000; and the late Mr Wombwell, the proprietor
of the extensive menagery, was equally wealthy. Many
other showmen have likewise accumulated fortunes, and
left at their death sums of money greater than those
accumulated in the publishing trade.

The gullibility of the public and the love of the marvellous call into action the inventive genius of a class of
people who are ever ready to turn the public craving into
a means of making money; and, in addition to what we
can make up at home, every portion of the globe is ran-
sacked in turn to find novelties for the showman: the
hippopotamus is caught, and hurried away from his
African haunts to the Regent's Park; the united twins
are taken from one of the distant Slave States of America,
and conveyed to Europe for the same purpose; and we
have good reason to suppose that an enthusiastic showman has started off to St Helena, in order to secure, if
possible, the great sea-serpent that has been seen so frequently of late disporting itself off that island. When a
showman has secured something with a look of novelty,
the next great point is to dress up a good story by which
to recommend it to public notice, or, as the showmen say,
get out "a stunning gag." Nothing is so attractive as a
marvellous legend of some kind or other; in fact, every-

thing connected with a show should smack of romance. Barnum was completely master of this art, and the history of how he "worked" the Feejee mermaid may be taken as a type of the quality of good showmanship, as devoted to this particular branch of the business.

The Feejee mermaid was one of Mr Barnum's most successful American speculations. This young lady was heralded to the public of New York by glowing descriptions and flattering criticisms in the leading papers of that city; and the ingenious exhibitor contrived numerous plans to increase the interest the press had created, and keep up at its full height what he designated "the mermaid fever." Woodcuts and transparent views were got up, portraying the mermaid at full length; and a pamphlet was issued under Mr Barnum's auspices detailing her history, and proving her authenticity. Editors and reporters were favoured with "private inspections," and went away honestly persuaded that what they had seen was a veritable mermaid. In fact, it was almost impossible to detect the hand of the *manufacturer* in the composition. This was a combination of the upper half of a monkey, with the lower part of a fish; and the monkey and the fish were so ingeniously conjoined, that nobody could discover the point at which the junction was formed. "The spine of the fish proceeded in a straight and apparently unbroken line to the base of the skull—the hair of the monkey was found growing down several inches on the shoulders of the fish—and the application of a microscope actually revealed what seemed to be minute fish-scales lying in myriads amongst the hair. The teeth, and

the formation of the fingers and hands, differed materially
from those of any monkey or orang-outang ever discovered,
while the location of the fins was different from those of
any species of the fish-tribe known to naturalists. The
mermaid was an ugly, dried up, black-looking, and diminu-
tive specimen, about three feet long. Its mouth was open,
its tail turned over, and its arms thrown up, as if it had
died in the greatest agony." The person from whom Mr
Barnum bought it informed him that it had been obtained
from some Japanese seamen, by a sailor in Calcutta ; and
not doubting that it would prove a valuable speculation,
Mr Barnum became its proprietor and exhibitor ; with
what success may be inferred from the fact, that "the receipts of the American Museum for the four weeks immediately preceding the exhibition of the mermaid, amounted
to 1272 dollars ; while, during the first four weeks of the
mermaid's exhibition, they amounted to 3341 dollars 93
cents."

For the success which attended the speculation, however, Mr Barnum was indebted in a great measure to the
notices in the New York papers, and the rumours regarding the history of the Feejee mermaid, which he caused to
be industriously circulated. On this point, he says in his
Autobiography : " I called respectively on the editors of
the *New York Herald*, and two of the Sunday papers,
and tendered to each the free use of a mermaid cut, with
a well-written description, for their papers of the ensuing
Sunday. The three mermaids made their appearance in
the three different papers on the morning of Sunday, July
17, 1842. Each editor supposed he was giving his

readers an exclusive treat in the mermaid line ; but when they came to discover that I had played the same game with the three different papers, they pronounced it a *scaly* trick."

Previous to introducing the mermaid to the 'cute people of New York, Mr Barnum contrived to create for it a wide reputation as a curiosity, by means of a very ingenious stratagem. A letter was sent to the *New York Herald*, dated and posted at Montgomery, Alabama, giving the news of the day, trade, the crops, political gossip, &c. ; and also an incidental paragraph about a certain Dr Griffin, agent of the Lyceum of Natural History in London, who had in his possession " a remarkable curiosity, being nothing less than a veritable mermaid taken among the Feejee Islands, and preserved in China, where the doctor had bought it at a high figure for the Lyceum," &c. About a week afterwards, a similar letter, dated from Charleston, South Carolina, was published in another New York paper. This was followed by a third, from Washington, published also in a New York paper, and expressing a hope that the editors of the New York papers would beg to have the mermaid exhibited in the "empire city," before its removal to London. Two or three days after the publication of this thrice-repeated puff, Mr Barnum's agent—who had assumed the name of Dr Griffin—was duly registered at one of the principal hotels of Philadelphia.· His gentlemanly and dignified manners, and his sociable temper and liberality, gained him "a fine reputation ;" and when he paid his bill one afternoon, previous to setting out for New York, he thanked the landlord for his courtesy, and offered to let him see something extraordinary : this was the Feejee mermaid. The host was so highly gratified, that he asked permission to introduce some of his friends, including certain editors, to view the wonderful specimen. The result was the publication of several elaborate editorial notices of the mermaid in the Philadelphia papers, which thus aided the press of New York in spreading abroad its fame. Of course all this work with printers' ink, as Barnum loved to call his billing and puffing manœuvres, was but the prelude to the one grand object, the exhibition of the mermaid, which was obtained as a great favour, and "positively for one week only," &c. The sequel may be guessed—the mermaid became ultimately a chief attraction of the American Museum.

This *working the oracle*, as it is called by professional people, is a most important feature of showman life. It is a kind of slang term much used by the class I allude to; and it may be translated as the art of getting people into the show, and of getting the exhibition so magnified in public estimation that it becomes the talk of the town and the theme of the press. The man whose business it is to work a show must have a peculiar talent, or rather tact ; he must be great in the art of palaver, have a ready wit, and be able to write out a first-rate bill, (or, at least, to know when a bill or placard is well written ;) and, like a good general, he must inspire all under him with confidence in "the concern." Barnum, who knows better than any other man how to transform a monkey into a mermaid, is a type of what is meant—his knowledge of the effect of printers' ink is undeniable. A good agent, or oracle-worker, is able to achieve a great success even with a bad subject, (*vide* the talking fish;) and for that he must possess in an eminent degree the art of hiding the nakedness of the land, and of covering up all imperfections. Such a man is worth any money, because a show may be ever so good, and yet fail from not being properly worked. A man may be able to paint a beautiful panorama, and yet not have the talent to describe it, or even to catalogue its merits in a glowing poster, fit to glare on the walls with the bills of other exhibitions. I have known several good shows that were failures till they got into the hands of the right man. A certain celebrated travelling wizard is immensely indebted to his secretary for getting up clever "sensations," and writing stirring stories about his performances. The best agents travel with or go before the most intellectual exhibitions, such as panoramas, conjurors, ventriloquists, &c. These gentlemen must make the most of everything that occurs, that can be turned to the advantage of the concern, whatever it may be. If a wild beast should chance to scratch the keeper's hand, the incident must at once be exaggerated into a "heroic encounter with a ferocious tiger," detailing minutely, how Signor Giacombo Frizelli, the celebrated lion-tamer, encountered a raging tiger, and how its fangs could not be loosened from his arms, till a red-hot poker was bored into the animal's mouth, &c., &c. There is always a mode of getting these little matters dressed up and inserted in the newspapers; the consequence is, of course, a rush to the particular circus or menagery where the exciting event took place. The people so love excitement that they will pay any money to obtain it, as we have all witnessed in the case of the gentleman who travelled with Van Amburgh, in order to make certain of being present at the moment when the lion should snap off that person's head. To make the most of such little incidents as a scratch from a tiger is "working the oracle."

There are men of position and capital, too, who are not above working the oracle, or taking a share in a good show or exhibition. Entertainments of various kinds travel the country at the risk of gentlemen in London, or other large cities, the exhibitors being paid a sure weekly salary, and attended by an agent who works the show with more or less effect. Provincial printers are noted for their *penchant* to speculate in exhibitions. A case which was lately before the Court of Bankruptcy at Birmingham let us have a peep into some of the speculations by which an amiable printer of that town had "dropped" a great deal of money. It requires much natural tact, as well as a great deal of acquired knowledge, to travel successfully with a show. Some towns are good for one description of show and bad for another. Thus panoramas "take" best in cathedral or educational towns, such as Lichfield, York, or Edinburgh—the latter city being particularly good for a "Holy Land" every two years, as a smart agent once told me. The genteel conjurors at high prices are also very favourably received in such cities ; while the bouncing necromancers and wizards hailing from particular points of the compass, who talk loud and hold lotteries, are most appreciated in manufacturing or commercial towns. Acrobatic exhibitions, menageries, &c., take best in the densely-populated manufacturing cities; and the rural population situated about our quiet English market towns are fond of " the horsemanship." All the likes and dislikes of particular counties or towns have to be studied, and a good manager will work his way from John o'Groat's to the Land's End, with a tact that will keep him clear of the places where he is sure to " drop his tin." He knows all the best places to visit, and the best time to visit them.

One of the best-worked shows of recent years was the exhibition of the Astecs—the bird-children from a mysterious city in Central America. The whole affair was, in the graphic language of the profession, " a dead sell." I had the whole story from a clever friend of mine, who was secretary and oracle-worker to a popular wizard, and it just corroborates all that I have already said. The children were found in America in a penny show, and were being exhibited along with a learned sow. They were brought to London, and a fine story about them was written in the parlour of a public-house by the gentleman I have referred to. This show was a great success, especially in the provinces; and the children are still travelling about, the grand story about their having been worshipped as idols in a Mexican temple still, no doubt, finding credence. The "What is it?" will recur to many. This was a nondescript impersonated by Hervio Nano, (or Leech,) who was a sensation-tumbler some twenty-five years ago. The exhibition was got up by Barnum.

Hervio was clothed in a dress worn for the purpose, and the show was very extensively placarded, each of the posters containing a picture of the anomalous animal; but, notwithstanding the best efforts of the astute speculator to "gull" the public, the exhibition was a complete failure, in consequence of the exposure of the hoax by Mr Mitchell of the Zoological Gardens, and Mr Waterhouse, the naturalist. The exhibition opened at ten o'clock and was closed by two! Poor Hervio Nano, the man-beast, afterwards committed suicide; and so, alas! did Mitchell. The Tom Thumb campaign is too well known to require recapitulation here, and the exhibitions of Earthmen, Zulu Kaffirs, and bearded ladies are too recent to require detailed notice.

# CHAPTER XIX.

HAMLET, ON HIS WAY TO LONDON, FALLS INTO THE DEN
OF A PUBLICAN ; AND PERPETRATES PANTOMIME IN
A SINGING - SALOON FOR THIRTY-SEVEN SHILLINGS
A WEEK, FINDING HIS OWN BEER.

WHO ever heard of a contented player ? No person.
Such a character would indeed be a *rara avis.* The very
principle that gives votaries to the stage repells all con-
tent. From the moment that the victim of Thespis rubs
his back against the scenes, " farewell the tranquil mind."
From that instant he is changed ; transformed as if by
the potent wand of harlequin, he becomes a being of a
different nature, doomed, during his theatrical existence,
to misery. Even if from the commencement of his
novitiate he " leads the business," he is miserable, and
never contented.

Here is a catalogue of a few of his sorrows :—The
manager does not make his name sufficiently prominent
in the bills; he ought to have a dressing-room to himself ;
he is not efficiently supported by the company, who are a
set of muffs ; his salary, considering what he draws, (who
fills the house, he should like to know ?) is an insult—it
don't keep him in gloves ; the wardrobe would disgrace a
booth—he never can get a dress fit to wear ; there are
not half enough of " sups." for the battle or court scenes ;

the *Gravedigger* will insist on spoiling his "business" over *Yorick's* skull by his "infernal mugs,"—how can the audience laugh at such buffoonery?—it only shews their want of taste; the low comedian's song attracted all the attention from him last night in the tavern; or, the criticism in the *Weekly Pepper-Box* has hurt his sensitive feelings: but, "no wonder," he says, "is it not written by a friend of Clarendon's," (Smithers is Clarendon's real name,) "and is not Clarendon my rival?"—and so on, through a long catalogue of discontent. It is the same with the young lady who "does" the juveniles. She thinks all the other actresses detest her; and, quietly speaking, she is not far wrong, as she, also, in her secret heart, detests them. The lady who sings, hates by instinct the leader of the band; he will spoil her best songs, and, of course, the band never keeps right time, and the violoncello drowns her voice altogether; in fact, the accompaniment is always too low or too high, or in a wrong key. Everybody naturally hates the stage-manager. "He is *such* a brute," Miss Fyggenson, (real name, Mary Ann Buggins,) who plays the breeches parts, says. Then, even that lady with the very, very short skirt, and the very, very pink legs, and the very, very suspicious-looking sandals, who dances, is not pleased. She has an ambition that lady, and when she is at home she rattles off long screeds of the fiery *Bianca*, the passionate *Juliet*, or the loving *Pauline*, or sings the song-snatches of the gentle *Ophelia;* in short, this lady, instead of leading the *figurantes*, would, if she could get leave, lead the business! The very prompter grumbles; for, as he says, when a muff like

Leon d'Arcy Latimer (real name, Simpkins—father a pork-butcher in Clare Court, Drury Lane) is stage-manager, what might he not aspire to? It's all cheek, says Mr Algernon Percy Splutter, (Splutter, by the way, is a famous stage name.) Cheek is the only commodity that is marketable now-a-days, and the great man turns up his eyes and shrugs his shoulders as he solemnly announces the fact.

And so the world wags on behind the scenes, every mite in that little kingdom considering himself the cheese itself. Even the call-boy, who has rather a *penchant* for low comedy, thinks, if he could only get a trial in *Benjamin Bowbell*, "wouldn't he just stun them—*rayther.*" Only let him try it, that's all. And so, as we can learn from these examples, there is no such thing as contentment among players. The very painter murmurs at the eternal use of old scenes made new. "No wonder the piece didn't take, my boy," he says; "how could it, with that d——d old rubbish of scenery?" and then, turning up his eyes, he quietly gives it to be understood, by the exercise of a little pantomime, that the management is going to a very warm place indeed; "and serve the management right, too," he says. He never saw such a thing before; "only think, we are reduced now to do one scene on the back of another—my eye!"

This discontent became no less a failing of mine than of others of the tribe, for, after a time, when the novelty of being a clown began to decay, I felt that irresistible desire for change which had always been a part of my nature. My longing, too, for a higher place in the drama

than a clown's, had, on the present occasion, something
to do with my resolution of once more attempting to gain
a position on the regular boards. I felt that I had it
within me to do something, and, like other great men in
their struggles with adversity, I resolved that out it must
come. I was determined that ambition should not, if I
could help it, mock my useful toil.

To effect this I determined to "cut" the sawdust, and
the motley garb of the clown. The poor clown, although
he appears a very funny fellow to his audience in the circus, has his trials and his sorrows—his jokes and jests
being often a mere coat of paint to hide a grief; and his
position entails upon him a great many *désagrémens* that
are hid from the outward gaze. His exertions at rehearsal are as severe as those of the other members of the
company, especially if he be a posturing clown ; for it is
only by the most constant practice that he can keep his
body up to the requisite point of flexibility, suitable for
tumbling. The jesting, spouting, swaggering clown, again,
has to be on the constant rack for new jests and anecdotes,
all of which have to be rehearsed and arranged with the
ring-master ; and if he hits upon a few good ones, and gets
a volley of laughter at night, (all his reward,) he obtains
as his *per contra* the envy of his brother clowns, and the
*chaff* and sneers of the other members of the company.
Who could think of entertaining particular consideration
for the man who wears the motley ? I somehow felt
rather diffident amidst the turbulence and vulgarity of the
place ; it better suits those who are native there "and to
the manner born ;" and, notwithstanding the "great fact"

of my salary's having twice been raised, I determined to leave Chirper, and seek fame in that great metropolis, "where success is fortune, and failure no disgrace."

Before proceeding to London, I got an offer, through a personage—a professional—whom I had become acquainted with in Edinburgh, which I did not think proper to reject, to sing and arrange a little pantomime for next Christmas in a saloon at Manchester.

As I was anxious to see as much variety in this professional way of life as possible, I thought a few weeks' engagement in a tavern-theatre would be something new, and so it was. The company, I found, consisted of a lady-singer, a comic-singer, a nigger-singer, a "sentimental vocalist," a *danseuse*, and a posturer. As soon as I joined, it was proposed by the manager that we should get up a little piece of some kind; and, to meet his wishes, I transmogrified "Robert Macaire" into a ballet, and, tolerably acted by the company after a considerable amount of drilling, it met with greater success than I anticipated.

My salary in Bobin's saloon was thirty-seven shillings per week, which was decidedly handsome ; only there was a considerable drawback in the quantity of liquor which the landlord expected us to consume. He made his money by the sale of the drink. There was nothing to pay directly in cash to see the amusements, but the waiter was constantly in the saloon, with "Give your orders, gentlemen, give your orders ;" and out of the profits of the ale, porter, and spirits which were sold, the landlord paid his rent and salaries, and banked a handsome yearly surplus.

Such places are now very numerous, and have greatly hurt the regular theatres. The drink is a decided attraction; and when a person wants a pint of beer, he goes to such a place as Bobins's, because there he gets more value for his money than elsewhere, never thinking that because he has a discount in the shape of amusement, that therefore that very circumstance attracts him more frequently from his home, and conjures a greater number of sixpences out of his pocket. The extension of these saloons must, in the very nature of things, damage the legitimate drama. Many of them are fitted up now with great magnificence, and the ladies and gentlemen who are engaged to perform in them are of unquestionable talent. Large salaries are very often paid in many of the saloons for the purpose of securing parties of name as performers; and in London such places are fitted up with great regard to style, and refreshments of a superior kind are supplied to the company at a moderate rate.

The person who procured me the engagement at Bobins's was an Aberdeen man, who had adopted a professional life. I had at one time been of some service to him in Edinburgh, when he was friendless and in poverty, and upon the occasion of my going to Manchester on my way to London I again met him, and we renewed our acquaintance. He at once repaid me a little sum of money which he had borrowed from me; and which, by the way, I never expected to finger again, and pressed me hard to join the company at the saloon in which he was engaged, and, as I have already said, I did so. The place was crowded every night, and a great sum of money must have been drawn, both for the performance proper, and also on account of the performance which took place after the general audience was dismissed. The lady performers of the saloon are also a great attraction for the money-spending young gentlemen, and for that reason managers endeavour to procure as good-looking young damsels as it is possible to get. The general salaries in such places are liberal, and regularly paid; and this fact gives another blow to the theatre, because, after young actors have had their dream of ambition out, and find how they have miscalcu-lated the effect of their being in the theatrical market, or, in other words, how few of their imagination-eggs bear chickens, money comes to be the one grand consideration with them, and they soon leave the regular boards to seek a comfortable engagement in the saloon.

# CHAPTER XX.

WITH the proverb of success or failure quoted above on
my tongue's end, I took leave of the salooners, and my
departure from the city of cotton, *en route* to London
where, in the due course of railway punctuality, I arrived
in safety. True to the old instinct, and unlike the Scotch,
nothing would serve me but a hotel—an expensive one,
too, in which, as in my old commercial days, it was my
use and wont to "take mine ease."

I was, fortunately for myself, not penniless, and had a
large stock of useful dresses and properties, which are, as I
have already said, an invaluable appendage to a young "professional." I was not long in London before I discovered
it to be a gross absurdity for an obscure player like myself to be living in style at Anderton's in Fleet Street.
Add to this the fact of my having been compelled to give
a loan of a few sovereigns to an evident pick-pocket, who
neither gave me an I O U nor an address, and the
reader will see another very good reason for a reduction
of my expenses.

I soon found out, too, in addition to my financial sorrows, that I had come up to London at the wrong time for an engagement. It was summer-time, and an awful hot one it was, and at that period none of the theatres were open. Week after week was passing on, and my stock of cash was fleeting rapidly away, but no engagement came. It was in vain that I rushed to the "Sporting Bear" every Friday evening, to read the first edition of that godsend to actors—the *Era*. It was equally in vain that I hurried with equal celerity to my lodgings to write to all the theatres which I saw were about to open, —no engagement came. Letter after letter was sent but it was a mere waste of postage. At last I was about to give up; in fact, I was nearly reduced to my last guinea, when an advertisement caught my eye from Andrew Gillon, the theatrical agent, now dead and gone, poor man.

I paid seven-and-six down before the great man would say one word to me; but the silver talisman had the desired effect. He opened his book of fate, and at last I was made happy; an engagement was offered, and the idea of again being employed, and perhaps at length having the chance of making myself famous, almost took away my breath. Gillon's announcement of the place and terms was exceedingly brief. A town in Essex was the spot—Crockby was the manager—utility was the business —and twenty shillings per week was the salary!

I packed up and packed off, happy as a king. I rushed to the station and booked myself for Romford; and after a walk of two miles, carrying a large bag containing my theatrical traps, I got in safety to the place ; but the manager had found it convenient, after a few days' experience, to make his exit from the cares of management, and rush up to London—in search of novelty, as he said—but, as it occurred to me, in search of a hiding-place. I found young Gordon, of Sadler's Wells, among the company — rather a respectable set — and he very kindly advised me to get away back to London with all the speed I could. Young Gordon was a Scotchman, and there was some little mixture of Scottish selfishness in his advice, as I afterwards found. The fact is, after "the illustrious manager" (Crockby) had "cut his stick," the company took upon themselves the cares of conductorship, forming themselves into a sharing republic, with Gordon as president, and were, as I afterwards learned, making a tolerably good thing of it, so that it was a matter of prudence to have a small company, as it afforded a larger moiety of cash to each individual.

The aforesaid Crockby, I soon found, was a little bit of a scamp. He had been a printer, but preferring the boards to a pair of cases, he became an actor. After the usual London probation of spouting - clubs, private theatres, and small country companies, he made a note of the fact that the manager had generally the best of it, and he resolved to go and do likewise. That is, seeing that the only persons who made money and lived well were managers, he fell upon the plan of managerial swindling, now so common. He scoured the country till he found out a few towns and villages with people in them green enough to serve his purpose. Then engaging the large room of the inn, a commodious barn—from time immemorial the arena of the stroller — or any other suitable building, he wrote to his friend the agent. The agent sent him down a company. If the thing succeeded, the actors and actresses got a few shillings; and if it did not succeed, they had to get out of the scrape and get home again the best way they could. Happen what might, the manager was all right. He changed the scene again and again; and so long as the agent sent him people to act, he put money in his purse, and laughed at the world, which he made his oyster, and opened at his entire convenience.

Some of the country managers are great scamps; I have met several whom I have not room to paint in detail. In a paper which I contributed to *Chambers's Journal*, I drew the following sketch of one of these gentry :—

In nine cases out of ten, he is a mere adventurer, with little or no education, low-bred and vulgar, with bullying manners, and a tendency to oblivion in all pecuniary transactions. I don't allude to the managers of first or second class provincial theatres, who are most of them respectable men. The specimen I select takes a country theatre as "a spec," goes to some dramatic agent, such as Suckem, and so collects a company. He hires a wardrobe from some Jew costumier, and by hook or crook gets himself and his company forwarded to the scene of operation. For the first week all goes well, the company obtaining the whole amount of their salaries. "Business," as it is called, continues brisk, perhaps even for a fortnight, and then a dismal change comes o'er the spirit

of the scene.   Some fine evening, it gets whispered about
that the manager is "nowhere;" and early next morning,
the leading lady, who is inclined to be stout, has the misfortune to be caught stuck fast in the rather narrow window of her apartment on the ground floor—a predica-
ment she has got into through a vain attempt to escape
the just demands of her landlady.   Her "properties"—
consisting of five silk stockings, a pair of black velvet
shoes, one and a half pair of white satin slippers, a much-
used suit of silk fleshings, one sandal, four skirts, an
old red silk train and a tinsel crown, with a box of worn
gloves and a white muslin robe—have been previously
spirited away by the leading lady's mamma, who accom-
panies her.   The low comedian of the company, who travels
only with a pair of tights and a few wigs, has been more
lucky; he never takes his "props," as he calls the articles
in question, to his lodgings, but always leaves them next
door to the theatre in case of accident.   After the esca-
pade of the leading lady, a miserable attempt is made by
the company, as a republic, to keep the place open for a
night or two ; but the mysterious disappearance of the
wardrobe creates a difficulty which no amount of ingenuity
can overcome ; in addition to that, the printer (a green
hand, newly arrived in the place) is wondering to whom he
is to look for payment of his bill ; while, to crown all,
the landlord has taken possession of the key of the theatre,
glad to get quit of the vagabonds without any rent, and
the place is peremptorily closed.   So ends a season which
is the exact counterpart of many more, and thus runs the
theatrical world its exciting round.

As a companion portrait to the foregoing, I present that of an honest manager struggling with adversity—it is painted by himself, and no touch from my pen could make it more graphic. As will be seen, it takes the shape of an address to his audience at the end of a disastrous season.

After the usual thanks to the "ladies and gentlemen" for their presence, he proceeds:—"At the conclusion, however, of a season which is well known to be about the worst there has ever been in this town, you will not expect anything very cheerful of me, especially when I tell you that I am very ill, that my wife is worse, and that we are both weighed down with turmoil, anxiety, and disappointment. I commenced my unfortunate season with an opera company for a fortnight, which was very unsuccessful. I then commenced with the dramatic company, which was still worse. . . . . Finding everything going the wrong way, I strenuously endeavoured to procure the visits of some first-class 'stars.' One, however, was in America, another settled for the time in London, and a third did not think this town would pay him—and those who did come, soon found such was the truth. With such stars as I could get, our receipts never exceeded £5, 1s., and were as low as £2, 17s. My friends, however, assured me that if I could weather the storm till Christmas, and then get up a pantomime, I might be sure of a reward at last. I tried the experiment; produced one—with much difficulty—that I believe gave general satisfaction ; but, alas! although there were one or two fair houses, the receipts fell during the *first* week of its run to £4, 13s., and during the *second* to £3, 1s. 6d. I unfortunately entered into a contract to pay the enormous rental of £225 for the season, of which—notwithstanding the bad business and general depression — £175 has been paid. (Cheers.) Finding it impossible to pay the last instalment, I made an appeal to the proprietors, and assured them that the £60 I paid down was sunk, that what money I brought with me was gone, what I had raised was spent, and what I had borrowed was unpaid—that having lost my all, my wife being so situated as to be compelled to give up her professional duties—with an anticipated increase to my family—my season at an end here, and nothing settled for the future elsewhere, I must throw myself upon their consideration, and—a good rental having been already realised—hope for a release. To all this I received no answer, but a brief inquiry about what *security* I could give for the balance. I replied that I had exhausted every resource, and could pay no more; but that I was anxious to do all an honest man could do—that there was a great holiday coming on the occasion of the Princess Royal's marriage, and I would get up a strong entertainment, and they might *put their own men at the doors and take the receipts*. (Cheers, and cries of 'Bravo!') Now, ladies and gentlemen, I know that not one man in twenty would have made such an offer, and I ask you if mortal man could do more? ('No, no.') Well, to that proposition I could obtain no answer; but all at once, while I was expecting one, I found the *bailiffs* in the theatre. But I had acted according to a hint I had received, very carefully removing all my best things, and safely disposing of my wife's dresses, upon the value of which I had heard certain parties had been calculating ; so when the bailiffs came in, they found little more than would pay for the distraint. (Tremendous cheering, and cries of 'Bravo!' and hisses from the proprietors.) It is to that fact, ladies and gentlemen, that I am enabled to appear before you this evening. I was therefore placed in a position to treat ; but no thanks to the proprietors if I am not now obliged to leave the town without one article of wardrobe, consequently, unable to take any other theatre, or even an engagement in one—for a wardrobe is to an actor what tools are to a mechanic—and as the result, in a short time, perhaps, to find my children wanting bread."

There was nothing for it, then, but to return to my old quarters in London, in Gough Square. This was where I latterly took up my head-quarters ; and as it was a cheap lodging-house, (threepence a-night, paid in advance,) principally used by the lower class of Bohemians, the reader will easily imagine that the lodgers were a very motley crew, fully illustrating the old proverb about misery making one acquainted with " strange bedfellows." Broken-down attorneys, dissipated printers, inspired, but drunken, musicians, bankrupt merchants, intoxicated doctors, and stuck parsons, were all here in one grand mass. A catalogue of the lot will be found in a future chapter. The common beds were in two large rooms, and I occupied a small chamber between these, with a window looking into each. I was thus, as it were, a kind of speaker to both houses ; and as the weather was warm, and sleep for divers good reasons perfectly impossible, we did nothing but debate. It was certainly amusing to see learned gentlemen, in very short night-gowns, arguing on all the questions of the day with the greatest fervour and ingenuity. One young fellow, a compositor, who always sat with a gin-bottle in one hand and his wages in the other, till the gin consumed the cash, gave a splendid oration on the Jewish disabilities question, in relation to the proposal to put Rothschild into Parliament. He spoke with great apparent ease, and was decidedly clever, but awfully drunken when he could get the means of buying beer. I learned a great deal among these fellows, and saw many a scheme put into execution for earning a livelihood that I had no conception of before. Thus, the drunken printer did penny-a-lining·at fires, riding to the scene of the "terrific conflagration" on one of the fire-engines—the dissipated doctor lectured in a hall in Farringdon Street on the destruction of the liver by drink—the broken-down attorney went about selling types to mark linen with—the stuck parson hung on at the courts as a letter-writer—the inspired, but "given-to-drink" musician assisted in a barber's shop—and the bankrupt merchant took orders for coals. Verily, "one man in his time plays many parts."

## CHAPTER XXI.

IS *THAT* A THEATRE WHICH I SEE BEFORE ME?   NO, SIR ;
IT'S ONLY A BOOTH.

ON my return from my bootless expedition to join manager Crockby, I went at once to " the agent," and told him
what had happened in Essex.

He swore a good mouthful of pretty round oaths about
my being very ill to please, and then, after very earnestly
blasting his friend Crockby, he turned up his book, and
told me, in the most patronising manner, that he had
something fine for me,—something very fine, indeed.

"Egad, my friend, you're in luck this time," said he.
"By the by, I am terribly thirsty ; would you oblige me
by going down for twopenny worth of rum, and mix it
with water ?—a-hem.   I'll give you the twopence again."

I did as I was bid, of course.   I got the drink, and, on
returning with it to Gillon's room, he told me that I was
to go off at once to the Turnham-Green Theatre, where
an engagement for the second low comedy awaited my
acceptance—salary twenty-one shillings per week, and
"sure as the bank."   This was encouraging, and I prepared at once to " bundle and go " with the greatest
celerity.

In due course, after a two hours' walk, I arrived at Turnham Green, and bounding joyously into the first public-

house I saw, after having had a glass of beer, I boldly demanded the road to the theatre.

"The road to the what?" asked the man at the bar, with a merry twinkle of the eye.

"The road to the theatre," said I, gallantly drawing my best sword from its crimson-velvet sheath.

"No such place here," was the reply, the man all the time trying to look as grave as he could.

"Are you quite sure?" I asked.

"Well, I think I am."

"Very strange," I repeated. "I'm a comedian, and my agent sent me down here to play at the theatre."

"Oh! he's done it for a bit of a lark."

"Not at all. I saw the letter from the proprietor."

"What's the name?"

"Sanger."

"Oh! Sanger's is a booth."

"A booth!—never!" and in went the sword to its sheath.

"Yes, it is."

"It must be a theatre."

"No, no! it is the booth you want, my boy; you will find it standing on the green behind this house."

"The booth!" said I, staring at him. "Then, Gillon has sold me!"

"Yes," said he, "you have been sold—I told you so; and you're not the first that Gillon has sold, either. We had another young man here to-day, but he just went back again."

There could be no doubt of it—I had been sold; *I*, the

future great man, had been sent to a booth, and that, too, by a "theatrical" agent.

"So, ho, then, Mr Gillon, you want to land me among the boothers, do you?" was my unspoken soliloquy as I abruptly left the public-house, where I had certainly given some amusement to the man at the bar. But I was determined I would not again be a boother, and resolved, therefore, to take no engagement at "Turnham Green Theatre."

I arrived at the booth about half-past six o'clock, just as the *corps* were dressing for the promenade. I got up the steps and went down inside. All were robing in a promiscuous style, after the manner of Hogarth's celebrated picture.

The company consisted of about seven or nine individuals, among whom I observed one very pretty girl, who dressed in a particularly splendid manner, and who, I was told, was also a capital actress. I stood a pot of beer, and had a chat with the gentlemen. I had scarcely, however, spoken above a sentence or two, when I was hailed as a fellow-countryman by a tall, sallow, thin, high-cheeked man of the name of Melville. He had been scudding about on the stage for upwards of thirty years, and I was told that he had been bred a lawyer's clerk in Edinburgh. Poor fellow, he seemed quite starved in these latter years of his life, and I cannot forget how rapturously he dwelt on all those dramatic pieces that had anything to eat set down in them.

"Ah! my dear boy, what a capital play that sheep's-head piece is,—dear me, what's this they call it?—ah! I recollect, 'Cramond Brig.' Oh, my precious eyes, how I delight in it! The sheep's-head is a delicious *morceau;* and then—oh, yes, I remember it well—the haggis affair, Allan Ramsay's 'Gentle Shepherd;' and then that's a capital piece with the leg of mutton in it—what's its name?—'No Song no Supper.' A prime leg of mutton with some good turnips is not to be sneezed at on a cold winter's night, I can tell you. But, sir, I do hate your sham feeds. Only think of talking on the stage about the glories of soup, fish, *entrées,* roasts and boils, dessert and wines, till, in your mind's eye, you conjure up a glorious banquet, and, at the end of a scene, leading out some fair countess to partake of its delicacies; and arriving at the side-scenes, not, alas! to dine, but only to rush away to a cold dressing-room, to change your wig, finding a note from your butcher, telling you that at last your credit's up, and no more mutton's to be had till the old scores are wiped clean out. O sir, it is melancholy that. These sham wine parties given by *Macbeth* and the *King of Denmark* are very trying to my nerves, Mr Capelton, I assure you. Sir, your imagination conjures up a glass of 'exquisite Constantia,' or even some rarer vintage, and then, sir, you lift the goblet to find it a thing of paste-board; faugh! it makes me sick to think of it. Thank the stars, the sheep's-head is a real thing! The very smell of it makes me ravenous. I remember once in my young days, sir, while playing with old Gunn in 'a fit up' at Gargunnock, that he always produced 'Cramond Brig' on the Saturday—it afforded us all a famous Sunday dinner, sir, as we had a large pot of broth made with the head and feet; these we eat on the Saturday night, the broth we had on Sunday. When the dressed animal was brought out on the Wednesday from Stirling, the head was at once bought by the manager, and a label stuck upon it to the effect, that 'this sheep's-head would be used in the play of "Cramond Brig" on Saturday night. God save the king.' O ye gods! for a glorious dinner of sheep's-head and trotters I would any day part with my best pair of tights!"

And so he went on in a similar strain about all the pieces in which there was anything to eat or drink. However, it was quite natural that a half-starved player should dwell with rapture on such rare delights. Good feeding might be scarce in the "Turnham-Green Theatre."

Many actors, however, are unable to partake of food upon the stage at all, and only make believe to eat or drink when the scene imposes such a duty upon them. Thus the feast is often removed from the stage untouched, to be greedily devoured by a lot of hungry carpenters behind the scenes. The haggis in the "Gentle Shepherd" is a great treat when it is good; but often enough in some of the Scottish theatres it is only a mess of oatmeal porridge, and not the real thing at all. Poor Melville had evidently enjoyed these delicacies in the good old times of Scottish acting, when they were pure and unsophisticated, and, as he said, had "no gammon" about them.

The "Castle Spectre" and "Fortune's Frolic" had been fixed upon as the entertainments for the evening I arrived. I determined to stay for the night and see the fun, but I was saved the trouble, for there was "no house." The business, however, had been good during the fair, and the shares had been respectable.  I was invited to " drop over to Ealing," in order to join the concern on the following day, and leaving them in the hope that I would be at my post at the time specified, I left once again for London.

## CHAPTER XXII.

GLIMPSES OF THE THEATRICAL WORLD, AS SEEN IN THE
PARLOUR OF THE "JEW'S HARP."

GILLON seemed anything but pleased at seeing the "Scotch ghost" again, as I was nicknamed. I had haunted him so perseveringly, that a number of people—I called them the curiosities of the profession—who frequented the "Jew's Harp," baptized me by that name, and it stuck to me like a burr all the time I went about the place.

This Gillon was a curiosity in his way; of a theatrical family, and himself an actor, but too lazy to bear the fatigues of acting, he commenced as agent between manager and player, procuring a company for the one, and a theatre for the other. He had evidently other irons than theatrical ones in the fire at the same time, and, in my opinion, some connexion with one of the candidates for the notorious borough of St Albans. Presents of all kinds of game were daily arriving; and I went frequently to a certain gentleman's chambers with mysterious packets, and brought back to Gillon's certain others equally mysterious, and for each of which I received a gratuity of one shilling, and very gladly pocketed both the money and—the affront.

I do not wish it to be understood that Gillon was an intentional rogue; but that his careless and slipslop style of doing business was productive of great inconvenience, not to say misery, to myself, and, doubtless, many others.

It was Gillon's mission to see the players "well bestowed," and he certainly had his work cut out for him. Any person, with even common powers of observation, might have had abundant food for speculation in taking stock of the visitors at the "Jew's Harp." It was a week or so before I could realise what it all meant, or rather till I found out that the intensely-seedy individuals, with tightly-buttoned coats—remarkable for the absence of anything white about their necks or chests, (linen was worn at that time, and not dirty-coloured flannel,) and with trousers strapped very tightly over black-lead polished boots, and having gloves of quite an indescribable kind—were players, were actors; in short, tragedians, comedians, in all the varied branches of the profession, as exemplified in light, low, eccentric, and character actors, juvenile tragedians, utility men, heavy fathers, low comedians, &c. Ladies, too, occasionally graced the scene, especially such as were, at the outset of their career, novices, who were not likely to be avaricious in the matter of salary. Gillon made most money by the introduction of sucking Hamlets to the boards. Stage-struck clerks who came to consult with him about engagements, first appearances, &c., were usually well supplied with cash, so that they were quite able to stand him unlimited beer or "bottoms" of brandy. Then he introduced them to dealers in wardrobes, theatrical bootmakers, wigmakers, and other tradesmen, having, of course, a *feeling* off each order. Gillon was always ready to receive money. Chief robber was now his *rôle*.

The first-floor room occupied by the agent was never dull. There was always something up; somebody was raising a company, no matter that it was problematical if it would pay. There were plenty of volunteers ready to try their luck, and be done again as they had been done a score of times before—young-lady novices who were dying to play the Beatrices and Rosalinds of the drama. Shop-girls or bazaar-keepers laid down their guineas and were persuaded to go down to the country for a few weeks without salary, just to fledge their wings and gain confidence. Managers are always glad to get a few good-looking and well-dressed women to fill up their scenes, and as they had them cheap they made no objection to stand half-a-guinea each for them, so that Gillon put money in his purse. There were other nondescript, hangers-on, inventors of patent thunder, producers of dramatic rain, theatrical tailors with a taste for acting, painters who could "go on" for little business, stage-carpenters, property-makers, &c., all and each of whom were in search of encouragement or employment; and all these circulated round the "Jew's Harp," and depended on Gillon to secure them engagements.

What puzzled me was, how they all came to be out of situations, and in such a hard-up state. I asked the agent.

"Well, you see," he said, "this is a bad time for us theatrical folks. There are few theatres open in the country just now, and managers don't care much for these old stagers,—they are without properties, and many of them, as you see, have fallen into 'the sere, the yellow leaf.'"

"But how are they all so shabby in their dresses?"

"Oh, you'll find that out some day."

"Can you not tell me—you must know?"

"In fact, my boy, these are what I call my worst lot; they have all some flaw about them—they drink, or want the necessary talent for their profession."

"Then why did they engage in it if they had no vocation?"

"Simply because they could not help themselves; most of that lot have been born in it, and know nothing else. We cannot all be stars, you know; and, besides, there are many who enter the profession, and having failed, have not the courage, or are too old, to seek a new way of life."

This little conversation gave me pause. With such a crowd of unfortunates in my path, how was I to get on, or make way? But, then, I thought these are only the black sheep of the flock—the men who are eternally sucking at the beer bottle, or sipping gin and water, and talking over their cruel fate, and wishing they were anywhere else rather than in this "bloody profession." Indeed, when I came to scan their faces, on which gin and water was legibly written, and make an inventory of the "properties," in the shape of wearing apparel, which they carried upon their backs, I could do nothing else than concur in the agent's remarks.

A brief notice of the career of one of these unfortunates, which I picked up in the parlour of the "Jew's Harp," will give my readers an idea of the whole. Bob Smithers (better known, however, as Alfred Henry Childers) was the only-surviving son of his doting father, and that worthy gentleman at one time had followed the profession of the bar, *i.e.*, been a publican, but afterwards became town-traveller to an extensive beer-brewer. After the age of infancy had passed over the head of our example, he was sent to a commercial academy at Newington Butts, in order to have a little learning flogg d into him. Bob was destined to be an attorney, as his father thought law the only business in which money was to be made. There are always, however, two people at least at the making of a bargain, and while the fond father was, in imagination, filling the woolsack with the person of his son, that precocious youth was thinking he would like much better to be a Garrick. He was oftener at the theatre than his chambers; and from being good at elocution at school, he came to be a spouter at a private theatre, where in time (at a cost of forty-two shillings) he was allowed to offer his "kingdom for a horse," under the supposition that he was *Richard the Third!* The applause on this occasion decided the question. Bob *would* be an actor. Stealing away his clothes, " he bade his father's halls adieu," and made his *debut* as a member of a family company in a provincial town, and from this date his career on the stage forms the usual story of the histrionic aspirant. He went about from one barn to another, on some rare occasions with a pound in his pocket, but oftener without a blessed coin. Bob knew not a few of those strange bedfellows alluded to by the poet. He was familiar with all kinds of beds, from the best room in the best hotel to the softest ridge in a bean-field, or the shady side of a haystalk. After long years of care and misery, he attained a slight name in the profession, and came to be recognised as a provincial "leading man." But what of that? Bob's ambition was gone —blighted. He had never known the comforts of an unbroken month's salary. His parents were dead, and the hundred pounds left him as a legacy had been squandered away in the vain attempt to get himself made a star. Thus left lonely and friendless, he had but two companions—the gin bottle and the pewter pot. Whenever he had a sixpence it was spent in the company of those dear friends, and when his own scanty funds were exhausted, he just sponged on all who would tolerate him. Next door to the theatre, Bob had his favourite seat in the parlour, and whoever liked to stand treat could have the benefit of any amount of theatrical slipslop, in the shape of song and anecdote. There was one bright spot in Bob's existence, which he loved to dwell on. He was an author. By some means or other he had concocted a melodrama, on the fame of which, when excited by liquor, he loved to give himself important airs. In the shape of pots of beer and "goes" of gin, "The Bloody Glazier; or, The Fatal Putty-knife," (the name of his play,) had been a perfect fortune to him. Drink at last fulfilled its mission, and ruined poor Bob. He became ultimately so besotted that no manager would look at him; and, coatless and shoeless, he was glad "to spout" in a taproom in order to wet his lips with his favourite "old Tom." Poor fellow! the parish workhouse and a pauper's grave ended his ambition.

So lived and so died poor Bob Smithers; and most of

the company I saw at Gillon's were of the same class. They had no high ambition to elevate their profession or themselves—their career was not even an effort for a living; entered upon originally from sheer vanity, it became too often, all through a lifetime, but "another way of starving." Of course, even among the kind of people to be seen congregated at Gillon's there are to be found exceptions to the rule I have laid down. I have a life-story of another aspirant for fame, who, after going through a succession of preliminary horrors, was rewarded with success. This gentleman has in his own graphic way told his own story—how at the early age of nineteen he had the misfortune to marry a widow with a ready-made family, which was like going into the battle of life with a millstone round his neck. Actors are prone to this sort of thing, and it often mars their advancement in life. The couple cannot always get situations together; if they do, the salary is less for the united pair than if they were two and distinct; but the husband has to fight the battle of two instead of one, as to parts, &c., and consequently is seldom out of hot water, and often out of an engagement. Then a large family is the consequence, and ambition becomes blunted or blighted in the submission to circumstances for the provision of food —for actors are also prone to sacrifice everything for their children. Our hero, anxious for employment, went about everywhere searching for an engagement; but it was ill to find. He could not go to a great distance for want of money, and, alas! he had but little to pawn. "O my prophetic soul, my uncle!" He walked to all the neighbouring towns where the shadow of a company was, but returned sadder than he went, and almost hopeless. Day by day he got deeper into debt; and poverty and debt are nearly allied to absolute misery. One day a ray of light crossed his dark path. But his own narrative of this circumstance is so graphic that he must be allowed to tell it in his own language:—

"I had heard that Mr Beverley of the Tottenham-Street Theatre, now called the Queen's—the father of that great scenic artist who now wields the brush where dear Clarkson Stanfield once held sway — was about to open the Croydon Theatre for a brief season. I applied to him for walking-gentleman—'Full.' For little business and utility—'Full.' For harlequin and dancing —'Didn't do pantomime or ballet; besides, didn't like male dancers—*their* legs didn't draw.' For the orchestra—'Well,' said he, in his peculiar manner, and with a strong expression which need not be repeated, 'why, just now you were a walking-gentleman.' 'So I am, sir; but I have had a musical education, and necessity sometimes compels me to turn it to account.' 'Well, what's your instrument?' 'Violin, tenor violoncello, double bass, and double drums.' 'Well, by Nero!'—he played the fiddle, you know—'here, Harry,' (calling his son,) 'bring the double—no, I mean a violin—out of the orchestra.' Harry came with the instrument, and I was requested to give a taste of my quality. I began Turtini's 'Devil's Solo,' and had not gone far when the old gentleman said that would do, and engaged me as his leader at a guinea a week. Had a storm of gold fallen on me it could not

have delighted Semele more than me. I felt myself
plucked out of the slough of despond. I had others to
support, board myself, and to get out of debt. I resolved
to walk to Croydon, ten miles, every day, to rehearsal,
and back to Shoreditch, on twopence per day—one pennyworth of oatmeal and one pennyworth of milk—and I did
it for six weeks, Sundays excepted, when I indulged in the
luxury of shin of beef and ox-cheek. The gentlemen in
the gallery pelted the orchestra with mutton-pies. At
first indignation was uppermost; but on reflection we made
a virtue of necessity, and collecting the fragments of the
not very light pastry, ate them under the stage, and, whatever they were made of, we considered them ambrosia.
At the end of the sixth week I had so pleased Mr Beverley
and his son Harry, that I was asked to give a specimen
of my terpsichorean abilities in a sailor's hornpipe for 'our
son's' benefit, with a view to an engagement for harlequin
at the new Queen's Theatre, Tottenham-Court Road. I
essayed the task, buoyed up with hope, dashed on the
stage, got through the double shuffle, the toe and heel,
though feeling faint, but at last, despite every effort, I
broke down from sheer exhaustion of strength, consequent upon a near approach to starvation; and the curtain
dropped on me and my hopes, and I burst into an agony
of tears. However, this mourning was soon turned into
joy; for Mr Beverley behaved like a father to me, took
me by the hand, and bade me cheer up, for he had
seen enough to know what I could do, and engaged me
as walking-gentleman and harlequin for his London
theatre, where I made my first appearance as Henry

Morland in the 'Heir at Law,' which, to avoid legal proceedings, he called 'The Lord's Warming-pan.' From the Tottenham-Street Theatre I went to the English Opera, now the Lyceum ; from there to Drury Lane ; thence to the Haymarket ; from there to Covent Garden, the Olympic, the Adelphi—and here I am, such as I am.

"During that long period, I did not, like Cæsar, thrice refuse the crown ; but I thrice left the stage, in despair of ever arriving at eminence, for, in my mind, not to be something was to be nothing. At the time I was called on, at a very short notice, to enact *Pompey* in 'Measure for Measure,' I had started and was doing well as a bookseller, being well versed in old and rare literature. Harley could not play the part, through a serious attack of ophthalmia. Every place in the theatre was taken, through the great cast of the piece, including the names of Macready, Liston, Richard Jones, Little Knight, Terry, James Brown, Gattie, Pope, Mr Bunn, Lydia Kelly, Mrs Harlowe, &c. After trying every one, both in and out of the theatre, except your humble servant, Mr Bunn, the stage-manager for Mr Elliston, thought of me, and the number of parts I had studied for him at an hour's notice when under his management at Birmingham. 'At all events he will be perfect,' said he, and the part was sent to me at three o'clock in the afternoon. I had gone to Paternoster Row in my way of trade, but my folks, thinking it a capital chance, returned answer it would be all right. I did not return with my blue bag full of publications until half-past five. When I was told of the circumstance I was horror-struck. I ran to the theatre.

No official was there.   What was I to do?   ' Set to work
at it,' was the reply ; ' you have done as much before.'
But not with Shakspeare, and in London.   I received a
very cold reception, but the audience warmed to me at
the end of my first scene.   At the termination of the
great tale *Pompey* has to tell, three distinct rounds of
applause greeted the poor unknown player ; and the
courage I had screwed up at this point sunk into my
shoes and I could scarcely carry them off.   The success of
the revival was complete ; all the great actors came round
me ; I was led in a sort of triumph into the first green-
room, which my salary did not entitle me to enter ; and
the press pronounced my performance the great hit of the
evening.   It is impossible for any one here to compre-
hend my excited feelings."

The hero of this little story is, happily, still alive—his
name is Benjamin Webster.

# CHAPTER XXIII.

SINGS THE SONG OF THE "FINE OLD ENGLISH MANAGER, ALL OF THE OLDEN TIME;" AS ALSO THE BALLAD OF "THE NOVICE SO GREEN."

I HAD also an opportunity, while hanging on at Gillon's, of seeing one or two of the old school of country managers, for London is still regarded as the common centre of the profession. Country managers—of whom there are about fifty or sixty, not including the directors of the few strolling companies still extant—always resort to the great metropolis to gather together their little band, and pay their annual round of visits to such of the theatres of London as have an open door, and play in the national tongue; at the present time there are about twenty of these, of various kinds and ranks. The country manager, and also the respectable country actor, have both of them a great liking for London. There they can enjoy a peep at that great theatrical world of which their little town is but the miniature. The respectable provincial manager has usually the *entrée* to the best of the London houses, because most of the London managers being actors, he receives an annual visit from them, in their capacity of "stars," and so keeps up a friendly acquaintance. He thus gets wonderful peeps into the inner circle of some of our London houses, and obtains ideas as to how all the

different "oracles" are worked which help to oil the
machinery of a London theatre.    He sees the great
man in his "sanctum;" finds out the true relation between the London dramatic author and the critic of the
daily paper, and sometimes stares to find them one and
indivisible.

The country manager of the old school—Mr Placide, I
shall call him—not being engaged to dine either with Mr
Buskin or Mr Roscius, his two most profitable stars, both
of whom are managers of London theatres, steps down to
Wych Street, to the "Sword and Tights," to enjoy a quiet
pipe before the parlour fills with its wonted company.
The organ of the profession, which he finds lying on the
table, opens up a new world to him: he recollects the
time, not many years ago, when the drama had no such
expositor; and he is more than astonished, as he glances
over the advertising columns, at the wonders with which
it is filled, never having known before that there were so
many kinds of public amusements competing for patronage.    What particularly strikes Mr Placide is the manner
in which the actors and actresses of the present day advertise and puff themselves; and how men, who are but
fourth-rate actors in a second-rate London theatre, pretend
that they are stars of the first magnitude in the provinces.
Then in every second advertisement he comes on the word
"professional," and determines to hate it, because it is a
new word to him.    He likes better the old word comedian,
or actor: "professional" includes, he thinks, all sorts of
horrors, such as niggers, bounding brothers, antipodean-
ists, and equestrian troupes.    "Ay, ay," says Placide to

himself over his pipe, " no wonder we managers can't make our salt now, with such entertainments surrounding us on all sides. Here is no end of concerts and exhibitions, where the public not only get amusement, but beer as well. What theatre, I should like to know, can stand against beer? Or, if we can beat the beer by means of either Buskin or Roscius, can we stand up against the performing monkeys, who are starring all the year round at the theatre; or, suppose we can even do that, how about the niggers in the concert-halls? A new Shakspeare could have no chance against the niggers—that he couldn't. Then, again, here in London we have the squalling Italians : there's Tamberlik going to get a cool thousand a month ; there's a palace been run up for them in five months' time. Who would run up a palace in five months for the British drama, I should like to know?" And Mr Placide, having vented these opinions quietly to himself, replenishes his tumbler, and re-adjusts his pipe, and has what he calls " another go in at the paper." But we need not follow him further. Suffice it to say, that he cannot tolerate the modern system of advertising at all. " Only to think," says he, " that men have such impudence —men I would not give fifteen shillings a-week to ! Advertising ; ay, it may be all very well for Mr Smythe—*I* can't afford it. Here is the thing for me ; and Mr Placide runs over the advertisement of the " Inauguration of the Dramatic College and Burial-Ground." " Ay, the grave will have us all at last ; I 'm glad to see that there is sense enough left in our actors to provide for this last scene of all. Truly doth Shakspeare say—

"Life's but a walking shadow; a poor player,
That struts and frets his hour upon the stage,
And then is heard no more; it is a tale
Told by an idiot, full of sound and fury,
Signifying nothing."

The organ of the profession, to which I have alluded, is the *Era*, a paper in which the theatrical world can be studied to the greatest advantage without moving from the fireside. What *Bell's Life* is to the sporting world the *Era* is to those engaged in the theatrical profession. In that journal we find the week's theatrical affairs detailed at full length. No matter what branch of the profession we desire to scan, in that paper we find the necessary particulars—all that is known about theatres, opera-houses, singing-saloons, tea-gardens, circuses, and exhibitions in general is chronicled, from the announcement " to proprietors of first-class concert-halls, gardens," &c., of the disengagement of that eminent nigger, Herr Guilden-stern, " the great original performer on ten tambourines at one time," to the astounding intelligence that Mr Waverley Mortimer Blank, " the renowned tragedian," is again, and for the third time, re-engaged at the Theatre Royal, Slashington. We can see, also, in the news-columns, that the walking-gentleman, who was advertising his services in the number of a fortnight ago, has been engaged at the theatre of Bagot-on-Shipston, where, we are informed, he has made a favourable impression on the Bagotonians; but we regret to find that " the heavy man," whose wife is useful in the "singing chambermaids," (their joint terms being very moderate,) is still out of employment. Poor gentleman! perhaps he is too heavy for the present state of theatricals, which are indeed tending decidedly to a lighter style than has marked their progress of late years. There is no want connected with the profession that cannot be supplied by the advertising columns. As an example of what is done, let us take the case of the London aspirant to stage honours ; in my own adventures I have pictured how the provincial fellow gets on. He will find from an advertisement that he can be " practically instructed and completed for the theatrical profession," by a gentleman who for twenty years has been " manager, author, and actor of the Theatres-Royal, Drury Lane and Covent Garden, Lyceum, Strand, Adelphi, Olympic, and Surrey Theatres." Or if the aspirant be a lady, here is her chance : " Miss Charming has returned to London for the season. She is prepared to resume dramatic instruction to ladies, and undertakes soon to render them competent to fill situations. Terms moderate. It is desired to form a company for the provinces, to commence about September, and those who evince aptness will be engaged." Supposing the stage-struck hero to have undergone the necessary cramming as to the "business" of the boards—that he has been taught how to kneel to a lady, how to cross from P.S. to O.P., and further, that the gentleman of twenty years' standing has given him hints on the expression of stage passions—that " madness opens the eyes to a frightful wildness, rolls them hastily and wildly from object to object, distorts every feature, and appears all agitation ; the voice sometimes loud, and sometimes plaintive, accompanied with tears ; " or that " affectation displays itself in a thousand different gestures

motions, airs, and looks, according to the character," &c. ;
supposing the curriculum of practical instruction to have
been achieved, the next business is to procure a wardrobe,
and an—engagement.  We presume, of course, that the
tyro, ere reaching this stage of his career has, like all
other novices, laid in a large share of burnt corks, so useful in the fabrication of stage-beards, eyebrows, &c., and
also a few hares' feet for the due distribution of the rouge
and pearl-powder, so essential to what is called the "make-
up " of all kinds of stage heroes.  The wardrobe is easily
managed, especially in London, and we presume it to be
from the great metropolis our novice is setting out.  Let
us suppose, also, that he has already applied to the theatrical agents in order to have his name placed on the roll
of actors wanting an engagement.  If his instructor has
not himself introduced his pupil to one, he finds the address of several in the *Era.*  Having " stumped up " what
the agent will facetiously designate the "needful "—about
half-a-guinea, more or less—his name will then be entered
on the books, and an engagement ought to follow in
due time.  The agent of course inquires carefully as to
his " props "—that is, his properties, in the shape of
dresses, swords, &c. ; and finding that the youth is unprovided with those indispensable articles of dress which all
actors are expected to find for their own use—as boots,
collars, tights, shape-hats, swords, &c.—the agent pretends
to glance at the *Era,* and then starting up from his chair,
he hauls off the youngster, exclaiming rapidly, " It's all
right, my boy ; come along with me to Sam Day's ; he 's
advertising again, and I 'll get him to do it at a moderate

figure for you;" and so the business of costume gets
settled ; and of course, as the agent is Day's friend, it is
but right for him to pocket a trifle of 10 per cent. or so
on the transaction. At this stage of the affair we may
almost hail our youth as a member of the theatrical world ;
he has now the *entrée* at the agent's chambers—agents'
chambers are usually to be found in a public-house—and
that gentleman very condescendingly partakes of the
novice's beer, and tells him stale anecdotes of the players
in return. In due time, the promised engagement comes
on the *tapis;* some Saturday morning, just as the novice
is getting restive, the *Era* announces that "Mr de Courcy
Smythe intends visiting London for the purpose of making arrangements for his ensuing seasons at the Theatre-
Royal, Slopperton, and the Royal Lyceum Theatre, Swindle-
ham ; and will be prepared to treat with acknowledged
stars, and professional talent for the regular company, on
and after the 20th instant: all applications to contain a
stamped envelope for reply, and to be addressed to L
Suckem, at the "Sword and Tights," Wych Street, Drury
Lane." The moment novice reads this, he is off to
Suckem's, at full speed, and insists upon that gentleman's
procuring him an immediate engagement in Smythe's
company. As Suckem does not see his way to any more
plunder, in the shape of beer or additional "goes" of brandy
and water, he reluctantly complies ; and in the course of
a few days, novice finds himself in the green-room of the
Theatre-Royal, Slopperton, an undoubted member of the
"profession," and certain to have his goings and comings
duly chronicled in the *Era,* for the edification of the public
in general, and the theatrical world in particular.

# CHAPTER XXIV.

GENTLE, KIND, AND DISCERNING READERS WILL FIND
THE SUBJECT OF THE FOLLOWING DISCOURSE IN MR
SHAKSPEARE'S TRAGEDY OF "HAMLET," ACT I., SCENE 5.
"O MY PROPHETIC SOUL ! MINE UNCLE !"

"Hope deferred maketh the heart sick," and I felt the
full force of the proverb, as day after day I lingered in
the great wen of London, without being able to procure
an engagement. My small stock of cash, growing "small
by degrees, and beautifully less," soon came to be denoted
by that round figure which usually signifies nothing. I
might have written home for a supply of what fast people
denominate "the needful," but my pride revolted at the
idea of that resource. I had left home only a few months
before to build up a fortune for myself; and to have written
then to my friends asking for money would have been to
have acknowledged myself vanquished. Perish the ig-
noble thought !—could I not die as Chatterton had died ?
Hundreds before me had fallen down, fainting by the way,
in the weary struggle for fame and fortune. Should I
turn coward ? Never ! Hope, in her brightest garments,
encircled by a halo of sunshine, had drawn me to London ;
cruel jade ! had she only done so to tantalise me ? Alas !
I thought, her blandishments are deceptive, and, handing
me over to misfortune, the hard-hearted dame is pre-

paring to hurl me into that abyss of despair where so many combatants in the world's strife have already despairingly fallen.

To live in London with a full purse is exceedingly pleasant; but I know of no position so melancholy as being confined to that city without money, and denied the chance of making it. That for a few weeks was the unfortunate condition in which I was placed. My money had been gradually expended, until at last there came a time when not having even one halfpenny to rub against a brother in exile made me very unhappy. This was anything but pleasant; indeed, it soon became offensively disagreeable. I had not had a great store of cash when I arrived in London, and having invested a considerable portion of it in articles of costume, and other properties, and lost a portion, as already mentioned in a previous chapter, I soon began to obtain an alarmingly-distinct view of the furthest-off end of my *petit* money-bag. Nor had I been so careful in hoarding it as I ought to have been. I frequently forgot that I was only a poor stroller, and therefore spent "the siller" with all the lavishness of old times, when periodical supplies were as sure as the bank; and, moreover, I had no idea that I should have been kept waiting so long for an engagement. There is no place where a limited supply of money sooner makes unto itself wings to flee away than London; but, to use a common phrase, money is but a sight anywhere. At any rate, my little store had melted insensibly away, and, before long, I was at what I may call the last scene of my purse; and what with little treats to my agent, given by way of general propitiation, in the hope that they might influence him to procure me an early engagement, and what with the just and unjust demands of my landlady, a rapacious "vidder, as 'ad nothink else to depend on," the last coin was speedily reached, changed, exchanged, and parted from.

At length, then, to make a long story short, I was penniless; and began to despair. The first thing I did was to rush in desperation to Gillon, to tell him that I could stand out no longer, and that I must have an engagement at once.

"It won't do, my boy," said Mr Agent, taking his pipe from his mouth, and looking coolly at me; "I can't *make* an engagement for you—and there's none in the market at present."

"No, there never has been for me."

"Well, I told you when you first came that all the Easter companies were made up; and that you would have to take pot-luck."

"Which is no luck at all," said I.

"Can't help it, my boy."

"Yes," said I, "but look at the expense I have incurred by your having sent me two or three times considerable distances on a goose's errand."

"Can't help it, my boy; you are so fastidious."

"Only as to the parade business."

"Oh, such things are quite incidental to this kind of life, my lad. But, I say, do order up a pot of beer, or some gin and water; I'm so thirsty."

"I can't, I have no money."

"What! no tin at all?"

"Not a copper."

"Where are all your fine *props?*"

"In my trunk, of course, where they ought to be."

"My eye! and you have no tin?"

"No."

"Then why don't you get some?"

I stared, dead beat at the fellow's coolness. Why didn't I get some? It was a question easier asked than answered. My eyes, I presume, looked my anxiety, and so he answered, "The properties."

"Properties are not money, are they?"

"No, but they are capital, and ought to be made productive when money is wanted."

"What do you mean?" I asked fiercely; "do you want me to sell them?"

"No, only to pop some of 'em."

"Pop them?"

"Yes. Send them to your uncle, he'll advance a few bob on them for you; he lives at the sign of the three balls, you know."

"Pop them! Never!" I scorned the very idea of the thing. It seemed to me, at the time, that to pawn my properties was to undo all that I had done; and as I looked on the trumpery paraphernalia of swords, tights, collars, caps, &c., I fancied it was these that made me the actor, and to send them away was to unmake me altogether. But I might as well have given in at once, for to the pawnbroker's I was ultimately compelled to resort. Some one has said that he believes there is not an actor on the stage who has not been compelled, sooner or later in his career, to pay a visit to that friendly banker, the pawnbroker. My fine stock of stage-properties soon faded away, left in security for various crowns and half-crowns kindly lent me by a venerable relative, of the *genus* uncle, in Fetter Lane; and still, during this painful course of disposition, there came no engagement. I was still blushing unseen, wasting my sweetness on the desert air of London, fretting myself to death in that mighty wen, but never all the time having the manly courage to look around me, and find out a new vocation.

*Facilis descensus averni;* in other words, a visit to the pawnbroker is the beginning of deeper misery. It was so with me, and it has often been so with others of whom I have heard or read. I need not minutely detail how shilling after shilling disappeared, or how my friend the agent enjoyed in "beer" his portion of my wardrobe, or how blank he looked when I had not a single article wherewith to propitiate mine uncle and raise new supplies. All this, I think, can be easier imagined than described,—at least the sensations I felt are beyond my powers of description. A time came when the landlady, with whom I had ever been punctual, began to look her opinion of my financial condition. Her terms of credit were exceedingly limited, and one day she emphatically declined to lay out a small sum for my dinner, and, in consequence, I went dinnerless that day, nor did I breakfast next morning. A small roll, purchased with my last halfpenny, was all the food I had obtained for the greater part of two days. I had left my lodgings with the determination of not returning till it would be time for bed. I did so, but when I came back the door was inhospitably fastened. I knocked, and the following little discourse with my landlady's woman of business soon brought matters to a climax :—

" Who's there ? " was demanded.

"It is I."

" And who are you ? "

" Capelton."

" Oh ! I'm so sorry, but we 'ave let your bed."

" Let my bed ! "

" Yes, as you didn't come 'ome at the usual time."

" And can't I have another ? "

" Ain't got another that's empty."

" Well, but you 'll allow me to come in ? "

" Can't do it, Mr Capelton."

" Well, but my trunks are all here."

" To be sure they is, but there's nothink in 'em."

" There's nothink in 'em " was a settler.

It was half-past eleven o'clock when this little dialogue was spoken, and I had not a place provided me wherein to lay my head for the night. I had not tasted food all that day ; but at the time of the parley I was so excited as not to feel at the moment that I was faint and hungry. Indignation at the heartlessness of the woman, who had hitherto been punctually paid, was, for the moment, the feeling that was most predominant.

Some folks think that, if starving be the order of the day, it is a matter of no consequence where the operation is endured. I differ from those people on this point. I found it more difficult to starve in London than I think it would be in the country ; because in London one is surrounded on all sides by the most tempting food-luxuries ; they are thrust, so to speak, on our vision, and assail our sense of smell at every turn of the street. In the country this contrast to the starving condition is wanting ; no doubt, there is good food enough in the country, and plenty of it, but it is not thrust on the general gaze as it is in London. There are no steaming eating-houses in the rural districts, no tempting ham and beef shops, no luxurious cake-saloons, seductive confectioners' shops, or tavern with open door inviting the wayfarer. In London, again, these abound, and the poor, starving, moneyless wretch feels the bitter mockery of the show, as he glances timidly, yet longingly, at the display. Would it be matter for wonder if he dashed his hand through the expensive glass, and ministered to his own wants ?

It had begun to rain heavily when I turned excitedly from the door of my inhospitable landlady, and rushed out of the little square into the busy thoroughfare of the Strand. It was a cheerless drizzling evening ; it had rained slightly but incessantly during the whole day, and now, when the curtains of night had been drawn over the vast wilderness of brick and stucco, the rain had gradu- ally dwindled away into a drizzle, and the atmosphere all around was choked up with that particularly well-known opaque substance which enters into the composition of a London fog, and through this molluscous haze came filter- ing the minute rain-vapour, a substance far less agree- able than the honest rain itself. After a while, I stood on Ludgate Hill, near St Paul's churchyard, and by this time it was about midnight. All the great marts of commerce, with which that neighbourhood is thickly studded, were closed—even the retail shops had, one by one, shut up their portals, and extinguished their burners. The lighted lamps shone dimly in the fog—each particular gas, like a wan spectre, threw out a funereal glow. The watchman had vanished; another cab had whirled rapidly past on its way to the *Times* office; the silence of the night had almost become profound; the heavy drops of accumulated vapour falling from housetops and projecting signboards made the only noise. Simmons's cook-shop alone gave forth signs of life, and at the window of this celebrated eating-house I had taken up my post on this raw and cheerless night. Does the reader ask why? Simply because I was starving. There, as if to tempt all who were in my condition, with but a thin film of glass between, were piles of those delectable viands held peculiar to the season. Well might the hungry stomach yearn at the sight! Well might that gateway of knowledge, typified in man's nasal organ, open wide its portals to admit that glorious combination of gastronomic odours which issued from the window-grating on which I stood! For a space of many yards around did that delightful incense permeate, filling all who came within its influence drunk with thoughts of good cheer. As preparations were made to close the eating-house—for even cooks must rest—I rushed eagerly forward to take a last fond look of the banquet, which seemed to grin at my empty purse, when, my foot catching upon the kerb-stone, I stretched out my hands to save myself, and in doing so I unfortunately made another stumble, and then a terrific crash proclaimed to all the street that I had fallen against the plate-glass window of Simmons's cook-shop, which, of course, was shivered by the concussion into a thousand atoms. What occurred then I know not. Doubtless Simmons rushed out, followed by his better-half, and shouted, "Stop thief!" Of course, so did his man, and the maid-servant no doubt would support her mistress. The watchman, doubtless, came puffing from his hiding-place, but too late to be of service ; I say doubtless, for all this is a stereotyped matter of routine, and so, in general, is the gathering of a mob, which on this occasion, however, was an impossibility, as London and its mob, the finest in the world, were either asleep or hiding from the elements.

I need scarcely say, that the instant I discovered what I had done, my legs were put to such capital use that I was out of reach in a couple of minutes. Up Fleet Street and along the Strand I careered at full speed, and never paused till I found myself leaning exhausted against the basin of the fountain in Trafalgar Square. My body was covered with perspiration, and my clothes were soaked with the rain. Breathless and excited, I sat down on a step to recover myself, quite heedless of the penetrating fluid which still continued to fall in a kind of sheet form. In a very short time I began to tremble from the united effects of the cold and damp, and to be affected by the check my sudden stoppage had given to the copious perspiration which issued from every pore in my body. Roused to the evil effects which might result from this state of matters, I forced myself to rise up and "move on," in order to prevent any bad consequences. Move on —but where to move on to was the question. Well, what did it matter where—along Piccadilly was just as good as anywhere else. All streets and places were alike to me —wasn't I penniless?

I went sauntering along Piccadilly, the water oozing out of my pumps, (a pair of dress shoes which I had been forced to put on, the soles of my boots not admitting of their being further worn at that time,) and the upper part of my trousers clinging to my limbs. These said trousers were a pair of canvas ones which I had borrowed from a tailor who was repairing those I usually wore. All my others were in pawn, and those I had on were made for a seafaring person—wide at the bottom and tight at the thighs. It is necessary to describe them particularly to explain what follows. As I went slowly along the trousers were incessantly flap, flapping about my ankles, and once or twice it occurred to me that the button of one of the legs hurt me. I stooped to examine the place, but there was no button. I then thought, "Oh, it is just a hard place of the seam—it's of no consequence." On I went again; but again the hard substance hit me. I stopped at the first lamp, and once more felt all round the cloth—there was a button, but it was inside of the seam, doubtless accidentally. Well, it can't be helped; I will walk more carefully, I thought, and it won't annoy me. But caution was unavailing; that button would bob against my ankle. At last, out of sheer ill-nature—and a starving man is easily excited—I seized hold of the hem of my unmentionables, and, by fair force, tore off the part containing the offending button and threw it down. After a brief moment, however, I felt an impulse to lift it up and examine it. I did so. "Bless me!" I exclaimed, "this is heavier than a button." Rapidly I tore off the canvas; there was something wrapped in dirty paper. I felt that it was a coin. But of what value? Ay, that was the question with me. I became more and more excited as I picked off the damp folds. At length it was uncovered, and held up to the glare of the gas. No, there was no mistake,—it was yellow. "Hurrah!" I shouted and danced for joy as I made the proclamation, "a sovereign! a yellow sovereign, and no mistake!"

# CHAPTER XXV.

ALTHOUGH, IN ACCORDANCE WITH THE PROVERB, I HAVE
BEEN ALL ALONG ANXIOUSLY TRYING FOR THE SILK
GOWN OF THE STAGE, I ONLY OBTAIN A SLEEVE—
IN OTHER WORDS, I BECOME A STAGE DOOR-KEEPER,
AND SO FIND OUT THE SECRETS OF THE PRISON-
HOUSE, AND FOR A BRIEF PERIOD HAVE MY BREAD
BUTTERED ON BOTH SIDES.

THE way in which I became for a brief period hall-keeper
at the Royal Arundel Theatre was another illustration of
the old proverb which condescendingly informs us that
great events occasionally flow from little causes.

Mr David Jones, the lessee, (better known in the profession as Davy Jones, from his so seldom having a shot
in his locker,) happened to be calling one day at the "Jew's
Harp" to see the agent. I was hanging on, as usual—my
sovereign being pretty nearly expended, for, even with
very strict economy, a sovereign won't last a very long
time—waiting, like Mr Micawber, to see what would turn
up, when I was unexpectedly appealed to to decipher the
signature to a letter which Jones had received that morning from a country actor. The autograph was almost
illegible, but I was able to make out the name, which
was a Scotch one—M'Pherson, to wit. My doing so, as it
turned out, was fortunate.

"Are you a good writer?" said Jones to me.

"I can write as well as I can decipher bad writing," said I.

"Good," said he; "I want a fellow like you very much to write for me. I don't want your London people about me, they always know too much."

To be brief, I agreed to go to the private sanctum of Mr Jones in the Arundel, to do "some writing;" and in all honesty I did much.

One evening, during the performance, I was sitting with Mr Jones in his private room, writing a confidential letter to his dictation, when Biggs, one of the painting-room boys, rushed in breathless to say that Faulkner (the hall-keeper) had taken another fit. "Another fit be ——," said Jones; but just as he had finished the exclamation, a second messenger rushed breathlessly into the managerial presence, shouting that old Faulkner had gone off in a fit of apoplexy. It was true; we all rushed into the hall, and there, in his great chair, sat the blackened mass that had once been old Faulkner. The only commentary on the event which I heard was that made by the call-boy, "It's rum and water as has done it," exclaimed that knowing youth. I said nothing, but had at the same time a shrewd idea that the rum was entitled to exclaim, like Coriolanus, "Alone I did it."

However, there was more in old Faulkner's death than met the eye of common observers. Jones was in an awful way about it—at times angry, and at times melancholy. Faulkner had been more than a mere servant to him, and had on more than one occasion been the means

of keeping the lessee out of serious difficulties of a kind
common enough to adventurers in London. The reader will
hear how I learned this, for, on the evening of the second
day after this occurrence, the manager, over a glass of
Moselle, said to me, "Capelton, I like you. You Scotch
fellows are altogether different from the English — you
are so close and prudent. I want you to do me a particular service. You shall become my hall-keeper." I
was petrified. I, Peter Paterson, a hall-keeper—I, who
had set my life upon being a tragedian—the thing was
ridiculous—preposterous—absurd! Of course it was,
and I indignantly refused the office.

It would be tedious to go over Jones's arguments, as
they all tended to one point—that I should accept the
situation without more bother. One little hint came out,
from which I put together a little story. Jones was a
bigamist, Madame Jones, the fascinating *danseuse,* (Mdlle.
Maria Talma,) was not his only wife. Then, besides, he
had creditors—what theatrical manager has not?—and
bailiffs were ever at the door; in fact, he wanted a confidential man to sit in the hall. He wanted a man who
would be a brother to him—would I be that man was
Jones's momentous question. To make a long story
short, I at length agreed, and thus filled the position of
hall-keeper in a London theatre for exactly seventeen
days, including two Sundays. At the end of that period
Jones got into trouble, the concern got into the Court of
Bankruptcy, there was another "man in possession" of
my chair, and I was down on my luck once more, waiting at Gillon's for a chance engagement.

Well, for the twenty-three days during which I served under the banner of Mr and Madame Jones, I was happy and rich, and obtained a promise of about eight pounds; and actually got, in one way or another, a sum little more than half that amount; but half of what I got was kindly borrowed from me by Madame Jones to pay a little bill for ballet shoes. She paid her "little" bills, but never her big ones. However, I lived like a fighting cock, as the call-boy said. To render it unnecessary for me to leave the theatre, Jones ordered the proprietor of a neighbouring tavern to supply me with whatever food I required.

I think I hear some of my readers suggesting that I would get to know a thing or two in this situation. There is no doubt about that; there is no situation in the world where a man can better study his kind than the hall-porter's chair of a London theatre. Let me, for instance, chronicle who called and who left notes—who wanted to pass the chair, who passed with impunity, and who waited in the lobby. Well, to begin at the beginning, Miss Bessy Gillman's friends were all admitted, she was the singing chambermaid, and her *friends* were well able to rent a private box. Her mother came with her, she was deaf, and, as ill-natured people suggested, blind as well. There was no end to the notes she received and the parcels that were left for her. One gentleman's servant came with a bouquet of choice flowers, another called in the course of the forenoon with a note; and about two o'clock there arrived at the stage-door a handsome olive-painted brougham to take Miss out for an airing. The friends of the principal dancing lady had the *entrée* as well. Many

were the parcels that arrived for Mademoiselle. One
gentleman supplied her with dancing shoes; another
presented her with occasional pairs of silk tights. Many
other gents had similar privileges. Most of the ladies
had friends who kept broughams in which they could
take an airing, so that in course of time the ladies of this
theatre had become notorious for fine linen, valuable
jewels, and tasty equipages; people even used to hint
that the ladies of the Royal Arundel Theatre were destitute of virtue; but that was mere spite.

The day at the theatre begins early. The first person
of interest who calls is the general postman, and there is
usually a great batch of letters. Look ye, now, these
bulky packets are "manuscripts"—*i.e.*, plays from persons who are anxious to shine as dramatic authors; it's
a chance, if Jones ever looks at them—they will be pitched
into a tin box, and there they will remain for some time,
when they will be taken away and sold as waste paper.
It is just possible that, by the merest accident, a good
comedy may be one day turned out of the box; but of
course Jones keeps a stock author, and does not rely on
outsiders. It would be bad policy to do so, because most
of the London playwrights are "on the press" as dramatic
critics, and it is the interest of managers to have them as
authors, or at least men of their clique, (they all praise
each other's productions.) When a man opens a theatre
in London, it is his first duty to subsidise these men, by
ordering a comedy from one, a drama from a second, a
burlesque from a third, and a farce from a fourth.* There

* "Most of our play and farce writers are 'on the press;' and a

is no use blushing at a name for this; it is a mode of bribing the press.

We have always a call about one o'clock from Boreas, the great burlesque writer. He and I are exceedingly friendly, and have often a chat together. He has just been through the Insolvent Court for the second time; and the hat has again been sent round for his brother's family, who have been left destitute by their fond but extravagant papa. Another man who calls here—an actor—has also had the hat sent round; everybody in the theatre subscribes, from his imperial highness the manager down to the call-boy. Year after year we have either a great actor or a great actress to subscribe for; or a benefit has to be got up, or the hat sent round, to relieve the sorrowful and declining years of a comic writer! As an instance, I may point out that when a very eminent comic actress left the stage, she was reduced to the greatest necessity, after having been on the boards for a long life-time, and having been in receipt of salaries that to some clergymen and literary men would be a perfect mine of wealth, her salary for years never having averaged less than £20 a week! And in addition she had countless benefits, starring engagements, and presents innumerable; but, for all that, she, too, was

shrewd manager takes care to select his authors accordingly, knowing that they form a clique, of which each member is bound to puff the other's production, because all in their turn need a similar favour. Still, however, the production of the new farce requires tact and 'management;' and there are numerous interviews between the author (translator, ought we not rather to say?) and manager, before matters get finally arranged, and the puff-preliminary is sent out. Outsiders rarely get a piece accepted; but when they do, what a gantlet of criticism they have to run."—*Chambers's Journal*, 238.

reduced to send round the hat. Some information on the important point of "how the money goes" with this class of people comes occasionally from the bankruptcy proceedings. A well-known London literary man acknowledged frankly to an income of something like six hundred a year, but ingenuously told the Commissioner that he attributed his insolvency to the fact of his income's having been insufficient for his wants ! This was a very philosophical way of accounting for his degradation ; but if many people were to adopt the same plan, the national shop might very speedily put up its shutters. It never occurs, we presume, to these Bohemians of art and literature, that the easiest and simplest plan of keeping out of the Bankruptcy Court is to live within their means ! They seem to fix a purely ideal income, and think they are ill-used if their little game be at all questioned—hence their frequent appearance in public both as insolvents and mendicants. What such folks do with their money is a mystery to me. Many will remember the case of a professional lady, a tragic actress of some eminence, now deceased. The affairs of her husband came before the Insolvent Court, when it transpired that she had for a few seasons been in receipt of an income of about £700 a year ; and had averaged for a period of about twenty years at least £500 per annum ; yet a subscription had to be raised for her. Here was a woman who, for a score of years, had been in receipt of a larger income than one half of the learned professors of our universities, whose husband added to her lucrative earnings by keeping a public-house, suddenly reduced to live upon subscriptions—and what was her excuse ? None that I can find. She had not had, like the poor professor, or the still more straitened clergyman, a high social position to maintain—she had had no fellowship in learned societies to keep up—no expensive books to purchase. No; she kept a public-house; and if a friend dropped in to have a little gin and water, the chances are, that he would not only pay for his own, but that he would most likely treat his landlady at the same time. It is painful to think that actors, actresses, and play-writers are so improvident a class of people.

Returning from digression, I may state that there are usually letters for everybody in the post-bag; it is my duty to put them up into a rack in the hall, so that all as they enter may claim their own. The ladies of the *corps de ballet* are always eager for their little notes; but *Honi soit qui mal y pense!* I say nothing against the ballet; in the aggregate, dancers are as virtuous as other women.

My principal duty is to keep out the duns. I know a dun at once—there is the handwriting of three of them. I never give madame these letters; they contain bills—large bills—she pays most of her small ones. This is from her shoemaker—he threatens a writ; her little feet, so handsome and carefully-tended, have walked her into debt. Listen to this catalogue :—

| | | | |
|---|---|---|---|
| 6 Pair of Pink Satin Slippers, at 6s., | . | . | £1 16 0 |
| 2 „ of White Satin Boots, at 12s., | . | . | 1 4 0 |
| 2 „ of Quilted Silk Dressing Slippers to match with Red Dressing-gown, | | | 1 1 0 |
| 2 „ of Black Silk Boots, at 15s., | . | . | 1 10 0 |
| 6 „ of Bronze Shoes, at 7s., | . | . | 2 2 0 |

Madame, you see, spares no expense for her feet. Her

*chaussure* is fascinating. Her hosier's bill is £70—all kinds of stockings, silk, lace, embroidered, striped, llama, coloured, and otherwise, testified to her exquisite taste.

About ten o'clock the company come in fast; there is a rehearsal at half-past. These dowdy-looking women are *figurantes*, or ballet-girls of the back row. The ballet-mistress follows. I don't like her face; as the Scotch say, her eye is "no canny;" and I always notice that girls whom she takes a liking to very speedily achieve the distinction of a brougham; but, as I shall speak of the ballet in my next chapter, I need not introduce the subject here.

Look at that beautiful creature—that is Miss de L——, the burlesque actress. I liked that girl very much when I first came here; her salary—this is not a large house, you know—might be £4, 10s. a week. Well, she was always neatly dressed, in a pretty merino gown, comfortable shawl, and warm boots, with a plain bonnet, and she invariably walked to and from the theatre; but now she comes in a brougham, with a liveried attendant; has five or six rings, mounted with expensive jewels, a silk dress, tiny boots of bronze kid or some other fashionable colour, and gloves of magenta; then there is always a gentleman in waiting for her, either in his private box or in the brougham. She lives at St John's Wood, and I don't like her now at all. She was led away by that woman.

I could write a long chapter upon the people that come here; and upon the company, their hopes and ambitions; but what I have said will serve for a sample of the material at my command. Here, for instance, comes a madman—he left a box here about six weeks ago, containing a new invention of his—patent thunder. It may be a good thing, but Jones won't look at it, he never has time, and my orders are to put the man off as well as I can. "Make way for the piano box," is being shouted along the passage—that is the slang for the exit of Jones. "He is abroad at present," is told to the numerous bailiffs, of whom there are always a couple hanging on about the stage-door; but he is snug behind for all that; and for a considerable time he will be able to make safe entrance and exit in that box.

During my brief connexion with the Joneses of "the Arundel," as it was familiarly called, I kept both my eyes and ears open, and learned a great deal about that world of Bohemia which is tenanted by such characters as Mr and Madame Jones. There came to the Arundel a Bohemian M.P. of great talent, who was a chief actor in the getting up of the "Royal Bank of Babylon," which, it will be remembered, grew rapidly, and fell with an awful crash. In fact, the affair was first promulgated in Jones's private room, and I wrote to the Bohemian M.P.'s dictation a rough draft of a prospectus of it, for which he tipped me a guinea. This clever Bohemian was a great projector, and in the end, when all was up with him, he made a mysterious disappearance, and covered his retreat by letting it be supposed he had committed suicide. By way of giving variety to these Confessions, I will introduce a couple of chapters, containing a condensed or bird's-eye view of the world of Bohemia, as seen by me during the various opportunities I had of viewing it.

To return, however, in the meantime, to my duties as stage-doorkeeper, I may state, by way of concluding this chapter, that I did not hold this office very long. Jones, when I became known to him, was on his last legs, as I have said; another *man* than myself was speedily "in possession" of my chair, and the landlord in a few days resumed his property. When Jones came before the court he made a funny speech about its being "still the same drunk, massa," and even spoke in favour of madame's extravagant millinery bill.

# CHAPTER XXVI.

## THE MYSTERIES OF THE BALLET.

As I have some knowledge of the ballet, it may interest my readers to be told of the joys and sorrows of the young ladies (and old ones, too, sometimes) who nightly attitudinise before the public in all the resplendency of silk tights and scanty skirts. As a whole, I have nothing but good to say of the *corps de ballet*; there are, no doubt, black sheep in the flock, as there are in other female flocks, but, as a body, they are a respectable and hard-working class of females ; and my experience of theatres, and it is considerable, leads me to put down the ballet wo-men as being as good, *cœteris paribus*, as any other body of working females. I might, indeed, considering the ex-traordinary temptations to which they are exposed, have said that they are greatly better. There homes are usually poor—often wretched. They are courted by the first in the land, sometimes even by princes of the blood-royal ; and although the sapient advice of the Jewish sage, " Put not your trust" in such, is undoubtedly worthy of all com-mendation, it must take far more philosophy than usually falls to the lot of frail womankind to resist the temptation with which they are so frequently beset from such quarters.

It is the case with the ladies of the *corps de ballet* as with acrobats and voltigeurs—they must begin their training early; the best dancers are those who have been educated from infancy to the business. No woman of mature age, unlearned in the art, can go upon the stage and expect to make a hit as a *danseuse*. I knew two young ladies, very accomplished in music, who made the attempt, and who were occasionally put to figure in the ballet; but they were very awkward and stiff, and no doubt, as I could see from their manner, felt ashamed of their scant skirts and long legs. Indeed a seven years' apprenticeship is not too much to serve for the acquisition of the art. The intense labour which a dancer has to undergo before she can achieve a reputation on the stage is not generally known. It is related of Taglioni, that after a two hours' lesson from her father she would fall exhausted with fatigue on the carpet of her chamber, and lie there till she was undressed, sponged, and resuscitated, being all the time in a state of insensibility. It is said that her father, who was her instructor, was in the habit of locking her with himself in the room in which she received her lessons, that he might not be overcome by the importunity of his wife imploring him to spare their daughter. But the old man was resolute; he was determined that she should be first in her profession, and such indeed she became. This was the price at which she bought the plaudits of the audience; and other aspirants who aimed at bounding into greatness by the suppleness of their limbs had to go and do likewise. Some years ago, in a French musical publication, the following account was given by a *danseuse* of the nature of the education which fitted her for the ballet :—

"Ah! sir, if you did but know how much courage, patience, resignation, and unremitting labour a poor girl must command—if you did but know what excruciating tortures she must submit to, and how many involuntary tears she must stifle even to become a mediocre dancer, you would at once be moved with terror and compassion. Scarcely was I seven years old when I was despatched to the class of M. Barres. Oftentimes I was sent early in the morning, with nothing in my stomach but an equivocal cup of coffee, without socks to my feet, or a shawl over my shoulders. I oftentimes arrived shivering and half famished; then commenced the daily torture, of which, however exact my description might be, I should fail in giving you a just idea. Banished from our code, torture has taken refuge in the class for dancing. Every morning my feet were imprisoned in a groove box, heel against heel, and knees turned outwards. My martyred feet accustomed themselves naturally to fall into a parallel line. This is what is called 'Le tourner.' After half-an-hour of the groove, I was subjected to another variety of torture. This time I was obliged to rest my foot on a bar, which I was obliged to hold in a horizontal line, with the hand opposite the foot I was exercising. This they term 'Le casser.' After these labours were over, you imagine, perhaps, that I enjoyed the charms of repose; repose for me, indeed! as if a dancer knew what repose was! We were like the Wandering Jew, to whom the Barres and the Coulons were continually crying out, 'Dance, dance.' After these 'tourners' and 'cassers' we were obliged, in order to escape from professional re-

primand or maternal correction, to study assiduously LES
JETES, LES BALANCES, LES RONDS DE JAMBES, LES ROU-
ETTES, LES CABRIOLES, LES PIROUETTES SUR LE CONTRE-
PIED, LES PAS DE BASQUES, LES PAS DE TOURNÉES, and,
finally, the ENTRECHATS À QUATRE, À SIX, ET À NEUF.
Such, sir, are the agreeable elements of which dancing is
composed; and do not believe that this rude fatigue lasts
only for a time—it is to last and to be renewed without
intermission.   On this condition only can the dancer preserve her *souplesse* and her *légèreté*—a week of repose
must be redeemed by two months of redoubled incessant
toil."

The ballet-girls at Jones's theatre were of all sizes—
from the age of six to the age of sixty!  It is a fact, we had
one old lady in the *corps* who confessed to being forty-
eight, and who was reputed to have seen three-score years.
As I have said, the children must be trained to the business; and stage-carpenters, and other workmen about
the theatre, are glad to allow their children to earn a few
shillings a week as elves, fairies, &c.   Some of those who
shew a peculiar aptitude for the saltatory art may in
time be apprenticed to a ballet-master, and come out as
regularly-trained dancers.   Their success is a matter of
chance; and many learn the art who have never been
qualified by nature for the calling of a dancer.   In Paris,
at one time, a very severe ordeal was undergone by all
who aspired to be *figurantes*.   I have read that they were
examined by two surgeons, successively; the object being
to determine whether their proportions adapted them for
the exercises of the dance, a lack of vigour in the ankles,

or fulness of respiration, unfitting them for the necessary physical endurance. If they were thought to be endowed with the necessary qualifications, they took their place among the pupils, and were educated accordingly. " M. Véron says that his anatomical knowledge enabled him to determine whether the applicant would make a dancer or not; and that he was able to prevent many from adopting the profession when they lacked the robustness necessary for it. A singer can frequently tell from the speech of persons whether they would be likely to make singers; and a dancer can likewise judge from the proportions and points of the body whether the ability of a dancer may lie within. When Duport was one day visiting Gosselin, a lute-maker, he saw two daughters, and noticed their feet. He examined them attentively, and told their father that they had eminent qualifications for *danseuses.* The plan of study that he suggested was adopted, and the girls afterwards became meritorious *artistes.*"

I have already hinted that the ballet people have hard enough work, especially when they are engaged in a heavy *spectacle* or very full burlesque. They will be weeks in rehearsing, and will require in the course of the evening to make several changes of costume, dance several dances, and execute a grand march. After midnight, in the cold and wet, they must trudge away home, to repeat night after night the same routine of labour, and all for a very small sum per week.

I always paid great attention to the rehearsals, both when I was engaged in them myself, and when I was a spectator. It is capital fun to see the rehearsal of a bur-

lesque—the stage-manager tearing his hair, the leader of
the band ill-natured, the leading comic lady laughing, and
all the underlings in a tremble.    The chief ballet ladies
are practising favourite steps in odd corners.    They are
dressed in a rather peculiar way—street-costume to the
waist, with ballet continuations—*i.e.*, white skirts of the
orthodox shortness, faded satin slippers, and gloves—
always gloves    Four or five are getting up in a tableau;
one of them assumes a look she never can feel, for at
night she must look a passion if she have it not naturally.
During the rehearsal all is dingy, but at night the place
lights up like magic ; and when the principal *danseuse*
bounds in at the third entrance, and the *corps de ballet*
rattle their tambourines by way of welcome, the scene is
indeed charming.    These young ladies in the faded dresses
and rather shabby bonnets are the persons who will in the
evening appear as the happy peasantry in the spectacle.
When the house is lighted up, and the scenes are set, and
the musicians are discoursing a flood of melody by means
of their fiddles, these girls will look charming in the dress
of the stage peasant—piquant little straw hats jantily
set on one side of the head, and adorned by a flaunting
ribbon, a neat gay cotton jacket, silk stockings, and thin
shoes.    It seems *de rigueur* for all stage peasants to dress
in satin slippers and silk tights.    In fact it is amusing to
note these and other stage incongruities ; such as ladies
travelling about bareheaded in evening costume in a dark
and dismal forest, or coming down to breakfast with bare
arms and a low-bodied dress.    I saw lately that a French-
man was astonished at the transformation effected by the

gay dresses and lights of the theatre. He had seen the ladies in the forenoon, who hung about in shabby dresses, pale and shivering from cold, transformed at night into gorgeous butterflies in gay apparel, happy and smiling as they bounded about the stage with their joyous tread and *dégagé* manner. The remuneration of this class of *artistes* is not very great. Mr Kean was considerate, and even liberal to the ladies of his *corps de ballet.* They never had a smaller salary under his management than a guinea a week; and, in addition to this, everything was found them, in the shape of skirts, shoes, stockings, and petticoats. At some theatres the salary of a ballet-girl is only eighteen-pence a night, and varies from that to two shillings. In some of the provincial theatres, I understand the wages are still less. A ballet-girl lately wrote to one of the daily papers about the remuneration given to her class. The following is an extract from her letter :—

"I know of several ladies engaged for pantomime only, who have to attend the theatre two, and occasionally three weeks before Christmas, many coming from a dis-tance, and who do not receive one farthing for this attend-ance. The salaries given by many managers, with a few honourable exceptions, are barely sufficient to keep life together. I know many in receipt of 15s., 12s., and 10s. per week; and I believe in a few theatres they give to their regular *ballet corps* even less than the last-named sum. I beg to ask you how it is possible that we can keep ourselves respectable upon such salaries ? There are many little things to purchase; and even those merely engaged for pantomime have shoes, stockings, and washiugs to pay for—the latter, as I said before, having to attend the heavy rehearsals gratis. No one knows what we have to endure during these hours, and hours occupied in trying dances; and as no refreshment is allowed unless you buy it yourself, how is that to be done upon the low salaries I have mentioned? I think it is high time the public should be made acquainted with the wretched pittances doled out to the poor ballet-girl; and I hope that, as you have invariably exposed everything that is unjust, you will allow this a small space in your columns. I feel assured you will receive many letters confirmatory of my statements."

As to the price of her dresses, a ballet-girl will have to pay from seven to ten shillings for a pair of silk stockings. These she attaches perhaps to the body of a pair of cotton drawers, the join being hid by the voluminous skirts which it is the fashion for her to wear. Complete silk tights, such as are worn by the principal dancers at the Italian Opera or her Majesty's Theatre, will cost from thirty shillings to three guineas. These are very elastic, fit like a glove, and yield to every move of the body. Ballet shoes used to be obtained only from Paris, but now they can be as well made in London, and the usual price is about five shillings a pair. Perhaps my readers would like to know the difference between the shoes of the ball-room and those of the ballet. The white satin shoes of the ball-room are made a little longer than the foot, the sole and upper being *flush*. The shoes of the ballet dancers are got up in the following style—they are made the exact length of the foot, in fact, they ought to fit without a wrinkle; the part of the shoe which encases the great toe has to be sewn over or darned, and the sole of the ballet slipper is always half an inch shorter than the upper, this allows the foot freedom to rest on the point. The only other difference between the two kinds of shoes is that those for the ballet are constructed with what is technically called more *spring*, causing the slipper to adhere more tightly round the top of the foot when the dancer is busy at her work. It will cost a common member of the *corps de ballet* about six shillings to furnish her with dancing petticoats, of which they generally wear five or six. A principal *danseuse* will put on as many as twelve, and use in their manufacture about forty yards of tarletan !

I fear the days of the grand ballet, as it existed in London at her Majesty's Theatre, are gone for ever. In the time of Lumley, the ballet was an institution, and the *pas de quatre*, and the *pas de fascination*, were the great witnesses of his success. Where are we now to look for Taglioni, Elssler, Cerito, Carlotta Grisi, or Lucile Grahn ? I fear they are for ever gone; and those distinctive styles of dancing by which they were distinguished, the "tacquete" and "ballonné" have gone also. These *artistes* are only visible in their palaces on the lake of Como, to which, as if by common consent, they have retired.

The questions of the ballet—the safety of its members from fire, and the general respectability of the body—have of late years elicited a great amount of newspaper controversy. The Lord Chamberlain has had a meeting with

the chief London managers on the subject; and various
new regulations for stage-lights have been adopted as one
result of the recent agitation caused by the death of Miss
Charles. Perhaps the best exposition of the mysteries of
the ballet that has yet been published has arisen out of
these circumstances. It has been " spoken by a dancer "
from the pages of *Punch*, and is as follows :—

" I Wish to address you a few words on a subject which
as come before the notice of the public a good deal lately.
Our Mananger says how it is cheefly the underclothing of
us Ladies of the ballet as catch fire, and if we won't
make them secuer from fire, *He* cannot help it. But *we*
all say the Mananger *can* help it ; as, If it is cheefly the
under-clothing as catch fire, and *not* the Dress which the
Mananger pays for *himself*, why dosent He *give* us petticoats secuer from fire ? A Mananger says that we won't
attend to these things ourselves, *He* can not help it. The
public will say " stupid Girls, it is their own fault ; " but,
my dear, they doen't quite understand it. Now, I want
to tell the public, that, we Ladies of the ballet, those of
them which are in the front Line (which I must explane
is neerest the orchestrar) get about 15 *shillings a week*,
and the ladies in the back line get 12 *shillings a week*.
Now, my dear, what have we got to do out of this salary ?
I will tell you, and the public shall say if it is fare to
expect us ladies to have to pay any more expences about
these petticoats than they do allreddy.

" Out of 15 shillings a week, which I used to get when
I was *younger*, but I am getting on now, and am put
into the back line with 12 shillings a week, and, my dear

it is hard indeed to save out of this for the time between the seasons *when I am not wanted*—there *will* be a time when I shall never be wanted any more—but we will not think of that *now*—as I was saying, out of 15 shillings a week, a Lady of the ballet has in the first to buy tights, fleshing Body and shoes. The best tights cost more than £2 odd, and so, very few of us can get *them;* but pink silk stockings sown on to cotton tops of whitey-brown thread come to *less,* and look as well from the front; but even on the *best,* you can not depend on them, as, unless you know how to mend them, and very few of the new ones do, they are almost useless to a lady who considers her position when they have once gone in *ladders.*

"You may not know what *ladders* is, but it is when the silk goes anywhere and then splits downwards, leaving little threads of silk like the steps of a ladder. Those which know no better *darn* the ladders, but where there's *one* there may be half-a-dozen of them, and then the tights would be darned all over, and the Mananger would complane of the *look* of the thing though he *dosent* find them himself, and if the lady dosent get a new pair *to please him,* she may be pretty suer of not getting engaged at *his* theatre again, and she couldn't go down to another in the westend with untidy things like that. So that is another expense. Of course when I say that *us* ladies cannot get the best tights, shoes, and fleshings, I do not mean that Miss Langham and Miss De Vere could not, who are in the front line. But we call them the Barroness, that is Miss L., and the Countess, that is little De Vere, and they come to rehearsal in white crape or

Paisley's shawls which cost *ten or twelve guinees a peace,* dressed up to the nines as we say, and *they* can afford tights and fleshings all silk and everything else, though they were the greatest scrubs at one time, and only do get *the same as us now,* 15*s.* a-week ; but *they* are exseptions, and are fetched away in broghums with corronettes or cockades, and if they doent receive *no salary at all* they would not care.

"Well the shoes comes next. Pink satin shoes is about 5*s.* 6*d.* a pare, the second best is 4*s.* 6*d.* But you ware them out very quickly, you know, and then we recover them with white satin or jane which also *adds to expense.* The tights must be washed onst a week at the leest, and then you pinksauser them for to keep the color. All this costes money, for pinksausers is 6*d.* and only does three pare, and then of course there's the soap for cleening. Well you can not always be covering and darning and mending shoes, which we do cheefly when there is a long rehearsal, and the call is at 10 in the morning, when we finish at 11, and are wanted again at 2 o'clock to practis a insidentle dance : and if we are to appear again at the night, there is not time ofen for us to go home and get a dinner, so we club together and send out for reddishes, bread and cheese and onions, for if we were working there all day, the Mananger dosent offer us anything ; and for rehearsals, sometimes for *three* weeks before *we are playing at the night, we never get paid at all,* as our engagement is not begin. Of course the Barronness and De Vere do not mind this, and *they* never need to send for reddishes ; and sometimes when I am

catchd in the rane going across Watterloo bridge to home,
its beyond that a long way, and been obliged to go without dinner, I have wished that I was De Vere or the
Baronness; for there is some excuse when you are very
*very* hungry and tirird to death. I doent think that *now,*
my dear, but used to when I was in the front line and
poor mother was in the wardrobe, and used to beat me.

" Then there is the fleshing Body, which is about 2
shillings. You cannot do with less than 4 petticoats
any one. These are the underclothing. The Uncumbus-
tabel Tarlartan, which is secuer again catch fire is 1s. 6d.
a yard, though as no boddy byes it, it is soled for 10½d.;
but it looks yellerish, not white : 2½ yds. it takes for one
petticoat about, so that the 4 petticoats comes to 8s. 9d.;
and these tarlatans will not last cleene very long : and *as
they will not wash,* you have to bye new ones again,
*which the Mananger wants us to do, and complanes that
we will not spend another* 8s. 9d. *out of our salary.* That
is why we do not get that stuff, for we would rather
stand *the chance* of burning, *than the sertenty of not
being able to live,* if we spend our salary on secuering our
clothes from fire. But they want us to dip our book-
muslin petticoats in Tunget of Soder, I think is the name,
when we wash them. 1s. worth of Tunget will cleene 3
petticoats; so that is 1s. 4d. a fortnight extra out of
salary, and then, *I think* it rots the muslin and the petticoats, which as cost 2s. 8d. a peace, and so must be got
new again, which we think the *Mananger might do, as
it is he as puts the fire near us, and not us as goes near
the fire,* though they do try to blame on us. It costes you

see about £1, 13*s.* 2*d.* to start any one of us ladies des-
ently, and I have told you what a *continnuel* exspense it
is on *us.* I have not said anything of my own averyday
dress, gound and shawl and boots, *which were very
quick;* and my lodging which I cannot get less than for
2*s.* a week, even in clubbing with another lady. Then,
my dear, one *must* dine sometimes evin if it is exspense,
and it dose not do to be exstravigant, but safe a little, as
when I am ill and cannot come to the Theatre, the Mananger *dose not pay me, but forfits every night we stop
away.* The doctor when I was lay up in bed was very
kind *for nothing;* and my landlady made me some broath
and talk to me, and I loved her; and she paid a man that
I bought a pair of shoes of for 2*s.* 6*d.* when he come
everyday for the money, as I was ill and out of work,
and she would not let me pay her again exsept by 2*d.* a
week. I can not be ofen ill. I have been fortenate to
meet with kind peeple; if you will forgive me for my
troubling you, and can get the Manangers to be more
kinder to us, I dare say there will come One Day, when
you will not be sorry for having said a good word for

" A Lady of the Ballet."

# CHAPTER XXVII.

INTERESTING TO JUVENILES, AS IT DETAILS THE ART AND
MYSTERY OF GETTING UP THE GRAND CHRISTMAS
PANTOMIME OF " HARLEQUIN AND THE TYRANT KING
GOBBLEMUPANDSKRUNSHEMDOWNO ; OR, THE DOOMED
PRINCESS OF THE FAIRY HALL, WITH THE FORTY
BLOOD-RED PILLARS."

As the Christmas pantomime * and the ballet are very
near of kin to each other, I shall, before proceeding with
my bird's-eye view of the Bohemians, introduce a sketch
detailing how these Christmas pieces are got up, and the
labour which has to be undergone to bring them to perfection. This will at least please the juveniles, who look
forward to the evening of the 26th of December as the
most joyous night of the year—for on boxing-night, as it
is called, a hundred pantomimes are conjured into existence in celebration of the season. A countless host of
little boys and girls are on that evening gratified with
their annual visit to the theatre, and witness, in a
paroxysm of excitement, the manifold delights of the
ever-after-to-be-remembered pantomime of "The Tyrant
of the Great Island of Grindhisbonestopowderwithapestlesir,
King Gobblemupandskrunshemdowno ; or, Harlequin and

* This chapter, and some other portions of this narrative, appeared in
*Chambers's Journal*, and are reprinted by permission.

the Doomed Princess of the Diamond Hall, with the Forty Blood-red Pillars," full of the usual tricks and transformations, and, if we may believe the bill, "resplendent with new scenery, machinery, dresses, and decorations."

I often wonder if my juvenile friends ever think of the enormous amount of industry which must be evoked before the pantomime can be presented to the audience— before the clown can knock down Piecrust the baker, or before pantaloon can rob the simple-minded butcher, who has been robbed every Christmas in every pantomime that has been produced in the three kingdoms, from the earliest period of their existence down to the present time. Even grown-up people have a sort of idea that the Christmas pantomime is a thing produced by accident, or that it is knocked together on the spur of the moment, just because people want a hearty laugh for their children on boxing-night; and also, *sub rosâ*, a little cachinnatory exercise for themselves. The pantomime is not, however, got up by accident, but is the result of intense labour, mental and bodily, on the part of all concerned, managers, authors, scene-painters, designers, carpenters, property-makers, costumiers, spangle and lace makers, and panto-mimists—that is to say, clowns, harlequins, pantaloons, columbines, sprites, harlequinas, ballet-girls, musicians, and supernumeraries of both sexes. The preparations for the pantomime may be assumed to commence in the large London theatres about the beginning of August, or even earlier, when " the house-author" and the manager determine what it is to be, and upon the principal ideas for which it is to be made the vehicle. As the autumn progresses into winter, *it*—having as yet no name, or the name being for a period a profound secret, the pantomime is always, by those interested, spoken of as *it*—gradually gets into shape ; scenes are invented, and tricks planned ; advertising tradesmen are arranged with, some of whom willingly pay £50 or £100 for a scene which advertises their goods—that is, a scene having a view of their premises, wherein the clown and pantaloon carry out a deal of practical fun with the articles in which they deal. The house-author, of course, only prepares what is called the introduction, or literary part of the harlequinade, which is usually made a vehicle for fine scenery, gorgeous processions, incidental ballets, panoramas, &c. Some one of the pantomimic corps usually takes charge of what, in technical phraseology, is called the "comic business;" but there are persons in London, such as the far-famed Mr Nelson Lee, who make it their special business, for a "consideration," to get up this department of our Christmas entertainments.

In the fulness of time, the pantomimic corps are summoned to the theatre—they have most of them been engaged since last season, if they are public favourites—and a time is fixed for the commencement of the necessary rehearsals. A troupe of fifty ballet-girls has been engaged for the processions and tableaux. Beverley, the inimitable scene-painter, has promised to do a couple of his finest scenes of fairy-land. Dykwynkin has promised designs for the masks and costume of the fifty guards of the tyrant king Gobblemupandskrunshemdowno ; and by and by things are so far advanced that the name of the piece is no longer kept secret; and the bill—the bill of the pantomime, with all its comicalities—is drawn up, and is very privately got into proof for the consideration and criticism of the author and manager; for, be it known, the bill is a most particular item of the pantomime, and has frequently been known to be a great deal funnier than the piece it professes to describe. But, previous to all this, when the author has got the piece into something like shape, the stage-manager assembles in the green-room those who are to take part in the acting or getting-up of the pantomime, and reads what is called in theatrical parlance the "opening," in order that the mechanists, tailors, artists, &c., of the theatre may each know what is required of him. For this purpose the necessary explanations are made, and the chief of each department is provided with a list, or "plot," as it is called, of everything which will be required in his line of duty ; and after this has been given him, there is no excuse for idleness ; so these heads of departments at once set to work, assisted by a swarm of *aides* of all kinds ; for the gigantic preparations will require every hour of their time, from the date of that reading till boxing-night, before the productions of these working *genii* can go before the public, with their fairy scenery, their comic masks, their elaborate dresses, and all the spangles and golden glitter which are incidental to the creation of a successful pantomime.

Let us imagine, then, that it is the middle of December, the best time for making the tour of that part of the house from which so many metaphors have been drawn—

Behind the Scenes. "Here we are," then, to use the Christmas language of the clown — having got safely through the hall, and passed, a difficult achievement, the Cerberus of the place—on the P. or prompter's side of the stage, at the first entrance. The curtain is drawn up; and the audience portion of the house is all covered over with calico, and looks cold and dismal enough without the happy faces whose smiling approbation will, in good time, light it up. A flexible tube conveys gas to an upright in the orchestra, where sits the leader of the ballet music looking over and trying his grand overture to the forthcoming Christmas novelty, while a *répétiteur* is busy scraping away at the Elfin Waltz, which a lady and gentleman, curiously-attired, are practising on the stage. The lady is dressed in an old pair of silk tights, dirty satin shoes, worn-out ballet skirt, a felt bonnet, and a warm cloth polka. "Is it possible!" exclaim our young friends'; "can that be columbine? and is that really harlequin?" "Yes," we reply, "that is the doomed princess, afterwards columbine; and her companion in the white trousers, pea-coat, and buff shoes, is the knight of the spangles—harlequin."* These are their working

* Some ignorant people are accustomed to assert that the pantomimic corps perpetually bathe themselves in oil, to keep their joints supple; but the great oiler of the joints of pantomimists is exercise, and the perpetual motion of their profession. A pantomimist does not live long, as the Herculean exertions which he has to go through soon kill him. It is said of Grimaldi that, even while he was a comparatively young man, his exertions had quite debilitated him. "Men were obliged to be kept waiting at the side-scenes, who caught him in their arms when he staggered from the stage, and supported him, while others chafed his limbs, which was obliged to be incessantly

clothes they have on; but wait till boxing-night, and what couple will be more resplendent! The cadaverous-looking trio in the prompter's corner, who are talking about some alterations of the comic business, consists of clown, pantaloon, and stage-manager. These men lounging on the other side are "supers"—that is the stage name for the wretched individuals who, for the sake of eighteenpence a night, will espouse any side of a dispute, and are perfectly indifferent whether they belong to the Montagues or the Capulets. On the present occasion, they are to act alternately, of course with a change of dress, as the retainers of the tyrant king Gobblemupand-skrunshemdowno, and of Prince Razorshanks, his rival in the affections of the Doomed Princess. That little, thickset, quiet man, with the intellectual face, is the painter or artist of the house; and the important-looking personage with whom he is talking is Mr Joints, the eminent mechanist of the establishment. Mysterious voices are sounding loudly far away up in the "flies;" while a busy carpenter is industriously opening up a "slote" at the back-part of the stage, and oiling a part of the work, to make it run well. We look through the long, narrow opening, and gaze at the wonderful region—the bowels, so to speak, of the place; what wheels, what ropes, what pulleys, what depths and depths there are, away far down below the floor, there, lighted by dim lights in obscure lanterns, and where men in fustian jackets and paper caps lie in wait for signals from above—tinkling bells, or

done until he was called for the next scene, or he could not have appeared again."

orders through speaking-tubes; while even the stage itself seems a perfect riddle of traps and openings, and a place of danger to the uninitiated. As we come off the boards at the P., or prompt side, passing the green-room, we see the door of the property-room, and although we are warned by a placard that there is "no admittance except on business," our young friends may venture in. What a scene! Just imagine a green-grocer's shop, a poulterer's and butcher's stall, a musical-instrument warehouse, an old-furniture depot, a china store, a hard-wareman's, all compressed into one moderate-sized room, and the reader will then have a faint idea of what a theatrical property-room is. The varied properties are piled away in heaps upon the floor, or on shelves, or are hung around on nails, most of them for use in the panto-mime; on the walls, especially, are grinning at us the gigantic false-faces, designed by the aforesaid Dykwynkin, and which are destined to be so provocative of mirth to the wondering Master Toms and Miss Maries of boxing-night.

We shall next visit the workshop where these things are made. That large mass of yielding clay can be easily moulded into the face of one of the tyrant king's guards. The mass, after the comic or terrific physiognomy has been shaped upon it, is smeared over with oil, so that a thin plaster-of-Paris mould can be taken from it. This, in turn, like a shape for moulding jelly, will be well buttered or greased, and then sheets of thin brown paper will be pasted in till the face acquires the requisite strength; then it is taken from the mould, and dried, preparatory to having masses of coloured wool or horse-hair sewed upon it, and the necessary amount of rose-pink bestowed upon the nose and cheeks, till it is fitted to pass as the head of one of Gobblemupandskrunshemdowno's retainers. Large quantities of vegetables are also in pro-gress—the great barrel full of saw-dust is for stuffing into these red cases, which, during the pantomime, do duty as carrots at the terrible "spill" or uproar which terminates each scene of the comic business. These fine-looking legs of mutton, loaves of bread, and sides of bacon, are all "got up" in this apartment, and, as the bill says, "regardless of expense;" as are also the tempt-ing pots of beer with the fierce foam upon them; also those miraculous chairs which change into pianos, and those wonderful beds which, with an utter contempt for the centre of gravity, will, the moment the clown lies down, mount to the roof of the bedroom; also those dummy figures of harlequin, policemen, &c., which are shot out of cannon, or are pounded to dust in a gigantic druggist's mortar, or are put once or twice through the clown's mangle, and then, by means of water, are re-made-up into their natural form. Everything required in the panto-mime in the shape of properties can be manufactured here, from the crown of the tyrant usurper to the rod used in the third comic scene—Dr Birch's academy—where the tall boy in the white pinafore, who brings up the rear of the boarding-school procession, comes in for a mock flagellation at the hands of a very starved-looking usher.

Next door to this wonderful workshop is the wardrobe,

where the theatrical dresses are kept. Those in a large establishment are, of course, very numerous and expensive, (the cost of the tartan alone for the dresses in "Rob Roy," for instance, was £150.) At present all hands are busy on the costumes for the pantomime; the dresses for the guards and the tyrant king are now in hand, made of real catskin, with the original hair on. Alas! how many poor cats will have disappeared from their homes and sympathising proprietors, to make up the requisite number of skins. Those young ladies, yonder, are busy sewing spangles and beads on the skirt of a dress intended for columbine to dance in. That pile of white-satin ballet shoes has just come from the shoemaker's; they are for the fifty pair of feet of the fifty young ladies of the tyrant's court, who dance and attitudinise that terrible bully to sleep. Observe, they are not squared off at the toes, like the white-satin shoes of society, but are beautifully rounded at the point, as the dancing-shoes of theatrical people invariably are. We will not venture even to guess how many yards of gold-sprigged muslin may be required for the fifty dresses of the aforesaid young damsels, but that enormous mass on yonder table is supposed to contain the full quantity. The green and red baize which lies about in careless confusion, will speedily be converted into tunics for the opposing pantomimic armies, who are to do battle for the rights and liberties of the Doomed Princess. The wardrobe and tailor's shop at such a period as this are perfect hives of industry, and with every person engaged, the order is "stitch, stitch, stitch," from early morn till the chimes ring out the midnight hour. Among the other costumes which are in progress, there is a dress for harlequin, made of beautifully-woven stuff, and patched all over with variegated pieces of silk. This style of dressing harlequin is exactly sixty-four years old, and was first introduced in the pantomime of "Harlequin Amulet," which was produced in 1800. Before that time, we are told, "it had been customary to attire the harlequin in a loose jacket and trousers; and it had been considered indispensable that he should be perpetually attitudinising in five positions, and doing nothing else but passing instantaneously from one to the other, and never pausing without being in one of the five."

The carpenter's shop is as busy a scene as the tailor's. The hammer and the saw are for ever sounding. "Flats" and "wings" are always being nailed into shape, and covered over with canvas, ready to go up to the painting-room. At the time of our visit, a being in canvas over-alls, wearing a paper cap, and having a neat little saw in his hand, is busy cutting out the shape of some foliage, or, as the operation is called behind the scenes, marking the "profile." Carpenters in some theatres perform a great many duties which are not dreamt of in extra-theatrical shops. We once knew a man who had been at some time or other connected with nearly every provincial theatre in Great Britain and Ireland, and who called himself a carpenter; but he could do anything: he could form a scene, stretch on the canvas, and, if it was for a chamber, he could paint it. He also officiated as a scene-shifter, and went on for "little business" at night. He

could make properties, and did not disdain to act the part
of tailor or check-taker when required. Once or twice,
upon emergency, he took a place in the orchestra; and
with an accordion he has sometimes officiated as the whole
band of a theatre rural. Yet for all his usefulness, he
never had a lárger salary than sixteen shillings a week.

We may now leave the carpenter's shop, and visit the
studio of the artist, which is situated at the top of the
theatre. The painting-shop is exactly over the back-part
of the stage; but it is a great way up. It is a long room,
and is filled with a profusion of light, by means of a
gigantic glass erection on the top of the house. In this
chamber we see the artist at work on the back-part of
"the tranquil lake in the empyrean fields of balmy delight." The canvas is astonishingly large; but it is quite
manageable, and can be lowered or raised to any required
height or depth by means of slight machinery constructed
for the purpose. The dexterity with which it has been
painted is quite wonderful. The immense surface having
been sized over, an outline of the landscape is traced out
pretty boldly by the principal artist; then it is more
minutely outlined in ink, and numerous portions of the
design, originally dashed off on Bristol-board in water-
colours, are shadowed forth on the large canvas;
all the principal masses of colour are at once washed
in by the assistant brushes, but the finish conferred
upon the whole is left to the principal artist, who
executes it with a skill and power which will obtain, we
trust, the high encomiums of the critics of the Sunday
papers, as well as the volleys of applause bestowed upon

it by the "discriminating" audience who are always sure
to assemble on boxing-night. The celerity with which
business is carried on in this department of the theatre
is quite miraculous, although aided, no doubt, by the
largeness of the canvas operated upon, which admits of a
perfect army of brushes being engaged upon it at the
same time, all directed, however, by the great master-
brush of the establishment. A considerable portion of
the labour in the painting-room is quite mechanical: for
instance, straight lines for cornices, &c., are traced on the
canvas by means of a tightly-drawn piece of cord, rubbed
over with dry colour, which is placed against the scene,
and then pulled out, and let down again, when, of course,
it leaves its mark. This and similar work can be done by
a labourer or boy. This elaborate scrolled scene for a
chamber in the tyrant's palace is done by means of
"pouncing"—that is, a small portion of the design is
pricked out on a sheet of paper, which is held against the
canvas, and then a bag of charcoal is dashed upon it,
leaving, of course, the outline to be afterwards finished.
This process is repeated till the whole of the large surface
is covered, and when finally perfected, it looks very well
indeed. When scenes are intended to dazzle and glitter,
as is usually the case in a pantomime, they are daubed
over with Dutch metal, the artist marking the places to
be so done with a thinnish kind of glue; and the bits so
prepared are either covered with gold or silver leaf, as
may be required.

So much for the libretto or introduction. The "comic
business of a pantomime," as it is called, that is, the fun

and frolic which succeed the transformation scene, is described, to those who are to take part in it, by means of a "plot," which is usually made out by the clown. Clowns, as a general rule, are not very grammatical, nor are many of them celebrated for their caligraphy. I happen to have by me a plot of the comic business of a pantomime, which I obtained from my friend Griffiths; and as it is a fair sample of these productions, I beg leave to print it just as it stands, spelling and all :—

### PROGRAM OF COMIC BUISNES

#### IN THE PANTOMIME

A cascaid at the fall of the Curtain by the caracturs;

(i. e., *after the transformation scene.*)

SCENE FIRST.—Poultry shop and Tailor shop—set.

*Dance by Harlequin and Columbine; then sprites to cross and Recross.*

Rabits and poultry on The stall with very larg Goos.

#### BUISNES.

Enter Clown and Pantaloon steeling goos (buisnes) enter tax colecktor with larg sumonds (writ) writen on it assecesed tax, then buisnes with the tailor, when he exits boy with pie.   Buis: Tax colecktor police and tailor and old woman (spill.)

This way of setting it down on paper conveys but a very inadequate idea of how effectively such business can be worked up by a clever clown and assistants.  He (*i.e.*, the clown) shews everybody what is to be done; and by going through the business once or twice, all become perfect, and so help to secure the success of the pantomime.

The famous old pantomime of "Mother Goose," which had at one time so great a run, having been recently reprinted, affords me a further opportunity of initiating my juvenile friends into the mysteries of their Christmas amusements. I may mention, that a "plot" is given to every one of the heads of departments ; thus, for the scene-painter for " Mother Goose," there was furnished a plot containing nineteen items—I give a brief selection from it :—

### SCENE-PAINTER'S PLOT.

*Scene* 1.—A village, with storm ; church with churchyard ; bridge, water, moving objects : Rainbow, cottage, and mansion. R. Tombstone with inscription, " In Memory of Zantippe, Wife of Bullface Bugle Esquire." Mother Goose on a Gander.

*Scene* 2.—Thick wood on one side ; entrance on the other ; thick foliage, and an owl posted on a branch L. Change to Mother Goose's cottage.

*Scene* 3.—A hall ; a clock with two faces to it ; one with a sportsman with his gun.

The next plot is made out for the carpenter, whose duty it is to furnish the necessary wood-work for the various scenes, &c. I will repeat from his plot the same three scenes that I have given from the painter's plot, to make my information as complete as possible :—

### CARPENTER'S SCENE-PLOT.

*Scene* 1.—Set village with storm ; water, bridge, with church and churchyard, tombstones. Cottage and mansion R ; with objects moving across the bridge &c.; mail-coach, waggon, small boats.

*Scene* 2.—A wood to change to cottage, &c.

*Scene* 3.—A hall ; panel to turn round ; trick-clock jump for harlequin, the clock door to open ; little harlequin is discovered ; trick-clock face.

We now come to the property plot, in which we find

the three scenes that I have selected, making still farther progress :—

*Scene* 1.—Thunder, &c.; stick for Mother Goose; favours for villagers; huntsman's whip; staff for beadle.

*Scene* 2.—Golden Egg. Goose.

*Scene* 3.—Three chairs; a knife and stick for pantaloon; a sword for harlequin; two pistols to fire behind the scene.

After all these have been seen to and provided, there comes the tailor's plot, in which we find a list of all the dresses that are required; and as among the characters there are an "odd fish," a fireman, a Jew, a cobbler, a link-boy, &c., the tailor would have plenty of scope for his ingenuity.

The first scene of the three I have selected for illustration comes out splendidly in the book of the pantomime, and is as follows :—

*Scene* 1.—A village, with storm, &c. Sunset; on the R. are the entrance gates to Squire Bugle's mansion, adjoining it Colin's cottage. A church, with churchyard in front, L. ; the perspective a distant view of a river and a bridge over it, (1;) moving objects both on the river and bridge, (2.) During the storm Mother Goose has raised, she is descending from the skies mounted on a gander; after the storm (3) the clouds disperse, and a rainbow is seen, the sun rises gradually, &c. &c., its golden beams are finely reflected in the window of the church.

A crowd of male and female peasants assemble, decorated with favours, to celebrate the nuptials of the Squire and Colinette.

This finishes our tour of the industrial departments of the house ; and if we have not adequately described the great labour involved in getting up the pantomime, we can give our readers another mode of judging of it by stating that the cost of getting up a great London Christmas piece at Covent-Garden Theatre a few years ago, was nearly eight thousand pounds; while the weekly bill for salaries and necessaries to keep it going was above seven hundred pounds! A London pantomime of any pretensions to magnitude or splendour will be certain to cost a couple of thousands; the competition is so great, that a manager must spend a great deal of money, or he will be outdone by others, and his house will fail in attraction.

But at length boxing-night—the night of nights to our young friends—arrives, and, having explored the region which lies behind the green curtain, and seen the details of which a pantomime is made up, we are now ready to see it as it appears to the audience. Before the curtain draws up, and during the time when our company are enduring what somebody has graphically called the purgatorial passage to the paradise of pantomimic delights, namely, the eternal "George Barnwell," or mayhap "The Stranger," we express a hope that our young companions, who are just about to enjoy their annual peep at the Christmas pantomime, are aware of the great antiquity of this their favourite entertainment. We beg they will remember, while laughing at the drolleries of Mr Clown, or while they are indignant at the buffets bestowed upon poor pantaloon, that pantomime was known to the ancients, and was practised in various forms by the Greeks and Romans—not, however, at all times as an amusement, but was resorted to in their great festivals and solemnities, as on the occasions of marriages and funerals.

Pantomimes were not got up in this country till the year 1702, when we find that one was produced at Drury Lane Theatre, called the "Tavern Bilkers." It was brought out by one Weaver, a provincial dancing-master, and was well received. In consequence of his success, he brought out several others; such as "The Loves of Mars and Venus," all of which were successful. It was not, however, till the advent of the Grimaldi family, in 1758, that pantomime began to be important. Mr Grimaldi, a son of the great dancer and famous clown, brought this kind of entertainment to a state of great perfection, and for many years assisted in the getting up of those pantomimes of the good old times about which we hear old playgoers talk so enthusiastically. Grimaldi was thus apostrophised by James Smith, one of the authors of the "Rejected Addresses:"—

> "Facetious mime! thou enemy of gloom;
> Grandson of Momus, blithe and debonair;
> Who, aping Pan with an inverted broom,
> Can brush the cobwebs from the brows of care."

But we are forgetting the present in these reminiscences. What a buzz there is when the curtain rises, and the tyrant king's band of Christy minstrels are seen, ay, and heard too, playing a serenade before the grand entrance to the palace. This morning, no person would have supposed it possible that the piece could come out at all; but here it is, ay, and a great success into the bargain, as might have been expected from what we already know of the preparations that have been gone through to insure its "going" well. "Could we not go behind to-night?" asks some one. Heaven forbid! we have more sense than to venture behind the scenes on the first night of a new Christmas piece. We know from experience what kind of treatment we should receive; how we should be knocked about at the various entrances of the stage, or perhaps shoved "on" *in propriâ personâ* in some of the mobs, without being called by the audience. The bustle and animation behind the scenes during the run of a popular Christmas piece can scarcely be described, and every available inch of space is blocked up with the necessary properties. Here a basketful of mock vegetables; there a lot of chairs; in another place, a heap of kitchen utensils. "Now, then, by your leave," and a fierce giant, carrying his head under his arm, twists you aside—not very ceremoniously. Then the shrill treble of a trembling fairy says: "Please, sir, will you allow me to pass?" Then the stage-manager asks some one who you are. Next, a carpenter condescends to inform you that it is very warm, and hints at "beer." "Take care of your feet!" shouts the prompter, and looking down, you see two gigantic warming-pans ready to be shoved on for the next scene. As you pass up the narrow path between the side-scene and the wall, in order to gain the door, harlequin and columbine, reeking hot, bound from the stage, and nearly overthrow you; while just as you recover your perpendicular, you receive a blow on the cheek from a soft turnip, and a furious knock on the shins from a wooden cheese.

It is said that the spell of pantomime is broken, and that this kind of entertainment will speedily be numbered among the things of the past. But the same thing was said a quarter of a century ago. Just at that date, a public journalist stated that "ingenious tricks, startling transformations, surprising feats of agility, grotesque masks, smacks, thumps, and tumbles, astonish without amusing, unless they are made to bear upon the action of the story. Wanting purpose, the wit of the concocters, the cleverness of the machinist, and the humour of the performers, are of no effect: strange, that those most concerned in the prosperity of pantomime will not see what is so obvious to everybody else!" Notwithstanding these predictions, we still find pantomime in vogue; and since some of the London Christmas pieces run for a period of sixty or seventy consecutive nights, drawing large audiences on each representation, we must conclude that there is yet life in that amusement.

# CHAPTER XXVIII.

IN WHICH I GIVE A BIRD'S-EYE VIEW OF THE WONDERFUL
BOHEMIANS OF THE MODERN BABYLON : SHEWING
HOW THEY "WORK THE ORACLE," AND PUT MONEY
IN THEIR PURSES.

CONSIDERING myself qualified to act as a *valet de place*
to persons wishing to know Bohemia, I shall here make
it convenient to introduce the Bohemians of London to
my readers.   First taking as a key-note to the chapter a
short extract from the " Mysteries of Paris."

" There are so many Bohemians in Paris.   ' Bohemians!
Refugees from Bohemia?'   You do not understand.   I
mean by Bohemians that class of individuals whose existence is a problem—their condition and their fortune an
enigma ; having no resting place; who are never to be
found, and yet are to be seen everywhere ; who have no
trade, yet live by professions; the greater number of whom
rise without knowing where they shall dine ; rich to-day,
dying with hunger to-morrow."

Notwithstanding the key-note which I have struck, it
is a little difficult to define with extreme nicety who are
and who are not Bohemians ; but there is an indescribable
something about the whole class, both high and low, which
singles them out for observation, and separates them from
the common herd of "highly respectable" men and women ;

and among themselves there appears to be a kind of free masonry in existence, which enables Bohemians to know each other; having their secret words and passes, they appear instinctively to come together; and, moreover, are all dead against that conventionality, the correct observance of which is recognised by "the world" as the best proof of respectability; for a true Bohemian has a natural love of licence, and an intense hatred of law and order.

The symbolical Bohemia is of unlimited extent; arms of it stretch out to all the quarters of the globe; its head quarters in Europe being London and Paris. But, as I may hint here, the empire is divided—there is a St Giles's and a St James's. The higher Bohemians are separated from the lower by personal splendour and the magnitude and cleverness of their operations, and by the sometimes extraordinary genius displayed in conducting them. Bohemia gives shelter to all kinds of clever rogues; men and women who live by their wits, and who can talk or "do" you out of your money in the most agreeable manner. Most Bohemians, too, have "a taste" in wines, a feeling for art and theatricals, and a keen relish for all kinds of illicit enjoyments. Many of the higher Bohemians are clever men or women, who, having been shipwrecked on the sea of life, are glad to drift on a raft of their reputation into a port of Bohemia, rather than sink into a state of damaged respectability; so that behind these educated gipsies' curtain of life we find displayed no commonplace world. It matters not which phase of Bohemianism comes up for review, or whether we drop upon St James's or St Giles's, all are alike feverish and hot;

with a terribly rapid pulsation ; and all shew the same contempt for "society" and its formalities. And as there is no limit to the ingenuity and ubiquity of these most polite rogues, it is not wonderful that there are commercial as well as literary and artistic Bohemians. Bohemian poets, Bohemian painters, Bohemian players, and Bohemian musicians, somehow or other seem natural. But there are great commercial houses in Bohemia also— "concerns" which rise, culminate, and fall in a single season—houses of curiously-embossed paper, which the public occasionally read about in that current history of the hour—the daily newspaper. Such houses are blown away even by the faintest monetary storm ; a bank tempest crumples them up like so many tea-bags.

The Bohemian commercial houses are originated by men of genius and figures, confined perhaps by some malignant influence to the rules of the Queen's Bench ; and after they flourish for a brief season in their suite of fine offices, we find their Bohemian accoucheurs "in bankruptcy," at a safe distance from those who want them —perhaps away in the remote Highlands of Scotland— at, say Tobermory. Any place, so that it be far from the inquisitive house of Mr Commissioner Holroyd. Of such, so long as the bank stands and the "tin" holds good, are your gay men who originate "will-o'-the-wisp" companies, and who have a speciality for getting up Bohemian banks and discount offices—indeed it is in these directions that their genius lies, and in such enterprises they have a way of seducing other men to aid them. Happy Bohemians! they are in clover. Then is the era of champagne suppers, unlimited turtle, and iced punch *ad libitum ;* Richmond dinners on Sunday at any price, or at Blackwall with whitebait additions ; or, more in public still, at the "Crown and Anchor" with Toole behind "the chair," and the gentlemen of the press in front of it. *Vive la bagatelle !* is the exclamation of the hour. Who ever thinks in Bohemia of a day of reckoning ?

Success in commercial Bohemia is but for a time. The bubble, no matter how dexterously it may be blown, will at last burst, and another nine days' wonder become evolved for public discussion. In literary and artistic Bohemia there are the same occasional flashes, or, as I once heard a Scotchman call them, " hungers and bursts." But in not a few instances the hungers have the best of it. We have all seen the picture of the "Distressed Poet;" and who is not familiar with the story of Chatterton, or of Richard Savage—two literary Bohemians of the last century ? And did not Haydon the painter take his own life ? And are there not left to us other painters of the same caste ? Men of genius without ballast, who murmur at the public support given to dwarfs, bearded ladies, and *artistes* of the tight-rope ; who talk big on this when they should be at work, and while doing so fly to that falsest of all friends, the brandy bottle, and so, asleep at the helm, get shipwrecked on the loadstone coasts of Bohemia. And are there not plenty of Bohemians in the green-room ? How long is it since that little story went the round ?—that little story of a poor comedian who was cheated and starved by a Bohemian manager, who fattened his paunch by eating up the salaries of his company. It is not so very

long ago.    The poor actor had to pawn his little properties
in order to obtain food for his dam and her pretty chickens,
and then, without the tools of his trade, his "properties"
—his kingly robes and tinsel jewels—he could not gain
employment, so that starvation was imminent.    To end his
days and his sorrows at one fell swoop he tried one night
to commit suicide ; and that which looked the blackest
hour in his life brought renewed joy and hope.    The
police caught him—his story came out in the police-office
—was graphically told in the newspapers, and public bene-
volence soon enabled him again to tread that *via dolorosa*
grandly termed the British stage.

But my readers would no doubt like to view the
*dramatis personæ* of the higher Bohemian world at rehearsal, preparing for that keen action which enables
them to live.    Undoubtedly they would.    Then out *lorg-
nettes*, for here is the curtain up, and there are the puppets
ready to make their *entrée*, and obey the behests of their
willing showman.    Who are all these?    Oh, these are the
characters of our first little tableau—a group of commercial Bohemians engaged in "getting up" a bank on the
joint-stock "dodge," as the projectors call their plan.
Their great difficulty, at the moment of exhibition, is to
obtain a few pounds to pay the expenses of the preliminary
advertisement.    In stage parlance, we have quite a picture.
For each of the *dramatis personæ* has just made the interesting discovery that the other is penniless ; and these
gentlemen who will presently figure in prospectuses as
men of great wealth, capitalists of the first water, have a
"leetle" difficulty of ten pounds—only ten pounds !    But

Bohemians never allow these petty obstacles to stand in their way, the sum required will be obtained. The prospectus will flourish in the daily papers, and in due course "a board" of Lords and Commons will be constituted. Wait but a poor fortnight and everything will swim with the tide. Various directors are bagged; the Earl of Calton Hill (an ancient Scotch peer) is secured as chairman; the O'Brolochan (M.P. for a Radical district in the north of England) obtains the deputy-ship; a grand building is erected; a manager is engaged, and at last business begins; that is, money comes in, and never goes out again, except in the pockets of the Bohemians, who have conferred upon themselves the order of the Golden Fleece. Thus the "institution" rises like an exhalation; but, like all the other creations of Bohemian architects, it crumbles and falls to pieces just as people are becoming familiar with it. And after the crash comes of course the usual howl of virtuous indignation at the gigantic swindle, and the tenfold sympathy with those who have been crushed in the ruins of the rotten building. And where are the directors? Gone, of course, like rats from a suspected ship. My Lord Calton Hill, himself perhaps a victim, is up the Rhine; the Radical member for Shoddyburgh is buried deep in the mountain fastnesses of Ireland; and the public wrath falls hot and furious on the luckless head of some silly official, who has to pay the piper in person. The law, having been outraged, must have somebody's scalp to hang up in the justice-room. But in a few months a new wonder will push aside even a Bohemian bank; the tears shed over it will be dried up; and so we may pull the trigger and change the scene.

I had at one time the *entrée* of the Bohemian Club. It was a grand place for wit, champagne, and devilled kidneys. It was frequented by all the great Bohemians. Boreas, the dramatic author, came there, so did Venom of the *Sunday Scourge*. Slop, the great scene-painter, and Davy Jones, the lessee of the Arundel - Street Theatre, were also on the list of members. So was M'Razor, the great Caledonian wizard, to whom I was at one time secretary. Bowl, the leviathan "bookmaker;" Spout, the theatrical critic; Beak, the well-known sporting reporter; Blucher, the champion of all England; Sir Belchington Spoon, the noble patron of the ring; and Habbakuk Crozier, the Jew diamond merchant; all rubbed shoulders at the Bohemian Club. "Motley's your only wear" might be said of all these—most of them had on a mask. See how they all get into action. The Earl of Calton Hill, always pushed for cash, contrives to suck a few pounds out of Crozier. "The O'Brolochan" comes in for a share of the "dibs;" and Venom, again, who is deuced hard up, as indeed he always is, "gets" a few sovs. from Sir Belchington, who thereupon commands that immaculate journalist to puff Polly Brigs, who used to play the singing chambermaids (in silk gowns, satin shoes, and diamond ear-drops, no theatrical chambermaid being properly made-up unless she is slippered and jewelled like a countess) at the Arundel. Blucher takes Sir B. aside, and puts him up to the very latest wrinkle of the sporting world; which is, that Tom Craggy

it has been arranged, is to be the victor at the approaching "mill" between himself and the Tiverton Pimple, and
in consequence the enlightened baronet is strongly recommended to *hedge* before any one else "gets the office."
M'Razor is bargaining with Davy Jones for a lease of
the Arundel, in which to set up his "Grand and Myste-
riously-mystic Magic Temple of the Golden Crocodiles of
the Nile;" and, as Spout has been secured by M'Razor
to *do* the bills and other mysterious announcements with
which the wizard delights to humbug the public, a great
season is confidently expected. And now it is midnight,
the theatres are closed, and crowds of visitors drop into
the Bohemian Club. Vamp has his Welsh rarebit and
his noggin of "hot with;" his new sensation drama of
"The Bloodhound of Breadalbane; or, The Withered Hag
of the Beech-tree Forest," has been a success, and Vamp
is high accordingly—he stands "sam" to the "villain" who
played in his piece, and who converses through a cold
caught evidently at a recent date in one of those canvas
caves in which he, as first murderer, delights to conceal
himself. The din and bustle as midnight is passing away
grow fast and furious. Bohemia delights to sup. Supper
is the favourite feeding time of these literary, artistic, and
theatrical lions, then they are indeed brilliant, and roar
with a delight that knows no stopping. A gentleman
in green-plush is ready to take orders; and devilled kidneys hissing in their fat, and the water of life sweetened
with sugar, and silver pints of stout, and small bottles of
Bass, and mutton cutlets, and broiled bones, and toasts
of Anchovy, and devilled biscuits, spiced port, mulled

claret, oysters, lobsters, and other crustacea are the order of the night ; and so the feast goes on till cockcrow gives warning of removal ; and many disappear from the club who wonder whether they will be able to sup there to-morrow night.   And so we again let down the drop, and prepare the next tableau.

# CHAPTER XXIX.

LADIES AND GENTLEMEN, THE CURTAIN WILL NOW RISE
ON THE NEXT TABLEAU, WHICH IS AS FOLLOWS :—

CALLING a hansom, we drive to the fashionable *quartier*
of the Bohemian St James's.   My Lady Calton Hill holds
a reception.   She has a mansion in her own right—
Baldrummy House, off Piccadilly—and to-night she is
at home, as usual, her great idea, under instructions from
her liege lord, being to keep up the influence in the
political world, and in the city, of her own and her husband's family.   It is a useless struggle, for my lord, except
for his coronet, would be in the Queen's Bench; as it is,
he is in Bohemia ; but *n'importe*, let us view the scene.
How splendid it all is!   Somehow the houses of the
Bohemian nobles are grander and more luxurious than
those of quieter people.   Here we have brilliant lights
reflected by gigantic mirrors, soft and yielding carpets,
gilded tables, and a perfumed atmosphere, with that
*sine quâ non* of society—noiseless attendants.   Then
there is a gay cavalcade of exquisitely-"toileted" ladies,
and gentlemen to match.   In the St James's region of
Bohemia there is a strong desire to indulge in the
sensuous.   The gentlemen cultivate their palate and
coddle their stomachs ; they delight in wine that has a
*bouquet*, dishes that have a *goût*, and in an atmosphere

that has been "Rimmeled," if I may coin a word.   So, too,
the ladies, lending themselves to the same feeling, are, if
anything, a shade over dressed ; rather gaudy in their
colours, but with faultless gloves and exquisite *chaussure*.
The latter, indeed, is with them a study : lace stockings
embroidered in colour, and of the finest texture, are
necessaries of life to my lady of Bohemia ; and my lady's
slippers must accord, perfect in shape, and of the finest
silk or satin ; they have but to shew their tiny shapes to
have at their little feet all the men of the age.   Did not
the handsome Madame Talaba keep a shoemaker to invent for her the most *recherché* slippers and boots ? and did
not the old Marquis of Calipash allow her two thousand a
year just for the pleasure of looking upon her tiny feet in
their silken and lace encasements ?—but that is nothing
in Bohemia.   It is in that region where novelists find
heroines who delight in a voluptuous *déshabillé ;* who,
when they are "in luck," have baths of crystal and
toilet-glasses from Munich; who wear ravishing bronze
boots, and invent new hats ; who ride in the park on
prancing steeds, or else drive pigmy ponies to the admiration of even the respectable world of London.   Such accessories combine to form a scene of splendour and gaiety as
enchanting as it is evanescent.   Look there!—that magnificent lady in the pink-silk dress is Lady Merryweather ; she was at one time a member of the *corps de
ballet* at the Arundel; (her father is old Jack Gong,
drunken Jack Gong, the hall-keeper at the "Falcon.")
My lady's maiden name was Matilda Gong, but Jones
brought her out as Mademoiselle Amelia Gongell—as

dancers with English names don't take in our theatres
—and, fascinated by her small silken-slippered feet
and elegant tights, old Merryweather elevated her to the
peerage, and a share of forty-seven thousand pounds per
annum. Her ladyship is not exactly *comme il faut.*
What need for her being in Bohemia if she were? But
we have not time longer to dwell upon her story, as other
fashionables of Bohemia are pouring into Baldrummy
House. "The O'Brolochan" and lady, the Hon. Lady
Verdant Gossamer, and Mrs Sparkle, the wit and satirist,
are each in turn announced. The lady was an actress,
in fact, is one still, indeed never more an actress than
now. Many were the choice stories that were told of Miss
Remington ; but they are soon forgotten, or dimmed in
lustre by the adventures of other heroines ; she still has a
fancy for the dice, and her ladyship, having now to live on
her wits, has all the address and courage necessary for a
thorough Bohemian. And now let us point out a group,
without particularising them, of the younger sons of Bohemia, who are anxious to make a lucky hit in the way
of matrimony—who will marry anything female that has
money in its purse, not objecting to a popular dancer or a
good concert-singer who has a large capital in her voice ;
their own capital varies from a few empty pomatum-pots
and two shirts, to a pound a week and three suits of
clothes per annum, the old ones to be given up on obtaining the new. Poor Patty Pirouette, the French *danseuse,*
seems unhappy. She is a *protégée* of that commanding
lady in the green-velvet dress; and she is dolorous because
Venom has just learned the history of a little adventure of

hers, which will not bear rehearsal in the public prints ;
but why weep for that, Mdlle. ?  Venom has a price for
which he can be bought—*his* inkstand is made of Bohemian glass.  Yes, get out your little velvet pocket-book,
and hand it over.  Tell him you want a criticism, and you
will obtain it.  In Bohemia—but nowhere else—journal-
ists can be bought and sold with vulgar gold ; elsewhere
the bribery is different, and must be "in kind."  Flexington
Treavor, the celebrated tenor, is in great voice to-night, and
is surrounded by a host of celebrities as he trills his best
ditties for the delectation of Bohemia.  Crozier, the Israelite,
who has to buy his invitations by lending his money to the
earl, walks about unnoticed ; one spark who "cuts" him
dead is in three hours thereafter cooling his heels in a
sponging-house.  Crozier never heeds the general neglect;
he adds it to the little bits of paper with the curiously-
embossed design in which he delights to deal.  Music and
dancing are the features of the reception.  The greater
Bohemians, as I have already said, esteem it part of their
code of life to have a taste, and they are generally very
fond of the drama and of theatrical people.  The countess
makes it a point of inviting all the operatic and dramatic
celebrities to her "At Home."  She pays them for their
trouble by taking a box at their benefits ; and she aids
them in becoming the rage in certain circles by her countenance and patronage.  Ices, coffee, wine, and cake are
handed round by the men in livery, and so the gaiety of
the evening moves in its feverish round.  Bohemian
members of Parliament — men who wouldn't strongly
object to selling their vote—drop in, and political combi-

nations that never can occur are freely canvassed. Her ladyship is great in politics. The enjoyment of the house is all the more fierce that to-morrow three or four of the guests will, for certain, drop from this St James's of Bohemia to the St Giles's of that pleasant country; and as a change of caste may speedily enough become the lot of all the brilliant company, so the hectic pleasures of the fleeting present are all the more enjoyable in consequence. Every to-morrow that dawns on the world of Bohemia brings its tide of evil. To-morrow the Bohemian bank collapses, and to morrow may witness the flight of its directors, and to-morrow may introduce "the man" into possession of many a noble palace of Bohemia; and so, as if harlequin had slapped the fabric with his magic wand, the scene flashes away, and the Bohemians seek out a new round of pleasure.

And now, let us ring down the curtain of our pretty little show, and examine the results of all the plotting and counterplotting which is so germane to the gipsies of art and commerce. And where, it may be asked, will we find an exposition of what has been achieved and what is going on? In the daily papers, to be sure—in the *Times*. In that wonderful second column of the advertising page, which is so evidently devoted to the professors of Bohemianism, and also in the police reports, in the leading articles, in the city intelligence, among the bankrupts, in the Insolvent Court, in the reports of the Master in Lunacy, in the suicides, elopements, assaults, fires, swindles. In the accounts of balls, races, meetings, fairs, dinners, &c., we shall find full intelligence of our friends in Bohemia. Take up the daily paper and it is certain to contain intelligence of one or other of the set we have been moving in—indeed, the chances are that most of our *dram. pers.* may figure in print with rare speed. Look here!—at a glance we hit upon two of our friends figuring in the second column:—" Parachute to Parallelogram—I have done the state some service, and they know it; but I intend to do a great deal more. Coventry, like Spitalfields, will not assist us, but the form must be gone through." Poor O'Brolochan! he is driven to correspond with his friend the earl through the second column of the *Times. He* has " done the state some service"—no doubt of it ; but for all that it will be the state's first duty to prosecute him, whenever it may be possible to put salt upon his hard-worked wings. And here, in the same paper which contains the plaintive appeal of Parachute, we have a *soupçon* of the later adventures of our friend Mr Jones, late of the Arundel Theatre. I copy the report :—

" The following curious case, which was heard at this court yesterday, will be found of interest not only to persons connected with our theatres, but also as an illustration of London life in certain Bohemian quarters. Mr Jones, the well-known lessee of the Arundel Street Theatre, was sued for arrears of salary by five principal members of his company. It appeared that Jones had become lessee of this tiny little playhouse without having had adequate means to carry it on, and the consequences are that he has fallen into arrears with his payments to tradesmen and the salaries of his company, so the principal actors resolved not to play unless they were paid every night in advance. This was agreed to by the manager, and for a few weeks the pre-payments were regularly made, and the play went on as usual. But on a particular evening—an evening which the manager for sundry excellent reasons best known to himself, had privately resolved was to be the last night of the season — Mr Jones contrived to be rather later than ordinary in reaching the theatre, thinking by this means to escape the usual pre-payment, as the company would be engaged in dressing; but there was to be no escape; the moment Jones arrived he was beset by his principal comedian and asked to fork over one sovereign. Poor Jones, he had but one, and how he was to pay three people one sovereign each, and the other two half-a-sovereign a piece, with that one coin was a feat in arithmetic that he could not perform—at least so at the first blush of the matter he thought. But Jones, as was stated in evidence, did manage to effect this wonderful bit of legerdemain. 'Fork out,' said the comedian, meeting Jones in the lobby. 'All right,' said Jones, ' I just happen to have enough for you five cormorants '— but we need not detail the 'chaff' which passed on either side, and which was all acted over again at the court. The 'tin,' (*i.e.*, the sovereign,) as the actor called it, was handed over, and so far all was well. The comedian who had been so fortunate as to secure payment went to dress, and had scarcely begun his toilet when the manager entered the room in breathless haste, and begged him to give him back the pound he had just received, as he required it very urgently just for a few minutes. 'Oh, no,' said the actor, 'you don't come that game with me. I 've bagged my bird, and I mean to keep it, I can tell you.' 'But, my dear boy,' said the manager, with inflexible gravity, 'consider what has happened, and don't be a brute. Poor Melville of the orchestra, has just been knocked down by an omnibus, and has sustained a compound fracture of his leg. I have sent him to the hospital, and that is his wife crying in my room; the money is for her, come now, be charitable—the doors are open, and you shall have your money in half-an-hour.' The appeal was irresistible—the comedian gave up his pound. 'Bravo!' exclaimed the manager, as he hurried out to pay away the sovereign to another member of the company, of whom, by relating once more the same sad story, it was borrowed again in a few minutes. The farce, as it appeared in evidence, was repeated till all were satisfied; and the result was that the clever but scampish manager contrived to leave the house, not only with a large share of the evening's receipts, but also with that bright particular sovereign in his pocket. Verdict for the plaintiffs, with full costs."

And now I have, perhaps, sufficiently illustrated the higher Bohemia—only there are still one or two of my friends undisposed of, and really the study of these spiders of an advanced civilisation is not without profit. Let me once more take up the *Times*. Here, *par example*, is an old friend of mine, Mr T. O. P. Saw-yer, barrister-at-law, (in the courts of Bohemia,) "in trouble" about a forged will. Committed, saith the magistrate. Guilty, say the jury. Two years hard labour, saith the judge; and so Mr Sawyer passes on; he was a great man at one time. Bless me !—here is Patty Pirouette at Bow Street;—it's all right, however. She is prosecuting a servant for stealing her pink-satin slippers; and it comes out in the evidence that they had been bought by some young swells from her "dresser," in order to their being used as wine-glasses from which to drain bumpers to Mdlle.'s health. Is not this a mad world, my masters?

And now I shall end this chapter, and pause for the present. The moral! Did some one ask for the moral? Well, to be sure, I didn't think of the moral; but I recollect when a gentleman, a friend of my youth, had concluded a story which he was telling about an ingenious robbery, he was asked by a lady, as there were several youngsters present, to point out the moral. "The moral, madam, is obvious," was the reply. "Seven years at the hulks."

# CHAPTER XXX.

## STILL IN BOHEMIA, BUT IN DEEPER STRATA; AMONG THE LOWER ANIMALS, IN FACT: SHEWING OVER AGAIN THE TRUTH OF THE ADAGE, THAT "ONE HALF OF THE WORLD KNOWS NOT HOW THE OTHER HALF LIVES."

I REQUIRE no text to aid me in describing the lower Bohemia. My own experience has been all too ample. As I have already indicated, some are born to an inheritance in Bohemia, while others drift into it by their own imprudence or impatience of restraint. The upper Bohemians, with rare exceptions, are not native and to the manner born, but become denizens of that kingdom by accident; but the lower class are mostly born to the joys and sorrows of that quaint and feverish gipsy life which is included under the general epithet Bohemian. A poor player like myself, a vagabond stroller, an acquaintance of mine, whose wife had been stricken down with fever of a malignant kind, went to the rectory to arrange with the parson for her funeral, and was upbraided by the clergyman for following so degrading an occupation.

"I cannot read the burial service over people of your class," said he. "It is disgraceful to see able-bodied men like you painting your cheeks, and making fools grin by your antics. How came you to enter on such a horrid pursuit?"

"Sir, I had no choice," quietly replied the comedian. "I was born in a theatre, and have been upon the stage ever since I was able to speak ; and so was my deceased wife, whom I now ask you to bury. We never knew any better."

The best way of bringing the lower Bohemians thoroughly before the mind's eye, is to describe them in the first instance *en masse*. Let us, then, suppose that, to see them, we have transported ourselves on Saturday evening to some one or other of our large manufacturing towns, and that we have taken up our position in a place where we can readily bring the motley band into a focus; and in such towns there is always some particular street where Bohemians hold a carnival. Business goes on briskly, and as we promenade up and down scanning the throng of people, we are nearly blinded by the blaze of naphtha gas which is in general use as an illuminating power, and almost deafened with the roar of the *marchands de Bohème*, who contrive to make a living by the sale or use of things that more solid men could only look upon with blank despair. In the street where we are supposed to be making our observations—and I acted in it, as assistant to a conjuror, for five weeks—there are at least one hundred and fifty different kinds of businesses carried on, and there are nearly as many modes of conducting them, and all the modes are, it need scarcely be said, significant of Bohemianism. On all sides we are surrounded by a curious medley of "operators;" organ-grinders with monkeys, posturers who can do their tumbling on a square foot of carpet, cheap Johns, quack doctors, and clowns, buzz around us; and there are shooting galleries, gambling-stalls, knock-'em-downs, theatres of ar with celebrated shipwrecks and movable storms at sea kept by Bohemians in velveteen coats; then there ar corn-extractors, with specimens, needle-dodgers, smal conjurors, and last, though not least, Massaroni, the grea lion-slayer, "direct from the hinaccessible wilds of the great Hafrican desierts." Let us listen for a moment to the hoarse yells of the "proprietors" of the gambling stalls, which are numerous, or the weighing-machines which are also numerous, or to the patter of the lady who owns the spirometer: there is a Babel of confused tongues sounding like "Walkupladiesandgentlemenwhiletheballsa-rollinandfortinsareabeinggivenforapennyapieceandseehajax defyinothelightninandhaveyourlungsatestedbythatwonder-fulandnewlyinventedhinstrumentthelearnedpigwhichwillte) agentshageorhowmanychildrenaladywillave," &c., &c. What a number of people do try their fortunes at the E.-O. table; and how curious it is that, as a general rule, they all lose their money; how rapidly the coppers are swept into the bank of the industrious owner. On the one side of the Copper Pandemonium, we have "The Royal Halbert Tubulier Shootin'-Gallery, at the unkimmen small charge of three shots for a penny." On the other side of the gambling-table there is a grand and "helegant" display of living serpents, which are *charmed* every five minutes, or as rapidly as the booth can be filled, at the low charge of one penny. There is much of this. It looks as if a dozen small country fairs had been rolled into one big one. A great number of the real show-folk are here putting off time till they can hit on a round of fairs that will require them to set off on the tramp. It is really amusing to witness the *sang froid* or impudence, we may call it either, of these diverting people. See, distinguished by the occasional shrill clangour of a gong, we have a personage who, if we take his own word for it, is the greatest man of all the assemblage. Behold him there, standing on an inverted tub, dressed in the faded remains of what has been a superb Hamlet shirt, grinding away at a barrel-organ, bowing, smiling, and proclaiming his style and title as the greatest conjuror of the age. The man, *par excellence*, who has conjured in the presence of all the crowned heads of Europe. But great as the conjuror may be, he is excelled by the quack, who performs his wonderful cure with an amount of "cheek," which only quacks have readily at command. He exhibits a splendid display of bottles, pills, herbs, cannisters, and tape-worms, which he describes in the most *recherché* language. But I "go in" personally for the school of mountebanks who are performing in the open-air. I have always had a wicked hankering after such people—their unnatural antics give me a sensation —there they fly about in their usual tinsel and velvet, their brows bound with victorious wreaths of red velvet, and their hair buttered down to their scalps as if it had been glued on. They twist and twirl their limbs into all kinds of serpentine convolutions, to the great wonderment of a large crowd, who seem puzzled at the "head springs," "fore springs," "lion leaps," "flip flops," &c., in which they indulge with so much fire and so little grace. The clown, of course, fires off the old jokes — poverty and starvation grinning all the time through the paint which bedaubs the poor fellow's face ! But we must leave off the general and come to the particular. Farewell, therefore, for the present, cheap John and street-juggler ! Farewell, flying-stationer, and you other gentlemen who deal in goods that are not for use, but only for sale !

Let us, before going further, have a glance at the domestic hearths of these Bohemians of St Giles's.

" Where do you live ? " I once asked of a Bohemian acquaintance of mine.

" Oh, we don't live, sir, we only exist."

" Yes, yes; but where is your residence ? " was our next query; and the answer was what might have been expected—

" We live wherever we can, sir."

Well-to-do showmen and rich cheap Jacks keep their living-waggon, and feast on fried steaks and onions when their business day is over. Other men travel with their little show on their back, and have no settled residence. And the other day did we not hear of a poor comedian of the Northern stage, who was living in the eighth flat of a falling house, and who only saved himself from sudden death by rushing to the street as the tenement came hurling into the Edinburgh causeway. This man, in the Theatre-Royal of Edinburgh, a comedian and a gentle-man, was playing for sixteen shillings a week—" passing rich on forty pounds a year ! " If we would know the residence of those of the Bohemians who have set up house-keeping, we shall require to explore dark and am-biguous passages, curious alleys, densely-peopled back

streets, and neighbouring mews ; in fact, we must explore
all kinds of places, where the ceaseless din of every-day
life, and the bustle incident to a dense population, are going on. And if we follow the Bohemians to their homes,
what kind of houses shall we find? "Can it be possible,"
some one exclaims, "that these Bohemians have wives
and children the same as the every-day people who gain
their bread by the sweat of their brow?" To be sure
they have ; and that half of the world which knows not
how the other half lives ought to be ashamed of their
ignorance. There are wonderful little episodes incidental
to the lives of this class. I do remember me of a poor
writing-master—a man who taught the art of caligraphy
in six lessons—who, to provide nourishment for a dying
child, chicken soup and wine ordered by the doctor, (ah,
these doctors, why will they insist on ordering wine and
other delicacies for poor people's children?) walked, or rather
dragged himself, one miserably wet morning before breakfast, a distance of three miles, in order that, by pawning
his blankets, he might procure these luxuries for his child.
But his toil was vain; there was a strike in the town, and
the pawnbroker's stores were glutted with blankets. So
here was an end to the affectionate soul's dream of wine
for his dying daughter. Every-day life teems with these
little tragedies, although we never know them. I recollect
a brief history that went the round of the newspapers
some years ago, which afforded us a glimpse of the domestic economy of these Bohemians. The person whose
history was given was a street clown. His wife had just
been confined, and his earnings on that day were only one

shilling and threepence—the street business was a curse, he said! He eked out his day business by singing in the public-houses at night, and his wife took in washing.

When I was starving in a cheap lodging-house in Pemberton Row, Gough Square, I became acquainted with a fellow in misfortune who was great at inventing for the newspapers occurrences that had never taken place. I was admitted to his confidence, and we once or twice contrived to set the town in a blaze. I was forcibly reminded of him at the time of the Waterloo-Bridge mystery, and guessed he had had a hand in that pie. I think my old acquaintance, Jim Blank, who had been a medical student, and was a contemporary of a clever gentleman-showman recently gone across the bourne, must have managed the matter from beginning to end. I was informed that about the date of that strange circumstance, my friend Blank had got married, and was rather in a flourishing way than otherwise. How it was all done, I can surmise. Blank, through the friendship of some of his old college chums, could easily procure the headless trunk of a human body; and the "liner," after encasing it in a suit of foreign-looking clothes, purchased for the purpose, would have it packed in a carpet-bag, and lowered from the bridge into the water. The body in due time is found, and the active reporter is thus enabled to grow many columns of matter out of the event for the morning papers; and straight the wonderful circumstance of a headless body, apparently boiled and perforated with stabs, being found on the buttress of one of the Thames bridges, takes rank (by the careful cultivation of the reporter) as one of the mysteries of the age, and spreads over the country with wonderful rapidity. But it is no mystery to Blank and his confederates; with them it is just a good "lark." I have no doubt whatever of the whole plot having been invented in a garret of Bohemia over a modest supper of bread and cheese and beer. The "penny-a-liners," as they are called, are not slow in seasons barren of fires or murders to use their inventive powers; and many are the "Strange Circumstance" and "Mysterious Event" which they have chronicled,—the real place of their occurrence having been, in all likelihood, a public-house parlour.

# CHAPTER XXXI.

WHICH CONCLUDES MY BOHEMIAN REMINISCENCES, AND
BRINGS ME TO MY LAST ENGAGEMENT.

THE class which I have been focusing in this lower
Bohemia are principally the out-of-doors class—indeed,
Bohemians of the lower world are chiefly workers in the
open-air; and they are to be seen in all seasons wandering
over the country, and grouping themselves at fairs and
races. One peculiar characteristic of this nomadic class is
their correct knowledge at all times of the whereabout of
each other. They can tell to a nicety all the chances and
changes of their career. If John Sangers be working a
stall in Vicar's Croft, Leeds, and George Sangers be shewing white mice at Musselburgh Races, Alick Chambers,
exhibiting his "hanky-panky" at Evesham, in Worcester-
shire, knows all about it. Even the changes from one
dodge to another are catalogued with the greatest certainty
by the 'cuter members of the nomadic race who are now
called Bohemians; if a man leaves a quack-pill affair
and takes up a natural-curiosity concern, it is all over
the country as quickly as the news of an arrival of
sprats at Billingsgate becomes known to the "costers."
This fact quite bears out an idea of mine, that among
the thorough Bohemian class there is a kind of intui-
tive freemasonry or mesmerism which admits of a quick

spread of all kinds of information pertaining to their craft.

In addition to the out-of-door phases of Bohemianism which I have endeavoured to portray, there is, besides, an extensive practice of "polite fraud" by means of advertising and letter-writing. In this class may be enumerated those begging-letter impostors, who, in spite of the Mendicity Society, carry on a thriving business and gain much money by an ingenious trading in fictitious woe. There is also a number of people who pass themselves off as graphiologists—fortune-tellers, people that conjure you by all you hold dear to "know yourself"—who can predict your future fortunes by examining a lock of your hair or a specimen of your hand-writing. Having myself been at one time in this line of business, I can speak with certainty on the large shoal of uncut postage-stamps which as a rule rewards the enterprising votary of this particular art of living. As a hint to those about to enter on a similar career, I may mention that I worked the oracle by means of a little volume entitled, "Le Corbeau Sanglant," a French work, which, according to the month in which you were born, depicted your future fortunes. My success was great, although I was working in a provincial town. I have had as many as thirty-five letters in one day; and there can be no doubt that those who set about this sort of thing in a systematic way, and who deal in hair-washes, graphiology, and toilet-powders, advertising extensively all the time, are able to enjoy a large income. Such people are adepts in the art of advertising, and are conspicuous in attracting attention ; these notices are usually headed "Your Destiny," or "The Future Foretold;" and they go on to say that "any person wishing to have their future life revealed to them correctly, with all events of life accurately portrayed, should send their age, sex, and nineteen postage-stamps to Howard Blank, Esq., 100 Bohemia Street." Another branch of this kind of business is followed by persons who are continually offering to tell you something to your advantage, in the shape of "valuable information gratis," or offering you "employment at your own home;" not at photography or mixing varnish, we are told, but "easy, profitable, and respectable," and suitable for either sex; and there are also Bohemians who, for a consideration, offer to confer upon us any amount of riches, who, for instance, in gratitude for a paid-down sum of £200, would willingly give us half the profits of a concern yielding its thousands per annum !

I cannot, in the brief limits of this chapter, go into all the shifts and dodges of the lower world of Bohemia; and there are some things I must not tell—points which, on the principle of honour among thieves, I must keep sacred. Nor can I at present enter into a detailed account of how I pulled the strings for a great conjuror, and procured admiring groups of generous citizens to present him with claret jugs and other trifling souvenirs at his own expense. Then, as to the grand prizes we gave away, it would not be fair to expose how we managed that the right person should always have the lucky number, and how, in consequence, the magnificent gold watch did duty in more towns than one. Nor shall I "split" upon the

conundrum dodge, and tell how it was all "arranged," and
how the jury were managed so as to hit upon the proper
conundrum.    These points of Bohemian life may form an
interesting volume upon some other occasion.    Meantime
I desire to close this part of my experiences by giving a
*catalogue raisonné* of twelve lodgers who dwelt with me
in the Bohemian lodging-house situated in Pemberton
Row, Gough Square, just behind Fleet Street, where beds
were let out at threepence a night, and where the company
was decidedly numerous if not select, and which I have
already partly described.

Number one of my fellow-lodgers was an attorney who
had been struck off the rolls for complicity in a fraud.
At the time I knew him he was a touter for business at
Bow-Street Police-Court.    He was most intemperate in
his habits.    Number two was a person who had been a
publisher's clerk, but had left the book warehouse and
thrown aside the collecting-bag for the stage, and who,
after hungering his life out in trying to grasp the Hamlets
and Othellos of the legitimate drama, was at last deriving
a precarious living by spouting comic stories at a public-
house.    I had seen this person act in a barn, where the
heading to the bill told the enlightened public that Mr
Orlando Howard was "starving for a few nights at this
theatre."    What a satirist the printer who set up that
bill must have been.    Number three was a disabled type-
founder, who went out every morning to a quiet street in
the neighbourhood of Russell Square, and wrote on the
pavement in chalk, in beautiful caligraphy, those very
pointed maxims, which tell us that "Hunger is a sharp

thorn," &c., and earned a few shillings by his labour. The fifth of the batch was a drunken compositor, who reported occasional fires or accidents, and who at times had to "eat grass" (*i.e.*, officiate for a regular compositor) in a newspaper office. He could, when employed, earn a handsome wage, which never, however, reached his pocket; he sat with the money in one hand, and the gin bottle in the other, till all was expended. Number six, a gold-beater, who, forsaking his own employment, had turned beer doctor, and wrote prescriptions for cocculus-indicus, to be administered to weak kilderkins. The seventh individual of our Bohemian society was a discharged bank clerk. What he did no one knew; but number five used to aver that he had seen him doing the Sheffield business, *i.e.*, selling knives with twenty blades, and other miracles in steel work. Number eight was in the advertising line, and sold a secret connected with the washing-tub, which, to judge by his correspondence, was largely in demand. The next in number was a doctor of medicine, from the Isle of Man, who drank hard all day in order that he might be able to lecture on temperance in Farringdon Street Hall at night. Number ten, a dissenting clergyman, formerly editor of a liberal newspaper, afterwards a teacher of writing on the six-lessons' plan, his pupils mostly being found in the neighbouring public-houses. Number eleven, the unfortunate owner of a Punch-and-Judy show—which being in pawn at the place where it was last exhibited, the pawner had walked to London, on his way to attend Greenwich Fair, in order to pick up a few pounds at something or other; and it is really wonderful to see the facility with which a thorough-bred showman can pick up a few pounds. Having gone down to the fair at Greenwich, I saw this man doing a large trade in coppers, with four pieces of wood he had set up in the " roley-poley " way; *i.e.*, three of the bits of wood were put on the ground, each having a penny-piece upon it, the fourth was used as an instrument to fling at the uprights, when, if the coppers fell outside a certain circle, they became the property of the person who threw —if otherwise, they were retained by the showman. This Bohemian came up to London on three different nights laden with penny-pieces, besides having a pound or two of silver. Number twelve was the Bohemian stroller, the writer of these revelations, about whom the reader already knows a great deal, and will know more immediately.

# CHAPTER XXXII.

"It never rains but it pours." I authenticate and sub-scribe to the proverb. Is it not a striking corroboration of the fact, that I, at the point of starvation—not having tasted food for a period of thirty hours—should all at once leap into the possession of a golden coin of the value of twenty shillings; and, better still, in the course of three days fall into a situation as secretary or amanu-ensis to a manager? "The secretary, afterwards door-keeper, by Mr Peter Paterson!"

Having a little money, I at once—that is, in the course of the few days I was idle—redeemed my properties, and, proceeding to my old lodgings, learned that a message had been left from Gillon wanting to see me. I called, and learned the pleasing intelligence of a new engagement having turned up.

It will be to the purpose of these Confessions that I should go into some details on the matter of this engagement, and which are as follow :—Mr Podger, the manager of the " Sheep's-head Company,"—so called, it is said, because the manager, when money was scarce, presented any strange member of the party with a sheep's-head for his Sunday dinner,—had just concluded a capital season at Shipston-on-Stour; and, his ambition—or rather the ambition of his family—being stirred, he bethought himself of having an addition to his very select party before he proceeded to the next small town on his circuit, which, in the present instance, was Beesham. This great event of an addition to the family was no sooner finally decided upon than a note was despatched, post-haste, to Mr Gillon, to send down a person at once to fill the new post ; and, what is more to the purpose, a post-office order for a sovereign had been enclosed to pay expenses ; the agent, however, only gave me fourteen shillings of that sum.

Gillon was quite excited when I called, all in a burst with his intelligence; and the moment I had entered his sanctum, his information welled out in the following style :—" An engagement—eight shillings a-night—Beesham—Podger's—Great Western Railway—Oxford—Coach—Beesham—Letter—Start to-day—A few bob sent to pay fares,"—at least, as well as I can recollect, these were the heads of the sermon which was preached to me on the occasion of this third engagement of Gillon's.

The small family companies, once so common in the provinces, are now nearly all broken up. Either the taste has died out which gave such little parties vitality, or the family concern has been disrupted from some particular cause—such as the death of one of the firm, or the desertion of one or two of the daughters, who perhaps marry the sons of some rival theatrical potentate. I have read of numerous family parties of strollers who had been known in particular districts of England or Scotland for a great number of years, who continued to pay their way and keep up an air of considerable respectability. But now the march of improvement has attacked these " strolling players ;" and railways afford such facilities for country bumpkins to visit large towns and see " the tragedians of the city," and the fine scenery and other equipments of large theatres, as to leave little store of admiration for the ancient comedians, with the old scenery and the older stock of plays, who have visited the same villages and hamlets for a time even further back than the memory of " the oldest inhabitant" can carry him. The railway also affords the same opportunity to the city actors to breathe the country air and play the last new farce in the town hall of Chipping Norton, or Beverley-cum-Tenterdon, where, by the exercise of a pretty little stock of impudence, they get up a few bespeaks from the mayor, " the member," and one or two persons selected from the more influential inhabitants of the place ; and after Chawbacon sees Horatio B. Middleton, of the Theatre-Royal, Birmingham or Warwick, how can he be expected to admire Tom Peterkin, who has not a tithe of the bustle and polish of the city player? Is not Chawbacon a man and a brother? and if so, is he not to progress with the age? Why should he be compelled to get his Shakspeare in a barn illumined by penny dips, or in the large room of the "Royal Oak," when his cousins Shuttle and Yarn have it at a regular house, with gas and all the other modern accessories of art and science ?   Why, indeed !

The manager to whom I was sent—old Daddy Podger —was the father and conductor of one of these companies, and had been known as such for years ; and although his concern was dwindling as to its ways and means, he still went on as gloriously and as pompously as if he had been manager of Drury Lane, or lord of the manor.

I went down to Oxford by the rail, after going by mistake to a station very near to Exeter.   I had alighted at the Didcot junction, and, after a long wait, I jumped into a train, fancying it was bound to Oxford, and did not discover my mistake till I had been an hour or so on my way, when, thinking that it was high time for me to be at the city of learning, I made a polite inquiry at a civil-looking gentleman as to the reason of our being so long in reaching Oxford.   His reply was accompanied with a broad and not very well-bred stare.   " Oxford !" said he, " why, you are far past the junction, and on your way to Exeter, and in a short time we shall be there."   This was " a heavy blow and sore discouragement" to a " poor player," having but a light purse in the pocket of a very thin pair of breeches.   There was no help, however, for my misfortune, and jumping out at the first station we came to, I sat me down and awaited the first up-train.

I remember well that my thoughts were none of the most pleasing as I sat ruminating, " chewing the cud of sweet and bitter fancies."   The folly of my conduct flitted occasionally at intervals across my wandering thoughts, and I almost resolved, after having out my Beesham trip, to give up this vagabondising life, be a good boy, and return to my mother. I saw that the golden dreams I had indulged in were slow in their realisation, and the knocking about in the profession which had already come to my share was pretty considerable ; besides, I had seen quite sufficient of its miseries to enable me to imbibe a strong distaste for the dark or salaryless side of the picture.

I slept one night at Oxford, where I met with a veteran campaigner, who had an immense store of theatrical anecdotes, which he was well pleased to retail to all who would listen ; and as he sent about the ale jug with great celerity, he had, in general, no lack of auditors. We had for supper that evening some of the delightful sausages for which the city of Oxford is famous, and I can testify well to their savoury excellence.

After supper, we—that is, the aforesaid campaigner and myself—indulged in beer, and, prolonging our crack till a late hour, regaled each other with theatrical *ana*, and stories of incidents connected with the histrionic profession. I make no apology for introducing here a small portion of our *noctes*, in the hope that it may while away, from the dull cares of the world, an hour or so of my reader's thoughts.

After retailing various of the *facetiæ* and funny anecdotes of actors and acting, which almost every person is familiar with, we came to speak of some of those sterner or graver incidents which belong to the history of the stage, as well as to that of most other institutions. The

following story, told by the person I met, is, I believe,
quite true in all but the names.

"The story I have to tell you," continued my Oxford
friend, "is one in which I happened to be a prominent
actor, being at the time one of the stock company of the
Beverley Theatre, New York. The most talented and
successful actor in our company was Mayfield—an honest,
open-hearted fellow, a great favourite, and to whom I was
often indebted for many acts of kindness. It happened
that, about the end of November 1840, a tragedian of
some celebrity came to play a star engagement at the
Beverley Theatre. He was a tall, pale, intellectual-looking
man—his *tout ensemble* being, in short, exactly suited to
the parts he took. His name was Charles Hartley. He
and Mayfield became intimate friends. Mayfield was
enthusiastic in admiration of his splendid talents, and
Hartley was simultaneously attracted towards him by his
kind and happy disposition. One night, as they were
quitting the theatre, they accidentally came in contact
with each other, and walked along together, conversing
in an animated strain, until they came to the corner of
Grand and Centre Streets. Here Hartley was about turning off in the direction of his hotel when Mayfield proposed that he should pay a visit to his house, which was
finally agreed to, and they again renewed their walk. He
was introduced to Mrs Mayfield, and in her agreeable
society the time passed away so rapidly that Hartley felt
much reluctance to depart. At length, however, he tore
himself away from their happy circle, and sadly proceeded
homewards to his hotel. I had occasion to call upon

Hartley next morning.  As I passed along the corridor towards his room I could see him through the crevice of the door, which stood ajar, leaning with his head upon his hand, evidently buried in intense thought.  Suddenly he muttered to himself—'It must succeed : failure is impossible, and the idea of suspicion folly.  *He* plays *Gesler*, *I* play *Tell*.  He, the tyrant, dies—ay, *dies!* and I, the hero, live, and shall be happy !'  The words had no sooner passed his lips, than he started to his feet, and, seeing me upon the threshold, came forward, with an exclamation of pleasure, to meet me.  Having transacted my business with him, I came away, and the incident of the morning passed from my memory.  A few nights after, however, Hartley took his benefit, and the first piece to be performed was 'William Tell.'  The theatre was crowded, and the curtain rose amidst a deafening round of applause.  The pale and agitated features of 'the star' were more than once the subject of remark in the theatre that evening : this, however, did not in the least mar the splendour of his acting, which all agreed was the grandest effort of his professional career.  The first and second acts passed over without any material variation in Hartley's demeanour, but as the drop-scene rose on the third act a perceptible change came over him.  Now he was firm and resolute, bold and determined, and seemed to pour out his very soul through the channel of his lips.  At length the last scene arrives ; the strong arm of *Tell* wrests the sword from the soldier's grasp, and with breast swelling and eye flashing with the intensity of his emotion, he rushes upon the tyrant *Gesler*, strikes the glittering weapon from his

hand, and, swift as the lightning flash, sheathes his sword
in the body of his victim. A faint shriek escaped the
wounded man, and the curtain descended on a tableau
never surpassed in the history of dramatic art. The
audience, perfectly enraptured with the natural beauty
and artistic skill of the actor, were vociferous in applause
and calls for Hartley. But, to the surprise and chagrin
of all present, no Hartley made his appearance; and
becoming at length exhausted with their frequent cheers
and shouts, the mass dispersed, entirely ignorant of the
*real* drama they had witnessed, and protesting against
the conduct of Hartley, and the obstinacy of actors in
general. The scene of consternation that took place on
the stage at the fall of the curtain is too harrowing for
description. Hartley assumed all the feelings of sorrow
and regret which such a dreadful *accident* was calculated
to engender in the breast of a man conscious of the act,
but innocent of the intent. The company considered the
occurrence perfectly accidental, as did also Mayfield himself. The wounded man was speedily placed in a carriage,
and driven rapidly to his home; but not, alas! before
the spirit of the sufferer had winged its flight to brighter
worlds. I at once conjectured that Mayfield's death
resulted from no accident. Taking it in connexion with
the words I had heard Hartley mutter in his room that
morning, I began to suspect that he must have premedi-
tated the murder. However, as there was no proof of the
fact, I never divulged my suspicions to any one. About
a twelvemonth afterwards, however, it was rumoured in
theatrical circles that Mrs Mayfield was about to become

the wife of Charles Hartley. Many were incredulous on this point, and stigmatised it as idle gossip; but certain it was that Hartley had proposed and been accepted by the beautiful widow. The appointed day at last arrived. The company were assembled—the bridegroom only was absent. Some hours passed, and at last it was resolved to send a messenger to his hotel to inquire for him, and to me that duty was intrusted. On entering the hotel I found the domestics all in a state of great consternation, and on inquiring the cause was told that the wretched Hartley had taken poison! I rushed to his room, and forced my way in. He was stretched out in bed; his face was of an unearthly colour, and his fingers were clenched as if in agony. He held out his hand to me and said, in a feeble voice, ' Mayfield is avenged!' His approaching union with the woman he had so madly loved and deeply wronged had preyed so heavily on his mind that he could endure it no longer, and in a fit of desperation he had swallowed poison, and buried his guilt and remorse in the oblivion of the grave."

"That," said I, " reminds me of a curious story that I once heard in Edinburgh. It was told me by an old man who had been one of the servants in the mansion of Lord Carleman, and who was himself an eye-witness of the incidents I will relate to you. About the beginning of 1835, then, Lord Carleman married a young and beautiful lady, the daughter of a neighbouring baronet. She was of a light, volatile disposition, and was vain and coquettish,—a circumstance which gave great pain to her husband, who was deeply attached to her. Well, about a twelvemonth after their union, a young military officer, who had formerly been on terms of intimacy with Lady Carleman, came to visit at Carleman House. His gay and thoughtless humour made him a great favourite ; but his attentions to Lady Carleman were observed with displeasure by his lordship. Major Blaze, however, would take no hint from any one ; and I believe that her ladyship secretly encouraged him out of a desire to torment her jealous husband. His lordship, meanwhile, said nothing to either ; but one evening, on walking through the garden that fronted the mansion, he observed the gallant major standing on the terrace in front of the house, talking to a lady, who, he thought, could be no other than his wife. He hurried on ; but ere he reached the spot the major bade adieu to the lady and disappeared. Some weeks elapsed, and the arrival of fresh visitors appeared to divert his lordship from the terrible thoughts that preyed on his mind. To vary the diversions of the party, it was proposed that amateur theatricals should be got up in Carleman House, and the proposal was willingly assented to by his lordship. A large hall in the mansion was fitted up in grand style for the purpose, and the rehearsals began. The first piece to be performed was ' Othello.' The cast was curiously enough arranged, so that his lordship played *Othello*, Lady Carleman *Desdemona*, while the major took the part of *Cassio*. The piece was gone through with great *éclat* until the last scene, when *Othello*, overwhelmed with jealous rage, smothers his young wife as she lies in bed. This part, Lord Carleman, wrought to desperation by his fit of jealousy, performed so admirably and naturally as to excite the wonder and approbation of all the guests; but imagine their horror and consternation on finding that it was, after all, no mere piece of acting that his lordship had gone through,—that Lady Carleman had, in fact, been murdered! A coroner's inquest sat upon the body, and returned a verdict of 'Accidental Death,' which saved both his lordship's life and reputation; but from that hour he became an altered man. The mansion was shut up, and his lordship went on the continent, where some years after he died."

"Allow me, before we part," said my friend, "to give you an account of a thrilling accident, resulting in the death of a clever girl, which occurred some years ago at Hull, and of which I was an eye-witness. It was a scene that I cannot forget. I was then performing in a circus, and the company was a very large one, numbering thirty-seven members altogether, including grooms. The cleverest and most beautiful member of the *troupe* was a Madame Woodford, a very great favourite with the people in Hull. She had an interesting and most lovely daughter, an exquisite dancer on the tight-rope, and the boldest rider in the company. La Petite Woodford, as she was called in the bills, might be about nine or ten years of age, beautiful as a *houri*, and full of grace. She was a favourite alike with the public and with her companions, and her feats of horsemanship were truly astonishing. She was doated upon by her mother, and when in the circle with her, her spirits were at their zenith. Poor creature, I never can forget how sad was her end! Dear little Petite, she was

killed by an accident in the circus. This melancholy
event took place shortly after we arrived at Hull. The
occasion was a benefit to one of the public charities of the
town, and the great amphitheatre was crowded to excess
—a perfect sea of human gazers. The house was very
large, and every seat was occupied. The performances
went on with great *éclat*, and they had nearly terminated
when the accident occurred. It was the time for the
entry of the mother and daughter. The mother entered,
riding on horseback, and the place resounded with deafening plaudits. She cantered once round the circle, and
then stopped. The folding-doors opened, and La Petite
bounded into the ring—a laughing 'thing of life and
light.' She courtesyed with inimitable grace to the audience, and, at one spring, leaped on to the horse, and hid
herself in her mother's bosom. The applause at this was
deafening. Away went the high-spirited black Barbary
courser, round and round the circle—at first slowly, then
quicker and quicker, till it rushed at a fearful speed.
The mother and child were exerting themselves tremen-
dously—they seemed as if they were actuated by the
same spirit, and had determined on this occasion to out-
do all their former doings. The audience were loud in
their exclamations of delight and approbation. The horse
paused an instant, then resumed its course with redoubled
speed—it was at its height—the girl was poised on her
mother's shoulder,—a moment more and she was on her
head. The horse darted along, gave an unfortunate
stumble, and in one second the girl was dashed against a
large beam, which, in the confusion, she had forgotten to

avoid : the audience screamed in afright—the girl fell into the ring a lifeless mass—the despair of the mother was terrible. Man, I shall never, never forget it. It was an awful circumstance."

"It was a striking scene, although a painful one," said I to my entertaining friend.

"It was, indeed," he replied; "but there are many such to be encountered on our voyage through life."

"Yes, undoubtedly there are; but there are comic scenes as well."

"Oh! such are always occurring, and oftenest to actors."

"So I believe; and I have witnessed a few incidents myself of a funny kind:" and, taking the opportunity, I repeated to him the story about the whisky, which I have already given; and, after a hearty laugh at the absurdity of the scene, he related to me a little anecdote of a personal adventure of his own, which was highly characteristic of the profession.

"The company to which I belonged at the period of this little adventure," said my friend, "had been starved out of the theatre, business was so bad. The manager, as is usual enough, had no capital, and our salaries were all in arrear. Such of the company as could manage it had left for London; and there was only a few left, who, in the hope of eking out an existence till something better would cast up, had rented a large hall, and were playing at half price. I was one of this hungry lot, and I can tell you that very frequently I was hungry enough. Even this miserable resource failed us; and one Saturday, being reduced to desperation and my last copper, I was wondering how I could obtain a dinner. Wandering about the town, looking the picture of 'pale melancholy,' lantern-jawed and woe-begone, I was astonished at being accosted by one of the leading men of the place, an upholsterer and undertaker. Would I take a glass of beer, he asked. Of course; I had no objection to that. We adjourned; and after a brief pause, out came the murder. 'You look miserable, my friend,' said the benevolent stranger. 'I have good cause,' said I. 'You are an actor, I think,' said he. 'Alas! I am; a starved one, too,' was my reply; 'with not the slightest chance of dining to-morrow, I assure you.' Then came another pause. 'Could you dine on five shillings?' asked Mr Undertaker. 'Dine on five shillings!' said I; '*dine*, did you say? Sir, I could feast—I could revel on that beautiful sum.' 'Very well; come to me to-night, and I will put you up to the way of earning it;' and how do you think it was to be done?"

"I don't know."

"By turning a mute, and performing at a funeral."

"A mute—prodigious!"

"Yes, a mute; it was amusing to find the way my new-found friend went about the matter; he seemed afraid I would not consent, and being, as I suppose, in a fix for a man, he determined to have me, if possible, to grace his funeral, which was rather a particular one. Well, I had often played a gravedigger for less money, and why not a mute; a starving man soon looses his dignity."

"And did you do it?"

"Did I do it! Can you ask?—was I not starving? and was not this five shillings a perfect godsend to me?"

"But were you not recognised?"

"I was ; and all the little boys in the town followed the funeral, grinning at me. I fancy that, hungry and melancholy as I really was, I looked comic. It was a rare lark ; but I got the five bob, and a dinner into the bargain, from my patron the undertaker."

# CHAPTER XXXIII.

IT was forty miles from Oxford to Beesham—a long walk,
but for some miles a really pleasant one—and I trudged
manfully along, with my sword over my shoulder, on
which was slung a bundle containing a small supply of
necessaries. I had previously sent on by waggon a large
bag containing the properties which I had redeemed with
the found sovereign. It cost me about a couple of shillings for porter and bread and cheese by the way, as I
generally had a slight refreshment at all the small towns
I passed.

At length, tired and dispirited, I arrived at Beesham, a
snug little market town on the banks of the classic Avon.
As may be supposed, I was well stared at by the inhabitants, who turned out in clusters to look at me as I walked
up the town; in fact, the immortal Gulliver himself
could not have made a greater sensation among the inhabitants of Lilliput than I seemed to make among the
wonder-struck Beeshamians. "He belongs to the 'show-
folk,'" was the universal shout—all denominations of cater-
ers for the amusement of the public being classed as "show

folk " by the worthy people of that ancient borough. It was the month fixed for an election when I got there, and the people were quite up to the ears in business. Bribery to a large extent, I speedily learned, was in full operation, and large prices were liberally given for the votes of the free and independent electors.

On making inquiries as to where the theatre was situated, or where I could find the manager, I could get no information. No one had heard of the theatre! It had not come yet. Podger was not even expected, but he might be coming for all that. This was poor heartening to a person who had travelled so far, and had built upon his engagement a fairy structure of surpassing grandeur.

Among other points which I had turned over in my mind, it occurred to me that eight shillings a night, which was Gillon's mode of describing the salary, would, when multiplied by six—the days of the week—amount to forty-eight shillings. "That is not so bad for a beginning," I thought, as I trudged along. "I will be able to save something off that, and get down the rest of my properties, so that I may cut a dash; and who knows," I thought further "but that, in the event of getting on well with the audience, I may get up a benefit, and so acquire a few pounds in cash, to keep me going all right and in that respectable way, as to dress and living, which I was lately hungering after." The reader must keep in mind that I had but very lately been in a starving condition, and that two pounds eight a week to a strolling player would be like the run of the Bank of England to a struggling merchant !

Therefore, not in the least discouraged by the remarks and stories of those of whom I inquired, I began to search for lodgings, and eventually took up my quarters in Vine Street, with a Mrs Russell, whom I found to be a kind, motherly person, and with whom I at once got on good terms. As soon as I arrived, I asked for something to eat, for I was hungry. Speedily I had a loaf of capital bread set down before me, and thus, with a piece of cheese, and some first-rate home-brewed, I made a hearty meal. I observed, however, that at every fresh *hunch* of bread I cut from the crusty loaf, Sophia, the daughter, nudged her mother's arm, no doubt to call attention to the fact of the poor stroller's having a good appetite.

I waited for some days at Beesham, with the greatest impatience, for the arrival of the Podger family, but they never came. Day after day sped away, but still no company of players arrived ; and, summoning up a desperate resolution, I resolved at last upon setting out in search of the manager of the renowned "Sheep's-head Company," and finding out what his intentions were as to a visit to Beesham.

"It is only twenty-four miles," said a person to me whom I had asked what the distance to Shipston-on-Stour was. The road was rough and long, through an uninteresting tract of country, neither varied by glimpses of fine scenery nor yet enlivened by town or village. When I set out the weather was exceedingly fine, and so it continued till I had got about half-way, when the clouds began to gather, and ominous drops of rain fell heavily upon the road, and forced me to think of looking for shelter. But as far as my eye could reach there was no appearance of a habitation of any kind whatever. The rain was soon falling with tremendous force, and in sheer desperation I took to my heels and ran till I reached the outskirts of an old farm-yard. Here I found a large rick of hay, with an erection of wood over it, which afforded a splendid shelter from the violence of the storm. On this bed of hay I gratefully laid me down. Wearied with a long tramp, and heart-sick with anxiety, in a short time I fell into a profound slumber, from which I was awoke by a gentle pat on the cheek. I opened my eyes on a vision of surpassing beauty ; it was the dark and pensive form of a handsome gipsy girl that presented itself to my astonished sight. I looked my astonishment full at her face. Her reply was a smile, and a very prettily-expressed apology for having interrupted my slumber. "I feared you would take cold lying there in them damp clothes; will you come to the fire, which is near at hand ? Our mother will give you a hearty welcome ; and you can then continue your journey. Are you a tramp ?"

This quite jumped with my humour, and the immediate and hearty assent which I gave to the proposal seemed to charm my dark-eyed friend. With great alacrity she led the way to the camp, which was about a hundred yards from the hay-rick where I had been found asleep. A gipsy encampment has been often described in glowing language by the poet, and in equally glowing colours by the painter. The present assemblage differed little from others of a similar kind. There was a large fire, as is usual, and on the glowing embers various messes were hissing, sending forth a delicious compound of savoury smells. When I explained that I was a comedian travelling to join a company, I was received with a very hearty shout of welcome, and invited to share in their hospitality; and wet, wearied, and hungry, I gratefully accepted the cordial invitation.

No doubt these gipsies hailed me as a kind of brother-in-trade. Your true stroller has much of the gipsy in him, and delights in a free and adventurous life. As one of the players once said, " Let me but get my eye on the first daisy of the season, and a fig for your managers." The supper was a gorgeous affair, and included most of the delicacies of the season ; at any rate, there was a great predominance of game, which I have no doubt these people considered it fair to capture and eat.

I made myself quite at home among the tribe, which numbered about thirty individuals, young and old. I must say, however, that I never before saw such hideously ugly women as these old gipsies—they were indeed " so withered and so wild in their attire," that they might have walked on to the stage, and danced round Macbeth's caldron without much trouble as to additional "making up." The merry song and the hearty laugh were kept up with great glee till an early hour in the morning; and I was glad when at last, by the gradual departure of most of the gipsies to their various tents, I was left alone with my host and hostess ; and spreading a great bunch of soft dry grass in a corner of the tent, I willingly extended my wearied limbs, and fell into a delicious repose. It was morning, and the whole community were astir before

I awoke. I was courteously saluted by most of my gipsy friends, and invited to partake of breakfast. It was a plentiful meal of poached eggs, cold fowls, a little brandy, new milk, fruit, and hot cakes made for the occasion. A king might have envied that delicious and splendid repast, which to me, with my keen appetite, seemed a feast to set before the gods.

I could not help recalling to mind, as the savoury steam of the previous night's supper danced in the light, the aspirations of the poor fellow at the Turnham-Green booth. Such a dainty series of repasts would have been to him a heaven of delight.

# CHAPTER XXXIV.

THE sun was high in the heavens ere I thought of taking
my departure, which I did amid the warm benedictions of
the whole gang, who warmly hoped we might meet again.
Returning all their kind wishes, I bent my steps to Shipston, which I found to be about eleven miles from the
gipsy encampment. I hurried on amid occasional showers,
and about two o'clock arrived at the appointed goal. I
soon found that the theatre was what is called "a fit-up,"
erected in the large room at the "Bell," a small hotel of
the town.

I was walking leisurely down the principal street of the
small town, when, seeing a respectable-looking yeoman-
like man, in a short brown coat, corduroy smalls, and
brown leather continuations, I accosted him in a civil
way, and asked him if he could tell me where I could find
the Podger family who had the theatre.

He scanned me all over, and then, raising his hat with
much politeness, but with considerable formality, said—

"Do I look like a player?"

"No, you certainly do not," said I; "I presume you are a country gentleman or farmer."

"Nay, you flatter me, young sir; but I know who and what you are by the cut of your beard, that is, if you had one, therefore I give you welcome. My name is Podger, sir, and I have trod the boards with the immortal John Kemble, sir. I have fenced with the great Kean, sir. I was the pet of the illustrious Dora Jordan, and here am I, sir, not too much like a player either; and I hope you will be comfortable with my family— they are all clever, sir, and all of them useful. Here come some of my daughters, sir; allow me to introduce you. Ladies give me leave—Mr Capelton, about to join."

Such is a slight idea of the grandiloquent manner of the chief of the "Sheep's-head Company," which consisted of—

Mr and Mrs Podger, the papa and the mamma.

Mr and Mrs T. Podger, the son and his wife, with their infant family.

Mr and Mrs Heathcott, a daughter and her husband.

Miss Caroline Podger.

Mrs Pearson, a daughter married to some poor stroller not acknowledged by the family.

Mr and Mrs Wood, a quaint old Scotsman and his wife, (a sister of Edmund Kean's,) who afterwards joined the company.

Mr Capelton, (my stage name,) the writer of this narrative.

The old gentleman played "the old men" of course— both serious and comic. He had been a useful actor, and in many parts a very good one, but now he was failing every day; he had lost his memory, and some of his characters suffered enormously from their very striking want of the author.

His son Tom fulfilled the "low comedy," and I soon found that he was a prodigious favourite in the whole of the towns visited by the family. He was decidedly clever in many of his parts, but very careless in acquiring the words.

Mrs Heathcott was a clever actress, and played the juvenile heroines with considerable taste and feeling. Her *répertoire* was far from extensive; but she was well studied in some of the best parts included in her line of business.

Her sister Caroline played the chambermaids, and generally gave satisfaction.

Mrs T. Podger was decidedly the cleverest of the family party. She took the leading business in the female line; and some of her assumptions were really splendid pieces of acting, and deserved a better fate than being thrown away upon the bumpkins of small country towns, few of whom had the soul to know much about the art of personation. Indeed—

> " For lofty sense,
> Creative fancy, and inspection keen
> Through the deep windings of the human heart,"

I never saw in any country theatre an actress who could compare with her. She was an affectionate mother, too, and had some clever children.

Heathcott was a pompous fellow, who, being short of

stature, tried to make up the deficiencies of nature by having shoes about an inch thick in the sole. He had talent, and was exceedingly useful.

I will speak of the Woods in another place, and in the meantime finish this chapter by continuing my narrative.

It being the company's last night at Shipston, I was at once pressed into service, and the small business I got to play on that evening helped to crush my

" Longings divine, and aspirations high."

To add to my other mortifications, the great number of visitors who came behind the scenes paid me not the slightest attention, and never offered the least share of the profuse hospitalities attendant on the last night of the season. I swallowed all this as well as I could, and treasured it up as one of those inevitable *désagrémens* attendant on the profession. I may mention that I got no money for my assistance on this occasion, and the shabby set even left me to pay for my "beggar's bed" and my breakfast next morning with my last shilling. I slept at the "Bell," where I had a bed in the common room, for which I paid threepence, and unfortunately I found to my cost that I was blessed with a number of companions that I had never bargained for ; but, as the saying is, "Misery makes a man acquainted with strange bedfellows."

The scenery at length was taken down, and the traps were packed upon a waggon, and the strollers commenced their stroll. The superiors rode in a spring-van, Tom and his wife and family travelled with the waggon, and I walked the whole distance. None of them had the civility to give me a cast forward on either vehicle, but I kept on as manfully as possible, determined not to be annoyed, whatever might occur. The distance by the road we took would be full twenty miles, and I had but three-half-pence in my pocket, which I spent on bread by the way; and this, with various draughts of water, which were obtained at almost every turnpike, formed the whole nourishment for this rather long pedestrian undertaking —long enough, in all conscience, for a poor half-starved actor-of-all-work.

As a hint to other strollers, I may be permitted to mention that during my walk I studied two parts from Sheridan's fine play of "The Rivals,"—these were *Fag* and *David*. I often used to study in the open air about the pleasant lanes around Beesham.

At last, as the shades of evening were beginning to deepen, I again arrived, footsore and wearied, at Beesham, and was cordially received by my kind and motherly landlady, who bathed my feet in warm milk and water, and treated me in as kind a spirit of love and affection as if I had been her own son.

# CHAPTER XXXV.

IT was perfectly evident that I was born, as far as theatricals were concerned, to

"Waste my sweetness on the desert air,"

for the parts I got to play were so disagreeable as quite to withhold from me the sympathies of the audience. I opened at Beesham in the character of an old miser, where I had to be discovered digging a hole in which to hide my treasure, and was then barbarously murdered by Heathcott; but I soon came to life again, and had to "double" a young part in the same piece—a gardener, I recollect, who saw me killed. I then performed some spooney part in the afterpiece, and was tolerated, but that was all.

The best of the fun, however, was the salary. I was to have forty-eight shillings a week; but I was three weeks idling about before I got anything at all, in consequence of the delay at Shipston, and the time it took us to "fit up;" and then after the first night I had half-a-crown, a sixpence, and three shillings handed to me, wrapped in a piece of whitey-brown paper. I opened the packet with some curiosity, counted the silver easily, and thinking I had dropped some of it, looked about.

"Was there not a sovereign among it?" said I to Tom, who had made me the payment.

"No," said he, looking with surprise at me; "it's all right—that is your share for last night."

"My share! oh, then, it is a sharing concern, is it?" thought I—and so it was.

"Dear me," I said, "I expected I was to have a regular weekly salary of forty-eight shillings."

"Forty-eight shillings!" exclaimed the astonished Tom.

"Yes," said I coldly.

"What, for every week?"

"To be sure—Gillon said so."

"Gillon the agent?"

"Yes; eight shillings a night were his very words, and that is two pounds eight a week, isn't it?"

"We only play three nights a week," said Tom; "that is, when we can get audiences so often."

"Well, but even that would be twenty-four shillings, you know, and Gillon"—

"D—n Gillon," said Tom, angrily; "he has been selling both you and us."

"Then I won't have even that?" asked I.

"Oh no; ours is a sharing concern," replied Tom, "and you must speculate with us."

Such is the way of the theatrical world. "Speculate with us!" This is too often the expression among the class; and the meaning is this—share with us so long as the business is not paying; and then, when it does pay, or, perhaps, as is sometimes the case, when it does even more than pay—you are put back at once to the salary and religiously kept to it. The speculation, *then,* is the manager's, and he takes capital care of the money. A manager never says, "Share with us" when he is getting large audiences; whenever such is the case, the actor very likely finds out that his services can be entirely dispensed with.

Six shillings for nearly a month's hanging on was no joke, and I let it be pretty freely known to the Podger family that such was my opinion. But, as old Podger most logically expressed it, "You could not extract blood from a stone," and so my complaint went to the wind. Even as a share my pittance was miserable, and not honestly dealt out, otherwise I ought to have had ten shillings on the first night; but these player people, especially when they have a family company, have little respect for the engagements they enter into with unprotected strangers. There are a few honest managers, but a far greater number who forget all about honesty and "that sort of thing."

In a short time I was pretty well starved. The only thing that I had a sufficiency of was study; and as all the pieces at Beesham were new to me, I had a bellyful of that. We got up a great many plays that we could not do anything like justice to, such as "Richard the Third," &c.; and the board that hung on one side of the passage which led to the playhouse was very significant— it was, "Mangling done here," and was put out by an old lady who kept a calender in a garret above the room which served us for a theatre. And this was sometimes vastly convenient, for when a thunderstorm commenced in any of the pieces, the mangle made a capital introduction to it.

As I have already said, we arrived about the election time, and, as a consequence, we had a bespeak from two of the candidates. As a sharer I was supposed to get my share in the bespeak, but I never found that it made one bit of difference to my empty treasury. The other, the defeated candidate, gave a sum of money, I believe, to the company, but none of it ever happened to come into my pocket. I fancied from this, and other circumstances of a similar kind, that Podger's morality and general notions of *meum et tuum* were very lax. It was evident he looked upon the cash which was thus received, not as a donation to the company, or as a salve to make up for the increased patronage which his bespeak would have produced, but as a donation to his family, to be solely spent for their own gratification. I never could forgive this; and when I was receiving a dole of one or two occasional shillings, I always thought of the member's five guineas, and cursed the Podger family, root and branch, with a great and hearty curse.

I may mention that Tom and I went out once or twice to the neighbouring villages to give entertainments. Tom exhibited a magic-lantern with dissolving views, &c., whilst I entertained the bumpkins with a slight exhibition of legerdemain—a few common tricks picked up from seeing the "Wizard of the North"—and we then concluded the performance with a few comic stories and songs, including a sprinkling of ventriloquism, in which I likewise dabbled.

My only pleasure was in hearing occasionally from a few dear friends at home, and in the perusal of the newspapers which they sometimes forwarded to me. A copy of the *Era* was a great treat. It is a regular actor's friend, and I looked forward to it with almost as much zest as I would have looked forward to a good dinner, could I have imagined such a thing to be then within the range of possibility. I was rapidly getting starved out of my romantic notions of being a great actor, and yet I felt no diminution of what I conceived to be my talent for the representation or delineation of character. But having to go day after day without anything like adequate food, with the consciousness of looking anything but respectable in the shabby-genteel coat which circumstances force you to adopt, soon deadens all exuberance of feeling, or any glow of enthusiasm which might prompt one to aim high and seek a first-rate position on the boards.

And, lest I forget, let me here thank my good friend, Mrs Russell, who was quite a mother to me during the three months I lived with her. I remember one Sunday, when, having had no salary for my week's exertions, I had gone up to my bedroom to have a hearty cry in bed over my hunger, she sent up her little boy with two apple dumplings from her own table. I knew what the boy was knocking at the door for, but my pride was alarmed, and I feigned to be asleep, while all the time the tears were trickling down my thin cheeks with the pain of the sheer hunger which was gnawing at me. I was not, too, despite my forbidding range of character, without some glimpses of success. The *Tailor* in " Cathe-rine and Petruchio," and one or two other little comic parts, went far to do away with the impression that I was a nobody who could do nothing.

During my sojourn at Beesham, Tom Podger being seized with a severe illness, a man of the name of Wood, his wife, and her son, who were " dodging" about in the adjacent small villages, were invited to come and help out the company. This of course added to our efficiency, but detracted from our already too scanty income, as the extra members of the *corps* made little difference in the number of the audience.

Old Wood was a Scotchman—a queer, dry, cynical fellow, who had seen a great deal of the world, and tasted many of its bitters. He carried about with him a huge and bulky manuscript volume of his life and adventures, which he had a great idea of publishing, and thought that if he could get it sent to *Blackwood's Magazine*, the pub-lishers would pay him handsomely for it.

Mrs Wood was a sister of the great Edmund Kean's, and she spoke with much bitterness of his neglect of her when he was in the zenith of his popularity, and fortune was showering her favours upon him. She told me one melan-choly story of a period when a London engagement of some importance was offered her while performing at Rotherham. She had no money, and could not get to London without it; but she learned that the great Kean was at Sheffield, and a ray of hope dawned upon her. Poor woman! hope flattered in vain, for, after a weary walk to Sheffield, the great man, instead of helping her, would not even see her. Perhaps at this very time he was earning his fifty pounds a night, and his sister could not get as many shillings to carry her to an engagement that might ultimately have crowned her with fortune also, for she had the family talent, and when I saw her the remains of a good actress were still visible.

When the family reached Beesham they were literally in rags and starvation, and as they had come far in the midst of a soaking rain, their condition may, as the play-bills so sententiously express it, " be more easily imagined than described." Perhaps, if Mr Charles Kean were to be made aware of his aunt's condition, he would help her a little. No doubt, as he is a charitable man, he will have many claims upon him; but a trifle would be a great deal to her, and " mercy is twice blessed."

I may finish this portion of my subject by stating that, in addition to playing several parts in each piece, I acted also as prompter, bill-deliverer, scene-dauber, property-maker, and bill-writer—verily, " one man in his time plays many parts."

# CHAPTER XXXVI.

THE AUTHOR AT THIS POINT RESOLVES THAT HE WILL
MUSE NO FURTHER ; AND THE READER, IN ALL PROB-
ABILITY, WILL BE INDUCED TO EXCLAIM, " FOR THIS
RELIEF, MUCH THANKS."

AFTER the Woods joined us, we got up " a grand series of
Shakspearian revivals ;" that is, we murdered " Macbeth,"
" As You Like It," " Romeo and Juliet," and others of
the great bard's works, after the approved manner of the
" habit-and-repute" stroller.   There was rare fun on these
nights, both before and behind the scenes.   Old Wood,
fancying that age and experience should carry all before
them, thought that, as a matter of course, he ought to
play *Macbeth*.   This, however, Heathcott would not
tolerate ; but Wood, in revenge, would come early to the
theatre, and picking out the best part of the ambitious
thane's attire, would either hide them or put them on as
part of his own costume.   Then would commence a series
of bickerings and sneers, which were bandied about at no
allowance—in fact, were "thick as leaves in Vallambrosa."
A storm was raised which would rage throughout the whole
night.   Heathcott scouted Wood as an old ass, and Wood
insinuated that Heathcott was a brainless puppy, who
should learn the words of Shakspeare before he attempted
to personate any of his characters, &c., &c.

Even in "family companies" the spirit of party and the demon of envy rage with exceeding strength. I was fortunate enough to preserve a tolerable neutrality; and in consequence of neither siding with the Montagues nor the Capulets, I was selected as a general depository for the criticism and observations of the different belligerent parties.

Their remarks would generally run as follow :—

*Mrs Heathcott.*—That isn't acting. Why, anybody could do that. It is a great pity Tom thinks so much of his wife,—she's not fit to play *Lady Macbeth*. She should stick entirely to the secondary parts, and leave me the choice of business. I can *play Lady Macbeth*, she merely goes through the words.

*Mrs Tom Podger.*—That woman's a fool on stilts. *That* is not acting; there's not one touch of human nature in that style of reading a part. Poor thing! she runs away on her stilts, and carries the author on her back; but she is to be excused—what can she learn in a few country theatres?

*Old Podger.*—God bless me, how these young folks do go on: in my young days the manager would not have allowed them to speak. There's too much vanity now, sir, in the profession,—boys and girls that are almost unfit to deliver a message now play leading parts. I worked my way up, sir, and so should all.

*Heathcott.*—I say, Capelton, did you ever see such a presumptuous old fool as that Wood? He's a regular stick. He act *Macbeth!* By God, sir, he couldn't do

*Rosse.* He quite foiled me with his *Macduff.* It strikes me he's not up in the part even yet.

*Old Wood.*—My eye, such murder,—such a style to play *Macbeth* in I never saw—did you? Good heavens he has no more idea of the part than my staff. Why, sir,' in the theatres I've been in, he would get the *Physician* to play, and good enough for him, in all conscience.

*Tom Podger.*—Blow me if these fellows don't murder the piece. I'm d——d if I couldn't do both parts my-self a great deal better.

*Mrs Wood.*—Any money yet? Isn't this shameful? We've been here a fortnight and have only got seventeen shillings.

*Old Wood.*—Never mind, dear, we've still one comfort —my manuscript.

*Mrs Wood* (flaring up in a passion.)—Faugh! your devil.

And so on till the quarrel would wax stronger, and there would be a slight skirmish, and poor Wood would reappear with a few slight scratches on his face. Mrs W. could not bear any allusion to "the manuscript," whilst the old fellow himself doated upon it, and thought that, some day or other, if he could only get it into *Blackwood*, it would make his fortune, and enable him to bid a long farewell to the stage, and all the "pride, pomp, and cir-cumstance" of strolling.

Among the one or two persons I scraped acquaintance with, while I sojourned at Beesham, was one whom I shall name Old Pistol, a hanger-on about the theatre, who was always met enjoying his pot of beer in the public-house parlour frequented by the company, which at that time was next door. Pistol, or "Old Pistol," as he was usually called by his cronies, was quite a character, and, according to his own account, had gone through more phases of life than any person on the boards.

"Ah! Pistol, you've seen acting in your day, you have," some one of the company would say—and such a peg as this simple observation afforded was quite sufficient for "O. P.," as Heathcott designated him, to hang a story upon.

"Yes, I *have* seen service, sir. By the powers, sir, before you had left your cradle, I had crossed swords with John Kemble. I have acted in every theatre in the three kingdoms,—I have. · I have played before royalty. I have been thanked by lords-lieutenant. Egad, sir, queens have smiled upon handsome Jack Pistol, sir—they have indeed, sir,"

"Well, Mr Pistol, you must have known a great number of the profession in your time?"

"I believe you, my boy. I know, or have known, every actor of eminence, sir, dating from the time of the Kembles. Why, sir, when a boy, I once fastened the sandal of 'the Siddons' herself—the great Mrs Siddons, sir. Yes, for the last forty years and more I have known all the great ones, ay, and all the small ones too. I have been actor, author, manager, painter, pantomimist, and leader of a band. I have travelled to all the fairs in the kingdom. I have had spotted men, white-haired ladies, mermaids, merry-go-rounds, wax-work, horsemanship, in-

visible girls, magic temples, and once a real rhinoceros;
and now, even at seventy-two, 'I am up to every move
and down to every dodge,' both ancient and modern."

Whether the one-half of Pistol's anecdotes were really
true or not I cannot tell, but, even old as he was, his
faculties were still alert, and he worked his way wonderfully. His purpose in hanging about wherever there was
a theatre was to make up occasionally a small company
for a brief stroll, and these excursions he managed remarkably well—if not great successes, they were sure to
be so well done as not to be great failures.

## EPILOGUE.

My race of folly now being over, I find I must draw my narrative to a close. The hard work, bad pay, and consequent starvation at Beesham began to tell rapidly on my health, and my gaunt frame and pale cheeks warned me that the career in which I had engaged must at length be brought to a somewhat hasty conclusion. The usage as to money matters which I received from the Podger family soon wearied me of actors and acting. I could see that the family party never wanted for all the comforts which good eating and drinking could confer upon them. Roasts and boils of the most tempting description daily graced *their* table, while I was glad to steal a few beans from a farmer's rick, or wander into a field and pull a juicy turnip wherewith to stay my hunger, which at times grew intense; and, to add to my numerous other miseries, my clothes were getting so shabby that I could no longer walk about the neighbourhood with the same degree of pride as when I first arrived in the place.

The following statement, copied from an old note-book, gives an exact account of my receipts during my engagement in the " Sheep's-head Company :"—

I arrived early in July. The first cash I got was to

| | | | | | |
|---|---|---|---|---|---|
| relieve my large carpet-bag from the carrier's, | | | | £0 1 | 6 |
| July   31, | . | . | . | . | . | 0 6 | 0 |
| Carry forward, | | . | . | . | £0 7 | 6 |

|  |  |  |  |  |  | £0 | 7 | 6 |
|---|---|---|---|---|---|---|---|---|
| Brought forward, | | . | . | . | | £0 | 7 | 6 |
| August 3, | | . | . | . | . | 0 | 5 | 6 |
| „ 7, | | . | . | . | . | 0 | 3 | 0 |
| „ 10, | | . | . | . | . | 0 | 5 | 0 |
| „ 14, | | . | . | . | . | 0 | 3 | 0 |
| „ 17, | (A Bespeak,) | | . | . | . | 0 | 9 | 0 |
| „ 24, | | . | . | . | . | 0 | 7 | 0 |
| „ 30, | | . | . | . | . | 0 | 5 | 0 |
| Sept. 7, | | . | . | . | : | . | 0 | 8 | 0 |
| „ 14, | | . | . | . | . | 0 | 8 | 0 |
| „ 20, | | . | . | . | . | 0 | 2 | 0 |
| „ 27, | | . | . | . | . | 0 | 1 | 0 |
| October 3, | | . | . | . | . | 0 | 2 | 6 |
| | | | | Total, | . | £3 | 6 | 6 |

For more than three months' service, including a journey of sixty miles there and back. The reader must make due allowance for these payments as they occurred in the service of the Podger family. I feel pretty sure that something like twelve shillings a week might have been got anywhere else.

A circumstance had also occurred, which, in the course of my sojourn, gave me some cause of alarm. I had ruptured a small blood-vessel somewhere about the lungs, and upon the occasion of any serious exertion I was sometimes nearly choked with a mouthful of blood. This was a warning not to be neglected, and the advice of a surgeon, who was so kind as to see me, was to leave off acting at once and for ever. I followed his advice, wrote home for some cash, went to London, and thence returned to my native city, looking, as many of my friends said, very like a skeleton ; and so ended my ambitious dream of becoming a great actor.

The reader must not suppose that, although I have been

*starved* out of the profession, I entertain anything like a grudge against it or its members. On the contrary, I always meet actors with pleasure, and indulge in theatrical gossip and small talk with decided relish. There are few members of the profession, perhaps, who have not suffered quite as much as I have done, indeed many have suffered a great deal more and said little about it; but it is surely proper that the unthinking youths, who look upon the stage as a mine of gold, should be shewn the fallacy of their speculations; and my humble advice to all would-be dramatic heroes is—DON'T GO UPON THE STAGE.

FINIS.